Radical Reforms

During the past decade international commentators and researchers have likened England to a science laboratory where the rate of experimentation has developed at a frenetic pace. Some governments have watched this situation with interest but from a distance, others have attempted to transfer policies and interventions across geographical and cultural boundaries. The current political climate would suggest this trend is likely to continue. Focusing on education as a major area of public policy in England, this book explores a decade of rapid and intensive modernization and draws out the lessons for those concerned with developing education systems across the globe.

In 1997 New Labour set out to transform the public sector in general, and education in particular. This book focuses specifically on reform in key areas:

- Standards and accountability
- Workforce reform
- Choice and diversity
- Every Child Matters and beyond.

The first decade of New Labour governments has produced reforms that are subject to debate with arguments that range from centralized interference in professional practice and the lives of children, through to recognition of major investment to create opportunities for inclusion and to modernize the system. Drawing on the framework which New Labour has developed to assess the approaches to and outcomes of interventions and the extent to which policies can deliver promised transformations, the authors present a critical account of reform by studying examples of policies, and conceptualizing the interplay of policy, practice and research.

This book will be of interest to researchers in education, education policy and school leadership in the UK and beyond.

Dr Christopher Chapman is a Reader in Educational Leadership and School Improvement in the School of Education at the University of Manchester.

Professor Helen M. Gunter is Chair of Educational Policy, Leadership and Management in the School of Education at the University of Manchester.

Radical Reforms

Perspectives on an era of
educational change

**Edited by
Christopher Chapman
and Helen M. Gunter**

 Routledge
Taylor & Francis Group

LONDON AND NEW YORK

First published 2009
by Routledge
2 Park Square, Milton Park, Abingdon, Oxon OX14 4RN

Simultaneously published in the USA and Canada
by Routledge
270 Madison Ave, New York, NY 10016

Routledge is an imprint of the Taylor & Francis Group, an informa business

Typeset in Bembo by
Keytroke, 28 High Street, Tettenhall, Wolverhampton
Printed and bound in Great Britain by
CPI Antony Rowe, Chippenham, Wiltshire

British Library Cataloguing in Publication Data
A catalogue record for this book is available from the British Library

Library of Congress Cataloging in Publication Data
Radical reforms: perspectives on an era of educational change/edited
by Christopher Chapman and Helen M. Gunter.
    p. cm.
   Includes bibliographical references.
   1. Educational change—Great Britain.   2. Education and state—
Great Britain.   3. Educational accountability—Great Britain.
4. Educational leadership—Great Britain.   I. Chapman,
Christopher, 1972–   II. Gunter, Helen M.
LA632.R328 2009
370.941—dc22   2008029008

ISBN10: 0–415–46401–3 (hbk)
ISBN10: 0–415–46402–1 (pbk)
ISBN10: 0–203–88411–6 (ebk)

ISBN13: 978–0–415–46401–7 (hbk)
ISBN13: 978–0–415–46402–4 (pbk)
ISBN13: 978–0–203–88411–9 (ebk)

Contents

Notes on contributors

Mel Ainscow is Professor of Education and co-director of the Centre for Equity in Education (CEE) at the University of Manchester. He is also the Government's Chief Adviser for the Greater Manchester Challenge, a £50 million initiative to improve educational outcomes for all young people in the region. Previously a headteacher, local education authority (LEA) inspector and lecturer at the University of Cambridge, Mel's work attempts to explore connections between inclusion, teacher development and school improvement. A particular feature of this research involves the development and use of participatory methods of inquiry that set out to make a direct impact on thinking and practice in systems, schools and classrooms. Mel is consultant to UNESCO, UNICEF and Save the Children, and is Marden Visiting Professor at the Hong Kong Institute of Education. Two recent books are *Improving Urban Schools* (Open University Press, 2006, co-edited with Mel West) and *Improving Schools, Developing Inclusion* (Routledge, 2006, with Tony Booth, Alan Dyson and colleagues).

Bill Boyle is Professor of Educational Assessment and the Director of the Centre for Formative Assessment Studies in the School of Education at the University of Manchester. He leads international assessment developments for the World Bank, Department for International Development and UNESCO, and since 1989 has been an adviser to the Qualifications and Curriculum Authority (QCA) on national assessment strategies in England. He has authored 75 practitioner and academic books and is currently involved in primary leadership research and development in Vietnam for the World Bank.

Joanna Bragg is Senior Researcher in the Centre for Formative Assessment Studies, University of Manchester. Since 1992, she has worked on a range of externally funded research projects. For ten years (1997–2007) she worked on the QCA funded School Sampling Project, subsequently the *Monitoring Curriculum and Assessment* project, and produced a series of reports, conference papers and journal articles that focus on curriculum trends (in particular allocation of teaching time and curriculum priorities), performance relating to disadvantage in primary and secondary schools and the impact of national testing on the school curriculum. Most recently, Joanna has been involved in research funded by the National College of School Leadership (NCSL), one project to examine New Models of School Leadership and the other to evaluate the longer-term impact of the Bursar Development Programme (BDP).

Christopher Chapman is Reader in Educational Leadership and School Improvement in the School of Education at the University of Manchester. Recent books include *Improving Schools through External Intervention* (Continuum, 2006) and *Effective Leadership for School Improvement* (RoutledgeFalmer, 2003, with Alma Harris, Christopher Day, Mark Hadfield, David Hopkins and Andy Hargreaves). Christopher is involved in a number of externally funded research and development projects focusing on issues related to educational leadership. He is grant holder for the NCSL longitudinal study of new models of leadership effectiveness and improvement in urban and challenging contexts. Christopher is also Programme Director for the MEd in Educational Leadership and School Improvement at the University of Manchester.

Alan Dyson is Professor of Education in the University of Manchester where he co-directs the Centre for Equity in Education and leads work on education in urban contexts. His research interests are in the relationship between social and educational inclusion and, particularly, in the relationship between education and other areas of public policy in urban contexts. Recent studies include the national evaluation of full-service extended schools for the Department for Children, Schools and Families (DCSF) and a study of school governing bodies in disadvantaged areas for the Joseph Rowntree Foundation. His publications (with colleagues) include *Schools and Area Regeneration* (Policy Press, 2003), *Housing and Schooling* (York Publishing Services, 1999), *School, Family, Community* (Youth Work Press, 1999) and *Improving Schools, Developing Inclusion* (Routledge, 2006). He also led the production of the *Open File on Inclusive Education* for UNESCO. Alan has worked in universities since 1988. Prior to that, he spent 13 years as a teacher, mainly in urban comprehensive schools.

Peter Farrell is the Sarah Fielden Professor of Special Needs and Educational Psychology, University of Manchester, and former President of the International School Psychology Association. He has directed or co-directed a number of projects for the Department for Education and Skills (DfES) and DCSF. These include projects on the role of learning support assistants, the education of children with medical needs, the relationship between inclusion and pupil achievement in mainstream schools and the role of educational psychologists. Two recent books are *Making Special Education Inclusive: From Research to Practice* (Fulton, 2002, co-edited with Mel Ainscow) and *A Psychology for Inclusive Education* (Routledge, 2008, co-edited with Peter Hick and Ruth Kershner).

Gillian Forrester is Senior Lecturer in Education Studies in the Faculty of Education, Community and Leisure at Liverpool John Moores University, and is Honorary Researcher in the School of Education, University of Manchester. Her main research interests are in education policy and modernization, teachers' work, performance management in schools and school leadership. Between January 2006 and December 2007 Gillian was Research Assistant to Professor Helen M. Gunter (School of Education, University of Manchester) on the Economic and Social Research Council (ESRC) project, *Knowledge Production in Educational Leadership* (KPEL) (RES-000-23-1192), which investigated the origins and development of school leadership in England.

Jo Frankham is Senior Lecturer in Education in the School of Education at the University of Manchester. Her interests include interpretive approaches to educational inquiry and researching sensitive issues. Recent work has included an ESRC funded exploration of the rhetoric of 'partnership research' with service users and Joseph Rowntree Foundation research with children and young people who have been permanently excluded from school. Her interest in networking was provoked by research on the ESRC Teaching and Learning Programme. Recent publications have appeared in *British Educational Research Journal* and *Journal of Education Policy*. Jo also leads the taught doctorate (EdD) in the School of Education.

Sue Goldrick is a Research Associate at the Centre for Equity in Education in the School of Education at the University of Manchester. Her main research interests include development and research processes involved in working with practitioners to achieve greater equity in education systems, educational improvement across school networks, teacher development, student voice, and pedagogy for diversity.

Helen M. Gunter is Professor of Educational Policy, Leadership and Management in the School of Education at the University of Manchester. Three recent books are *Leaders and Leadership in Education* (Paul Chapman, 2001), *Leading Teachers* (Continuum, 2005) and *Modernizing Schools: People, Learning and Organizations* (Continuum, 2007, co-edited with Graham Butt). Helen's main area of research is in knowledge production in policy studies and educational leadership. She is grant holder for the ESRC project, *Knowledge Production in Educational Leadership* (RES-000-23-1192), and she is researching the origins and development of school leadership in England.

Dave Hall is Senior Lecturer in Education in the School of Education, University of Manchester. His research, linked to a series of externally funded research projects, has mainly focused upon the relationship between schools, teaching and socio-economic context and educational transitions. His publications have recently featured in the *International Journal of Inclusive Education, British Journal of the Sociology of Education, Journal of Education Policy* and *Journal of Vocational Education and Training*. Dave is also Programme Director of the MA in Education at the University of Manchester.

Andy Hargreaves is the Thomas More Brennan Chair in Education at the Lynch School of Education at Boston College, MA. He was the Simon Visiting Professor in the School of Education, Faculty of Humanities, University of Manchester in 2007. He has authored and edited more than 25 books in education, which have been published in many languages. His book, *Teaching in the Knowledge Society: Education in the Age of Insecurity* (Open University Press, 2003) received outstanding book awards from the American Educational Research Association and the American Library Association.

Andy Howes is Senior Lecturer in Education in the School of Education at the University of Manchester. Recent books include *Improving Schools, Developing Inclusion, Reforming Education?* (Routledge, 2006, with Ainscow, Booth and Dyson et al.) and *Improving the Context for Inclusion* (Routledge-Falmer, 2009, with Sue Davies and Sam Fox). Andy's research is in the area of teacher development, pedagogy and social justice. He is grant holder for the ESRC project, *Facilitating Teacher Engagement in Inclusive Practice*, and he is involved in a number of other funded inclusion-related projects. He also coordinates the Educational and Professional Studies programme in the Secondary Postgraduate Certificate in Education (PGCE).

Kirstin Kerr is a Leverhulme Early Career Fellow in the Centre for Equity in Education, School of Education at the University of Manchester. Her research explores the complex webs of factors that create inequities in disadvantaged communities, how these impact on education, and how multi-agency working can be developed in response. Kirstin's work also involves supporting Local Authorities and Education Improvement Partnerships who are seeking to develop new strategies to address local inequities.

Olwen McNamara is a Professor of Teacher Education and Development in the School of Education at the University of Manchester, where she is Director of the Primary Initial Training Programme and Executive Director of the Teach First Northwest Programme. Her research interests are practitioner focused with a particular emphasis on professional learning and mathematics education. She publishes widely in these fields and her books include *New Teacher Identity and Regulative Government* (Springer, 2005, with Tony Brown), *Practitioner Research and Professional Development in Education* (Sage, 2004, with Anne Campbell and Peter Gilroy 2004) and *Becoming an Evidence-based Practitioner* (RoutledgeFalmer, 2002).

Nadine Mearns is an Educational Psychologist with the City of Liverpool. She has for five years provided advice and practical support to a Sure Start Local Project, a Sure Start Children's Centre and a Multi-agency Early Years Special Educational Need (SEN) assessment service in the city. Her doctoral thesis (University of Manchester, 2007) examined the subjective experience of Early Years professionals employed in a range of multi-professional contexts, including both Sure Start and SEN project teams. She has previously published work on Computer Assisted Learning – 'Using computers in the home and in the primary school: Where is the value added?', *Educational and Child Psychology*, 18, 3, 31–46 (with D. Moseley and T. Harrison, 2001).

Denis Mongon is a Senior Research Fellow at Manchester University and Senior Associate at the Innovation Unit. His current research interest is in the role of schools in their communities, in particular, the poor outcomes for white working-class students, new forms of management and governance for the range of children's services and the contribution of schools to local regeneration. His teaching career was in Inner London, mainly with 'disturbed or disaffected' young people and he has since held senior posts in several local authorities and worked for a range of national agencies on policy development.

Daniel Muijs is Professor of Pedagogy and Teacher Development in the School of Education at the University of Manchester. He has conducted a wide range of research in the areas of school and teacher effectiveness and leadership. He is joint editor of *School Effectiveness and School Improvement* and active in a number of professional bodies in the field. Books written include *Effective Teaching, Evidence and Practice* (Paul Chapman, 2001, with David Reynolds) and *Teacher Leadership: Improvement through Empowerment?* (Open University Press, 2004, with Alma Harris).

Carlo Raffo is Reader in Equity in Urban Education in the School of Education, University of Manchester. Carlo's main area of research is in the area of education and poverty and educational equity in urban contexts. He is grant holder for the Joseph Rowntree Foundation project, *Education and Poverty* – a critical review of theory, policy and practice and has been involved in numerous other externally funded projects that focus on schools and education in areas of urban disadvantage. His publications have recently featured in the *Journal of Education Policy*, *British Journal of the Sociology of Education* and *International Journal of Inclusive Education*. Carlo is also Programme Director of the Ed.D and coordinator of the Urban Contexts pathway.

John Smyth is Research Professor of Education, School of Education, University of Ballarat, Australia. Three recent books are *Critically Engaged Learning* (Peter Lang, 2008, with Lawrence Angus, Barry Down and Peter McInerney), *Teachers in the Middle* (Peter Lang, 2007, with McInerney) and '*Dropping Out*', *Drifting Off, Being Excluded* (Peter Lang, 2004, with Robert Hattam). He is the grant holder for two Australian Research Council projects: 'Individual, institutional and community "capacity building" in a cluster of disadvantaged schools and their community' (with Angus) and 'Enhancing school retention: school and community linkages in regional/rural Western Australia' (with Down). He was the Simon Visiting Professor in the School of Education, Faculty of Humanities, University of Manchester in 2008.

Rosemary Webb is a Professor in the School of Education at the University of Manchester. She has published extensively on aspects of primary education. A recent book is *Changing Teaching and Learning in the Primary School* (Open University Press, 2006). She has had a varied career in primary education as a teacher, professional officer at the National Curriculum Council, lecturer and researcher. She is a past chair of the Association for the Study of Primary Education (ASPE), initiated the British Educational Research Association (BERA)/ASPE Special Interest Group (SIG) on Primary Teachers' Work and is currently its convenor

Mel West is Professor of Educational Leadership and Head of the School of Education, University of Manchester. His work, principally being in the fields of school management and school improvement, has taken him to many countries including Iceland, Laos, Chile, Hong Kong, China, Puerto Rico and Malawi, working with a number of international agencies including the British Council, Department for International Development, Organization for Economic Cooperation and Development (OECD), UNESCO and Save the Children. In the late 1980s he was one of the architects of the influential *Improving the Quality of Education for All* (IQEA) programme. A recent book is *Improving Urban Schools* (Open University Press, 2006, co-edited with Mel Ainscow).

Charlotte Woods is Lecturer in Education within the Management and Institutional Development group of the School of Education. Charlotte has worked on a series of funded research projects for NCSL in connection with the development of School Business Management capacity nationally via their Bursar Development Programme (BDP). She is currently working with colleagues in the School of Education on a three-year investigation of the longer-term impacts of the BDP within the context of current reforms.

Abbreviations

ASPE	Association for the Study of Primary Education
BDP	Bursar Development Programme
BERA	British Educational Research Association
BEST	Behaviour and Education Support Team
BIP	Behaviour Improvement Programme
BSF	Building Schools for the Future
CACE	Central Advisory Council for Education (England)
CATE	Council for Accreditation of Teacher Education
CEE	Centre for Equity in Education
CPD	Continuing Professional Development
CSBM	Certificate of School Business Management
CTC	City Technology College
CVA	Contextual Value Added
D&R	Development and Research
DCSF	Department for Children, Schools and Families
DENI	Department of Education, Northern Ireland
DES	Department of Education and Science
DfE	Department for Education
DfEE	Department for Education and Employment
DfES	Department for Education and Skills
DSBM	Diploma of School Business Management
EAL	English as an Additional Language
EAZ	Education Action Zone
ECM	Every Child Matters
EiC	Excellence in Cities
EIP	Education Improvement Partnership
EP	Educational Psychologist
ERA	Education Reform Act
ESRC	Economic and Social Research Council
FE	Further Education
FSES	Full Service Extended Schools
FSM	Free School Meals
FSR	Fifty Schools Revisited

GCSE	General Certificate of Secondary Education
GM	Grant Maintained
GTC	General Teaching Council
GTCNI	General Teaching Council for Northern Ireland
GTCS	General Teaching Council Scotland
GTCW	General Teaching Council for Wales
HE	Higher Education
HEFCE	Higher Education Funding Council for England
HEI	Higher Education Institution
HMCI	Her Majesty's Chief Inspector of Schools
HMI	Her Majesty's Inspectorate
ICT	Information and Communications Technology
IEA	International Association for the Evaluation of Educational Achievement
ITE	Initial Teacher Education
ITT	Initial Teacher Training
KPEL	Knowledge Production in Educational Leadership
KS	Key Stage
LA	Local Authority
LAA	Local Area Agreements
LEA	Local Education Authority
LIG	Leadership Incentive Grant
LMS	Local Management of Schools
LPSH	Leadership Programme for Serving Heads
NAO	National Audit Office
NCC	National Curriculum Council
NCSL	National College for School Leadership
NDPB	Non-Departmental Public Body
NEET	Not in Education, Employment or Training
NESS	National Evaluation of Sure Start
NIS	National Indicator Set
NLS	National Literacy Strategy
NNS	National Numeracy Strategy
NPQH	National Professional Qualification for Headship
NQT	Newly Qualified Teacher
NVQ	National Vocational Qualification
OECD	Organization for Economic Cooperation and Development
OfSTED	Office for Standards in Education
OfSTIN	Office for Standards in Inspection
ONS	Office for National Statistics
PA	Personal Adviser
PANDA	Performance and Assessment
PAT	Policy Action Team
PAYP	Positive Activities for Young People
PGCE	Postgraduate Certificate in Education

PISA	Programme for International Student Assessment
PMSU	Prime Minister's Strategy Unit
PNP	Primary Needs Project
PNS	Primary National Strategy
PSHE	Personal, Social and Health Education
PTA	Parent Teacher Association
PwC	PricewaterhouseCoopers
QAA	Quality Assurance Agency
QCA	Qualifications and Curriculum Authority
QR	Quality-Related
QTS	Qualified Teacher Status
R&D	Research and Development
RAE	Research Assessment Exercise
RATL	Raising Achievement/Transforming Learning
SAT	Standard Attainment Tests
SBM	School Business Manager
SCITT	School-Centred Initial Teacher Training
SEF	Self-Evaluation Form
SEN	Special Educational Need
SES	Socio-Economic Status
SIG	Special Interest Group
SIPs	School Improvement Partners
SITE	Standard for Initial Teacher Education
SLT	Senior Leadership Team/School Leadership Team
SSAT	Specialist Schools and Academies Trust
SSP	Specialist School Programme
TDA	Training and Development Agency (for Schools)
TIMSS	Trends in International Mathematics and Science Study
TLRP	Teaching and Learning Research Programme
TTA	Teacher Training Agency
TVEI	Technical and Vocational Educational Initiative
UCET	Universities' Council for the Education of Teachers
YA	Youth Apprenticeship
YFP	York-Finnish Project
YJP	York-Jyväskylä Project

1 A decade of New Labour reform of education

Helen M. Gunter and Christopher Chapman

Introduction

In 1997 New Labour set out to transform the public sector in general, and education in particular.[1] From the outset this involved significant input of resources into schools combined with high-profile targeted interventions aimed at improving educational standards, often in the most socially deprived areas. Early targeted interventions included *Education Action Zones* (EAZs) and the *Excellence in Cities* (Office for Standards in Education (OfSTED) 2003a) programme,[2] and then the *Leadership Incentive Grant* (LIG) (DfES 2003a).[3] These were followed by a second wave, including national strategies for literacy and numeracy (OfSTED 2003b),[4] the introduction of the *Every Child Matters* (ECM) (DfES 2003b) agenda,[5] and then *Education Improvement Partnerships* (EIPs) (DCSF 2008a).[6] These initiatives have tended to be underpinned by attempts at curriculum and leadership development, a broadening of agendas and the promotion of cross-school collaboration such as *Federations* (DCSF 2008b).[7] More recently, the reform has shifted its focus to organizational structures and the workforce, leading to radical systemic changes to the type of schools such as *Academies* (DCSF 2008c) and *Trusts* (DCSF 2008d),[8] and the composition of the workforce, known as *Remodelling* (DfES 2003c).[9] These policy interventions have been implemented rapidly, with policy-makers arguing for a 'boldness of reform' and 'quality of implementation'. Michael Barber (2007) as an architect of New Labour education policy conceptualized this approach to educational reform as outlined in Figure 1.1.

For Barber (2007) the aim was nothing short of transformation articulated through the goal of a world-class education system, with an emphasis on simultaneously securing high standards and personalization. Such a strategy continues to be contested, and can be polarized, with discourses which stress the opportunities created, while others reveal the erosion of professional and public sector values. New Labour uses a 'score card' approach to measuring the impact of transformational reforms, and we intend to go much deeper and wider than this. By 'we', ourselves as editors and our co-writers (and colleagues), we mean those involved in producing a portfolio of work with valid things to say about educational reform. Drawing on a programme of research undertaken by

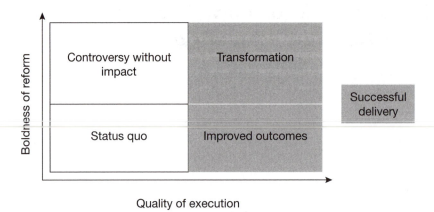

Figure 1.1 The map of delivery (Barber 2007: 83)

members of staff in the School of Education, University of Manchester, we present a critical account of reform by studying examples of policies, and conceptualizing the interplay of policy, practice and research. Hence while the language of New Labour is about 'new', 'modern' and 'transformation', we intend to show that there is much in common with the direction of travel set by previous administrations, not least through the dominance of neoliberal values, thinking and espoused practices. Hence radical change to the *roots* of the public sector system is about the protection and extension of market processes and practices in ways that are more functional than socially critical (Raffo et al. 2007). The book will not only examine the strategic aspects of reforming the public sector through major policy initiatives but also move inside the policy process through examining evidence and analysis that is close to practice.

Policy context

After a decade of New Labour governments, Tony Blair (2007) spoke to the Specialist Schools and Academies Trust and outlined the importance of education that had been the mantra of 'education, education, education', in 1997:

> Good education makes a difference. Good teaching changes lives. Educate a child well and you give them a chance. Educate them badly and they may never get a chance in the whole of their lives.
>
> (Blair 2007: 13)

New Labour had wanted to invest in public sector services, and recognized the need to improve the status and impact of education if they were to keep parents and the taxpayer onside. He gave testimony to the achievements of this 'investment for results' (Blair 2007: 1) policy by celebrating outcomes:

- 'English 10 year olds are now ranked third in the world'
- 'Funding per pupil has doubled'
- 'The success in specialist schools has been remarkable'
- 'More than 1,500 previously failing schools have been turned around'
- 'We have achieved the best ever GCSE [General Certificate of Secondary Education] and A Level results'

(Blair 2007: 7)

He professed the belief that both excellence and equity can be achieved, and that this is through two forms of ongoing restructuring: first, systemic diversity with a range of providers such as Academies and Trust Schools; and second, responsiveness to learning needs through personalization. And so, 'what was once monochrome is now a spectrum offering a range of freedoms and pathways' (Blair 2007: 11). While in 1997, to paraphrase New Labour catchphrases, standards mattered more than structures, by 2007 structures through restructuring of the ownership of education (e.g. private ownership of Academies) and the growth in non-departmental public bodies (e.g. NCSL) re-emerged within the strategy.

The approach taken has been recognized by New Labour as centralized regulation, where the need for top-down performance management has been justified through the outcomes identified combined with the need for rapid change (Prime Minister's Strategy Unit (PMSU) 2006). Hence the 'Blair generation' of children who went to primary school from 1997 could benefit (Miliband 2004a). Blair along with Adonis (Adonis and Pollard 1997) and Barber (1996) conceptualized, controlled and secured the type, order and pace of educational reforms (Beckett and Hencke 2005). Complacency, low performance and rent-seeking behaviour by 'professionals' were identified as barriers that had to be overcome, and so the emphasis was put on eradicating failing schools, teachers and bureaucrats. Major changes took place as outlined in *Excellence in Schools* (Department for Education and Employment (DfEE) 1997a) and based on six principles:

1 Education will be at the heart of government.
2 Policies will be designed to benefit the many, not just the few.
3 The focus will be on standards, not structures.
4 Intervention will be in inverse proportion to success.
5 There will be zero tolerance of underperformance.
6 Government will work in partnership with all those committed to raising standards.

(DfEE 1997a: 5)

And further policy texts were generated to develop the detail, for example national literacy and numeracy strategies, performance management, training and headteachers as leaders (DfEE 1998a). The approach was to directly intervene in strategically determining the purposes of schooling, the tactical day-to-day operation of schools, and the work of teachers and headteachers in curriculum design, teaching, learning outcomes and assessment. Attention was given to 'failing' schools and resources were targeted on areas of deprivation with Education Action Zones and Excellence in Cities, and those with low attainment through schools facing challenging circumstances (Reynolds et al. 2002).

Barber (2007) outlined the rationale and detail of reform implementation through a 'delivery chain' from Whitehall to school that became known as 'Deliverology':

> The crucial concept was the delivery chain. Again, it is not more than a blinding flash of the obvious, but none the less important for all that. The best way to think about it is to imagine what is implicit when a minister makes a promise. Supposing a minister promises, as David Blunkett did, to improve standards of reading and writing among eleven-year-olds. Implicit in this commitment is that, in one way or another, the minister can influence what happens inside the head of an eleven-year-old in, for example, Widnes. The delivery chain makes that connection explicit.
>
> (Barber 2007: 85).

The working of the delivery chain depended on minimizing interference so that what has been determined centrally is secured without direct resistance or indirect obscuration. Hence New Labour put in place a legal framework requiring compliance (e.g. DfES 2004a), a guidance framework simulating compliance (e.g. DfES 2004b), a training regime seducing compliance (e.g. DfEE 1998a), and structural arrangements staffed with advisers and consultants based on contractual compliance (see Gunter and Forrester 2008). New Labour has been able to co-opt a range of people who it could trust to deliver either by being brought in to lead reforms or to work locally to ensure compliance (see Clark 1998; Collarbone 2005; Hopkins 2001; Munby 2006; Reid 2007; C. Taylor 2007) or to supply policy information and strategies (e.g. DfES/ PricewaterhouseCoopers (PwC) 2007).

The delivery chain also required performance targets to be underpinned by data collection and analysis at key 'links' in the 'chain' either at national level with the Prime Minister's stocktaking meetings or locally with headteachers examining student outcomes with staff, inspectors and School Improvement partners (SIPs). Barber (2007) outlines his case for the public collection and analysis of data and the rank ordering of schools:

> Not everyone in public services likes league tables, but I love them. I have spent much of the last decade advocating them, usually in front of sceptical or even hostile audiences of headteachers. They make the evidence about performance public, they focus minds on the priorities they encompass, and they make sure, in whatever system they are applied, that something is done about the individual units at the bottom of the league table –

whether they are schools, hospitals, police forces or local authorities. This is why I never accepted the idea put forward by many in education that, once we had a measure of value added or progress, this should replace the raw data. I have always advocated the publication of both indicators. The value-added figures show what contribution individual schools are making, which is important; the raw figures reveal where the biggest challenges are in achieving universal high standards and focus the system on those challenges, which is even more important. By laying bare the problems, league tables drive action. The fact that school failure has been much reduced (though there is still a lot more to do) and that the gap between the lowest-performing schools and the average has been narrowed owes a great deal to league tables. In fact, there is no more powerful driver of equity.

(Barber 2007: 96)

The micropolitics of convincing Whitehall politicians and civil servants, combined with unrelenting direction of schools and the profession, is key to Barber's strategy, and even though New Labour insiders such as Hyman (2005) saw the challenges this created at school level.

In the run-up to his resignation as Leader of the Labour Party and hence as Prime Minister, Blair made sure that his legacy of achievement combined with an agenda for what still needed to be done was made public. For him, the data show not only success (see above), but also the need to retain the permanent revolution of change. The argument being made is the need to shift from the top-down performance regime towards users shaping reforms (see PMSU 2006): 'but recently we have moved increasingly from centrally driven approach – necessary to address the worst of the problems we inherited – to try to make change self-sustaining by the use of incentives, user choice and contestability of service' (Blair 2006: 2). Central to the *Every Child Matters* (DfES 2003b) agenda is questioning the nature of provision through separate services (schools, welfare, health and security) and separate professions (teachers, social workers, doctors and police) with particular expertise. Trends suggest that schools as they have traditionally been conceptualized together with teachers, support staff and a headteacher are open for fundamental change, with restructuring leading to a range of provision (e.g. all-through schools, federations) and a workforce that may be more concerned with executive delivery based on generic leadership skills than on educational professional *teacher* determined leadership (see Butt and Gunter 2007). Consequently, emphasis remains on choice, diversity of provision, the targeting of resources linked to choices, and workforce changes that produce a flexible response to consumer choice attitudes and practices:

Throughout the process of reform, there are certain maxims I have learnt. Put the consumer not the producer first. Learn from those at the frontline actually doing it. Question the system as well as just work it. Back public servants who take risks and tough decisions. Experiment and innovate.

Money matters but it is never about money alone. Break down barriers between public, independent and voluntary sectors – they are often more about history than service. Let me put this another way: public services are not a monument, to be erected and then admired. They are living organisms, planted in the soil around them.

(Blair 2006)

Research context

The decade of New Labour affords the opportunity to undertake a rigorous examination of the reform process. We are aware of the challenges of doing this as educational research has faced direct attack in England regarding its assumed utility (Ribbins et al. 2003), control by government and its agencies over funding (Weindling 2004), researchers who have experienced political interference in commissioned projects (Gunter and Thomson 2006a). Those who seek to open up a dialogue and/or to generate alternative strategies have been labelled 'naysayers and doubters' (Miliband 2004b: 9), and *The Independent* (Cassidy 2008) reports on the official response to research produced by the 2008 Cambridge University Primary Review on the damage done by too much political interference in primary school teaching and learning by reporting that:

> A spokeswoman for the Department for Children, Schools and Families dismissed the research as 'recycled, partial or out of date'. 'We do not accept the claims,' she said. 'We are currently engaged in a review of the primary curriculum, as set out in the Children's Plan, which will build on a decade of success in raising standards – success that has been validated on numerous occasions by independent experts. The Government does not accept our children are over-tested.'

(Cassidy 2008: 2)

While we realize that our scholarship will be subjected to necessary and welcomed peer review, we are also aware that this book is a political document and as such it could be sucked into media and government debates about reform. Our research and commentary can speak for itself and we look forward to making a contribution that not only charts what has happened but also puts into the public domain evidence, analysis, thinking and ideas that can enliven our polity.

In planning and producing this book we are aware that we are part of a field of researchers who are concerned to examine changes to the public sector and education in particular. Anniversaries such as a decade in power by one political party provoke such analysis, not only to take stock but also to produce perspectives about the antecedence of reform ideas and strategies together with trajectories regarding where things are going and how a change of Prime Minister and/or government might impact. Over the decade there have been research studies of New Labour (e.g. Rawnsley 2001; Seldon 2007) and education (e.g. Coffield et al. 2007; Driver 2006; Lawton 2005; Strain and Simkins 2008; Tomlinson 2005; Walford 2005). Some studies of education have focused on particular themes such as neoliberalism and privatization (e.g. Ball 2007), impact of the layering of reforms over time on schools (e.g. Gewirtz 2002) or particular policies (e.g. Beckett 2007), while others, such as this book, have been pit-stop accounts, where the opportunity has been taken to examine what is happening and what it might mean (e.g. Fielding 2001). It is out of the scope of this introduction to undertake a full analysis of such rich and important texts, but overall the balance sheet does show gains made as a result of New Labour policies and investment. For example, Fielding (2001) identifies:

> Within the overwhelming majority of the contributions to this volume there is genuinely felt goodwill and substantial admiration for the degree of commitment and tenacity shown by the Labour administration: this is a government that clearly cares about a positive, challenging educational experience for all students. Where critique is offered it is done with a view to furthering real, responsive and responsible education policy and practice that has an emancipatory, not an inquisitorial, intent. It is offered in the spirit of genuine dialogue which is the *sine qua non* of real, responsive and responsible democracy.
>
> (Fielding 2001: 7)

More recently, Coffield (2007) concludes an analysis of the New Labour reform model (PMSU 2006) as follows:

> We welcome the improved performance of the education system since 1997 which is visible, for instance, in the marked reductions in the numbers of failing schools and local authorities. Investment has also increased significantly over the same period: funding per pupil has doubled, as has the number of support staff, and there are now 36,000 more teachers than ten years ago . . . We are also in agreement with the basic aim of the government to improve still further the quality of the education service.
>
> (Coffield 2007: 62)

Texts which report on practitioner experiences show that gains have been made locally as a result of particular policies. The collection of papers by Butt and Gunter (2007) on workforce remodelling report headteacher accounts of how renewed investment in information and communications technology (ICT) and the workforce has enabled important changes to take place that is improving standards in teaching and learning. An unpublished survey of headteachers in the North West of England from the School of Education, University of Manchester (see Appendix) shows that the majority of headteachers agreed that the following have had a positive impact: the emphasis on learning rather than teaching, greater flexibility in curriculum development, the national strategies, investment in ICT, buildings and reducing class sizes, use of Performance and Assessment (PANDA) data, target-setting, increased accountability for performance, school-to-school collaboration, national training programmes for heads, *Every Child Matters*, investment in pre-school education and student voice. Indeed, the study reports one headteacher saying: 'For all its faults, the present Labour Government has had an enormous positive effect on education in Britain. Memories are short if those in education can't remember the temporary classrooms and general lack of investment under previous governments.' Certainly, within this book we intend to give recognition to such gains, whether financial investment, process developments and/or outcomes, and we will consider how the spaces created by reforms have enabled opportunities to be created and seized. We take the view, like Steer and Coffield (2007: 1), that as 'critical friends' we do want to make a contribution to the policy process and our work shows that learners are at the centre of our value system and research design. We also want to respect those who have worked hard in these modernizing times to make improvements in their own and others' work. We do not wish to discount this or to trivialize it. However, we want to relate assessments of personal and local gains into a wider picture, and so we will examine how perceptions of gains may misrecognize the underlying trends that are doing longer-term damage to education as a public service. We see our role not only to disseminate what we have found out, but also to speak with and for practitioners and students, and to speak back and against policies that are missing the point or more worryingly doing visible damage.

Headteachers in our study (see Appendix) identify serious concerns. Policies encouraging competition and marketization are seen as problematic. The emphasis on competitive bidding for resources, use of performance tables and private investment in education are negatively assessed. The General Teaching Council (GTC) is overwhelmingly seen as a failure. Some heads also commented that the sheer volume of policies had been problematic: 'too many policies in too short a time to ensure that policies are properly embedded' being a typical comment. Similarly, one respondent commented that 'Headteachers feel justifiably "initiative-ed out"'. What this raises are issues that the wider research community have identified, but there is a more substantial critique of reform that moves beyond technical implementation towards philosophies, values and assumptions. For example, while the collection of papers by Butt and Gunter (2007) do show local gains, there are wider and bigger picture concerns about how workforce remodelling has challenged, weakened and begun to eradicate the role of Qualified Teacher Status (QTS) in the teaching and learning process (Gunter and Butt 2007c), and research by Gunter and Forrester (2008) identifies the shift away in New Labour policies in 1997 from headteachers as school leaders towards generic effective leaders (see DfES/PwC 2007) of localized educational provision. Hence headteachers may be working hard to handle rapid and complex reforms and through this may create the conditions of their own demise (see Chapman et al. 2008; Gunter et al. 2008). Further, while both Fielding (2001) and Coffield et al. (2007) do recognize gains, they also identify the problematics of New Labour reforms with technical implementation through to deeper matters of ongoing damage to the public domain. Tomlinson (2005) encapsulates this nicely:

> no government up to the turn of the century came near to resolving the contradictions involved in greater investment in education and training for all, in a society that still regarded educating the working class and socially excluded with ambivalence and had not yet managed to come to terms with the moderate success of welfare state education. The status division between academic and vocational education persisted. Expanded secondary and tertiary education, which allowed more people to acquire credentials, created anxiety among the middle classes, who feared increased competition and manoeuvred for the positional advantage . . . Disadvantaged groups found raised hurdles and moved goalposts in the struggle to acquire qualifications. The increasingly competitive nature of education meant further control of the reluctant, the disaffected and those 'special needs' groups who were unlikely to join the economy at any but the lowest levels, but whose presence might interfere with the prescribed education for the majority.
>
> (Tomlinson 2005: 8)

The issues raised are ones that are enduring with a body of evidence and conceptual analysis that demonstrates the need for urgent and ongoing attention and engagement.

There are essential continuities with the previous Thatcherite administrations which can be masked by the investment that took place post-1997: first, *neoliberal* modernization based on the protection and advancement of the market in the design and delivery of services that are in the name of the public but are increasingly for private individuals and beneficial to private interests; and second, *regulatory* modernization based on top-down determination and control of national strategy located in the belief dispositions of elite policy-makers, and local implementation where tactics on how to secure reforms (e.g. meet national standards) within context are subject to national performance management based on a pseudo-science of targets, data and evidence. While calculators add up the investment, it is noted that much public money has gone into private hands (Ball 2007; Beckett 2007) and

> the growth in spending on education has over the course of two terms of a Labour government fallen behind transport; is only just ahead of policing and public order; and is less than one percentage point above the long-term growth rate in education spending.
>
> (Driver 2006: 275)

So there are questions to be raised about the beneficiaries of such an investment: children or private philanthropists, and about how government manages the overall investment in modernizing the economy. In Bobbitt's (2002) terms, living through the replacement of the welfare state with the 'market state' where people form human capital as the aggregation of individual consumer choices: a person invests and wins or loses. This is seductive, but as research shows it advantages already advantaged groups (see Ball 2007; P. Woods et al. 2007), and while the language is about choice and diversity, in reality such practice reinforces power structures and sorts and re-sorts people accordingly. This fracturing of the *public* with its ideas and ideals of the citizen, collective and social responsibility, has in our view serious consequences, which researchers must address.

These are important matters producing questions that go to the heart of the public domain and the interrelationship between the state and the economy. Like Fielding (2001) we do see the two main questions as being: 'What is education for?' and 'How might we best achieve our educational purposes?' (Fielding 2001: 9–10), and like Coffield (2007) we don't think the New Labour government has got a model that will deliver their answer to these and other questions we might want to raise. Notably, we want to open up the overemphasis on functionality in educational reform where change can be conceptualized as rational and capable of technical delivery, and scope the opportunities to develop a rationale and series of narratives that are more socially critical (Raffo and Gunter 2008). In doing this we don't intend to reinvent a golden age but we do want to reimagine an approach that conceptualizes and treats all those in the system with trust and respect. We know from research (Gunter and Forrester 2008) that New Labour has invested heavily in headteachers as local deliverers of national reforms (see e.g. DfES 2004a) but we also know that they are both appreciative of this and troubled by it. We know that teachers and children have been excluded from reform decisions and have been objectified as the beneficiaries of a modernization project decided at a distance from where they live and work, and by people who do not necessarily engage in those lives and work. Research shows that this is damaging teachers, children, and ultimately schools and families (Smyth 2006) and that there are alternatives to this through working with teachers and students in policy-making that is educational and professionalizing (Fielding 2006; Hollins et al. 2006; Thomson and Gunter 2006). A key issue that we intend to take on, and will be returned to in the final conclusion, is how those actively involved in education, as teachers, support staff, children, parents, community members and taxpayers, can be enabled to participate and be accountable in ways that stimulate creativity within and about teaching and learning. This directly challenges the school as a self-managing firm conceptualized and legislated for by the previous Thatcherite administrations and sustained and strengthened by New Labour, and begins with people working within and for public service.

Contribution of this book

This book does not intend to supplant what is currently in print but to supplement the emerging evidence about what has happened and what the wider trends indicate. In the School of Education at the University of Manchester we have a team of researchers who have worked on the New Labour reforms since 1997 and so are at the forefront of these matters. We have a research programme that embraces all the major areas of New Labour investment: workforce preparation and training; curriculum strategies; accountability and inspection; leadership; inclusion; *Every Child Matters*; collaboration and multi-agency working; standards and testing; extended schools; workforce remodelling; education and poverty. There have been commissioned projects funded by national and local agencies, as well as independent organizations such as unions; and we have held esteemed grants such as the Joseph Rowntree Foundation and the ESRC. Uniquely we have research evidence and critical analysis on the major reforms of the past decade, and we can confidently say that the University of Manchester is leading the way in areas of education policy analysis, urban education and disadvantage, inclusion, school effectiveness, educational leadership, and school improvement. A major contribution is being made to understanding and explaining how public policy is formed, understood and experienced. We can comment upon and provide new insights into what the New Labour lexicon of choice and diversity, standards and accountability, and modernization and communities actually mean in practice for those working within this culture of change.

Nevertheless we present a health warning: first, the projects and research reported are not part of a grand scheme but have emerged on the basis of planned research by individuals and teams together with the opportunities that have presented themselves for commissioned research; second, while we are a School of Education with agreed goals we are not a uniform group with the same ontological and epistemological positions, interests, methods and ways of working. Scholarly work does not need a uniform vision and a mission but it needs the conditions in which ideas can develop and working with a range of practitioners in local settings can flourish. There is evidence in this book of research for policy and about policy, people take different positions regarding the politics of reform. In many ways the book is illuminative of 'productive pluralism' that one of us has advocated (Gunter and Fitzgerald 2008) where a range of work is seen as legitimate within the field of educational research and policy studies in particular. This presents challenges as it could seem that 'anything goes' and hence contradiction and inconsistency are validated and the book becomes at best a pot-pourri and at worst a scrapbook. We would challenge such a characterization because we set out to represent a range of knowledge claims and arguments with the intention of demonstrating that within a democracy all can make a contribution to dialogue and that a vibrant School of Education is a place where this can be productive. We can agree and disagree, sometimes simultaneously, and this forms a healthy and necessary culture for intellectual work and argument. Some, in Young's (2008) terms, are involved mainly in 'political' debates, others are more involved in 'theoretical' debates, while some move between the two. What matters is that we need to recognize what we are doing, where the border is, and our particular terrain in a university as distinct from a non-departmental public body (NDPB). In this sense we try to model the type of polity that we would wish to see sustaining education policy-making, where a range of voices is heard and that decision-making which necessarily involves selection and position-taking is transparent in the relationship between the state, public policy and knowledge. We don't pretend to do this well all of the time, and we would expect that this is understood and respected by readers because our individual and group projects grow over time and in context.

Following this introductory chapter is an opening scoping account by Andy Hargreaves, who was the Simon Visiting Professor in the School of Education in 2007; his contribution to the School and to the book is to provide an insider/outsider perspective. During his career Hargreaves has developed a deep understanding of education systems and educational change. In this chapter he draws on his extensive knowledge to reflect from a position across the Atlantic on decent developments within the English context.

The book is divided into four broad clusters of chapters. The first examines a central mantra of New Labour education policy regarding Standards and Accountability. There are three chapters: Muijs and Chapman examine the interconnection that has been made by policy-makers between improvement and functional accountability, where they examine the rhetorical claims of New Labour, Webb focuses directly on primary schools by comparing developments to those in Finland. Bragg and Boyle draw on a decade of data to examine what the National Curriculum and testing has done to curriculum design and the experiences that children have as a result. Within the context of this regime of accountability testing

The second cluster examines the escalation of central intervention by New Labour, but begun under the Thatcherite administrations, into the composition and training of the education workforce. Forrester and Gunter examine the leadership imperative as a keystone to the New Labour reform process where headteachers were identified as local implementers. Woods examines the role of school business managers in the workforce reforms in regard to their role and training. Finally for this grouping, McNamara provides an overview of what has taken place in regard to the preparation and accreditation of teacher training, and how this is playing out in three out of the four home nations in the UK.

While national standards and personal accountability are key features of the New Labour decade, this is juxtaposed with choice and diversity within this book. The third cluster has three chapters: one by Mongon and Chapman that describes the restructuring of education with a range of provision such as specialist, academy and trust schools. Howes and Frankham take head on the 'network' word, and critically examine what it could mean, and problematize its conceptual development and use. Similarly, West and Muijs confront personal-ization, and track its development, not least its use and misuse with a current rebranding by the New Labour governments.

The imperative to ensure that all children are safe and central to reform and professional practice is the focus of the final cluster. Here the *Every Child Matters* agenda is examined by three chapters, beginning with Dyson, Farrell, Kerr and Mearns, who examine the construction and operation of multi-agency work in the new children's services. Hall and Raffo tackle the evidence base for the relationship between education and poverty, and how New Labour policy has targeted its resources. Finally for this grouping, Ainscow, Dyson, Goldrick and Kerr present how in the Centre for Equity by using a Development and Research Approach, they are working with schools and wider stakeholders.

The book concludes with two chapters. John Smyth was the Simon Visiting Professor in the School of Education in 2008, and together with Helen M. Gunter has studied the underlying rationale for New Labour strategy and policy. They examine in particular the testing and accountability regime and show the links with neoliberal values, thinking and practices. They present an alternative agenda to the dominance of the market and call for politics to be restored as the means by which decisions, not least public decisions about resources, are agreed. Finally, Chapman and Gunter return to the key themes of the book, and examine how the identified trajectories seem to be working their way through and what the prospects are for the next decade. Unsurprisingly, they present an agenda that is based on returning to educational matters in regard to the starting point for reforms.

2　Labouring to lead

Andy Hargreaves

Introduction

This book comes at the end of a decade of Labour government in the UK. It has been a dizzying period. Under the banner of modernization, where Old Labour and old ways gave way to New Labour and modern thinking, England especially has undergone remarkable social and economic change.

Middle-class UK, like many other developed economies, has seen unprecedented prosperity. Even moderate earners have turned into property owners and speculators, boosting consumer spending and incurring increasing debt with the almost sure knowledge that ever-rising property values would cover their credit. Disposable income and inexpensive travel changed twentieth-century England into an EasyJet society where stag nights in Vilnius or romantic trysts in Vienna gave almost everyone feelings of affluence and aspiration. But now the boom is over, house prices are falling and the credit crunch is on. From now on, we're going to need more knowledge, creativity and innovation to stay ahead, not a blow-out of spend, spend, spend! Blue-sky Blair has given way to Brown. Some city centres have become night-time nightmares; knives are the new must-have accessory of adolescents and among 21 countries surveyed by UNICEF (2007), the UK ranks dead last in child well-being. Cheaper foreign travel has not cultivated greater generosity towards immigrants. In society and in education, it's time to put the culture of booze and bling behind us and to search for something more innovative, inclusive and inspirational instead.

At the end of the twentieth century, this is what New Labour claimed to be about. They called it the Third Way. Tony Blair wrote a pamphlet on it. Bill Clinton called an international meeting of world leaders in Washington to discuss and develop it. Theoretical guru and former director of the London School of Economics, Anthony Giddens, devoted a whole body of work to it (Giddens 1998, 2000, 2001).

The Third Way proposed a set of principles and strategies that stood between and beyond two preceding and competing directions:

- Extensive state investment in welfare, medicine, transport and energy resources, housing, municipal services, pensions and education that had characterized the three decades after the Second World War.

- Full or partial privatization of these services along with market competition for and among clients and providers of them.

Despite providing social services and opportunities for everyone, Giddens (1998) argued, the social state had expanded far beyond what its creators had first envisaged, it had become unsustainably expensive, and it had fostered long-term dependency and even irresponsibility among hard-core recipients. The market, meanwhile, had not only promoted individual initiative and responsibility, but also made social safety nets unacceptably threadbare and created self-centred cultures of individualism and divisiveness. The professions had great freedom and autonomy in the First Way, but in the Second Way, they were more subject to government interference and market forces. What the Third Way promised was more creative combinations of public, private and voluntary solutions, top-down with bottom-up initiatives and professional engagement that did not extend to unrestricted licence, in order to further the goals of economic prosperity and an inclusive social democracy.

The antecedents of and promise of the Third Way have been strikingly apparent in educational strategy – the centrepiece of Labour's reform agenda. These patterns are not completely peculiar to England but are also characteristic of a number of other Anglo-Saxon countries especially. The argument in this chapter is that the Third Way of Educational Change has become a distorted and disfigured version of what it ideally promised to be and that is in need of supercession by a Fourth Way, or in some ways, 'true' Third Way if we are to achieve the greater economic competitiveness and social cohesion that the Third Way originally promised.

The First Way

In the context of the United States and Canada, Ivor Goodson, Dean Fink and I, along with other colleagues, in our project on *Change Over Time*, investigated the experiences of educational change over thirty years in four innovative and four traditional secondary schools (Hargreaves 2003; Hargreaves and Fink 2006; Hargreaves and Goodson 2006). Periodization of these cases in terms of identifying moments of dramatic change, or significant turning points within these schools, revealed patterns somewhat similar to the First, Second and Third ways of policy, and these patterns have their parallels also in England, albeit with a slightly different chronology.

From the 1960s until the late 1970s, this research has shown, teachers worked in an era of optimism and flexible innovation, for which many of those still working in the system felt profoundly nostalgic. Some, especially those who had been drawn to more innovative environments, were nostalgic for the professional freedom and flexibility to develop and adapt curriculum to fit the diverse learning needs of the children in their classes in pursuit of a world-changing social as well as educational mission. The present emphasis on standardized curriculum, excessive testing and intrusive inspection, they felt, had taken away this Golden Age and stolen their mission from them. Another group of teachers, more often in traditional schools, were equally nostalgic, but for different reasons. They too resented the loss of autonomy, but to teach traditional subjects, in the ways they chose, irrespective of how students responded to it, or how it meshed with the preceding and succeeding curriculum. These teachers hearkened back to an age of smaller secondary schools, where underachievers left early, all the others could learn and Christian hymns could be sung in assembly without thought for religious diversity. The age of optimism and innovation may not have been one of lower standards, as some claim, but it was certainly one where quality was subject to the lottery of school leadership among individual school heads. My first solely authored book, *Two Cultures of Schooling*, based on research in the mid 1970s, depicted how huge differences could exist between traditional and progressive middle schools in England, for example, and how the teaching varied dramatically even within these middle schools, depending on whether teachers were recruited from ex-primary or ex-secondary backgrounds, and on how the schools were led (Hargreaves 1986).

The theories of change-in-action during this First Way could start innovation and even spread it among enthusiasts. However, the skill base of teacher education rested more on intuition and ideology than on evidence, and there was no leadership development to create any consistency of impact or effort.

The interregnum

After the First Way, a transitional period set in – an interregnum of complexity and contradiction. From the late 1970s to the mid 1990s overseas and the late 1980s in England a declining economy quelled the thirst for innovation while encouraging a focus on market-driven competition among schools. Common educational standards and assessments (around which competition would be based) emerged as a way to create more coherence across the system. At the same time, people continued to preserve some of the ideals of the First Way. The results were complex and often contradictory.

In North America, outcomes-based education and standards-based reform tried to build common understandings of and commitments to more challenging learning defined in terms of very broad standards, but teachers struggled to translate these guidelines into practice. Portfolio assessments were paralleled by standardized tests, interdisciplinary initiatives ran alongside subject-based standards, and partly selective magnet schools (similar to specialist schools) also had to include students with special educational needs.

The theory of change-in-action was designed to increase standards and develop higher order knowledge by getting teachers and schools to address them together, while leaving enough room for intelligent professional judgement and interpretation in practice. The more innovative schools that had leaders who could help teachers interpret the complexity together, succeeded in maintaining their missions while still addressing the standards. The traditional schools, however, drifted into decline as their leaders overprotected their staffs and shielded them from the reform requirements until it was too late. Here, teachers complained when the standards were too general and confusing and when local districts responded by making them too specific and detailed. The problems were not in the standards but in how many leaders and their school communities failed to make sense of them. This theory-in-action lacked investment in the system-wide professional development and leadership development that was required to build the strong and intelligent learning communities that could interpret the standards and define their purposes together (Hargreaves et al. 2001).

In the UK, much of the 1980s was marked by efforts to create more consistency and coherence in the curriculum and develop a new educational consensus. Following on from the Great Debate of the 1970s, this age witnessed many efforts to establish new directions and also stronger coherence, but the efforts and effects were also often contradictory. The Keith Joseph period of the early 1980s witnessed animated and passionate discussions about the need to dramatically reform secondary schools, David Hargreaves (1982) provided outstanding intellectual leadership in drawing together conservative and radical definitions of community along with different forms of achievement to inspire reform in the Inner London Education Authority and elsewhere. Her Majesty's Inspectorate (HMI) devised seven then eight areas of curricular experience as a way to try to define the basis of balance, breadth and coherence (HMI 1983a). And energetic initiatives took place in secondary and especially vocational education within a number of local authorities where Records of Achievement blazed the trail for what we now call assessment for learning; where the Technical and Vocational Educational Initiative (TVEI) and City Technology Colleges (CTCs) created the modular curricular options that were the forerunners of personalized learning, and where personal and social education programmes also proliferated, laying the groundwork for their reinvention in the form of Personal, Social and Health Education (PSHE) and mentoring schemes in the present. My books on *Curriculum and Assessment Reform* (Hargreaves 1989) and on *Personal and Social Education* (Hargreaves et al. 1988) documented these developments and their effects.

In this time of potential paradigm shift, great local education authorities (LEAs) with leaders like Robert Aitken and Tim Brighouse worked with the complexity and seized the moment to push forward progressive innovations that benefited all kinds of students in a responsive, challenging and authentic way. Weaker local authority leadership, however, turned modules into curricular chaos and Records of Achievement into time-wasting paperwork and bureaucracy. The problem of educational leadership in England at this time was therefore at the LEA level, where once more, there was no investment in or attention to improving its quality and consistency.

The Second Way

Frustration with years of inconsistency, coupled with political and public nostalgia for tradition, competition and certainty, helped propel many nations into a strident Second Way of standardization and market competition. Fuelled by free market ideologies and fanned by the parallel presence of increasingly autocratic state control, many Anglo-Saxon governments, with lesser or greater degrees of resources and support, imposed prescriptive and sometimes punitive reforms in the shape of increased competition between schools fuelled by public rankings of high-stakes test and exam results.

- Prescribed, paced and sometimes scripted curriculum content in more narrowly defined areas and goals of learning.
- Periodic inspections and management walk-throughs to boost skill development and enforce classroom compliance.
- Political targets and timetables for delivering improved results.
- Principal removal or even school closure when failure persisted.
- Teacher training that was increasingly moved away from the academy towards on-the-job training in schools.
- Replacement of broad professional development by in-service training on government priorities.

In England, this Second Way was most evident in the creation of a detailed National Curriculum in 1988, the pervasive impact of Standard Attainment Tests (SATs), the intrusive influence of OfSTED and the strict demands of the timed and scripted National Literacy and Numeracy Strategies, along with increasing privatization of services, public rankings of school performance, increased parental choice between schools and reduction of local authority control.

Opinions vary about the necessity of this national strategy. Some, like Sir Michael Barber, have regarded it as a necessary device to develop a sense of urgency, secure public support for educational investment and move the profession in a common and accountable direction. Others claim that the same goals could have been achieved by less punitive, prescriptive and pejorative means. Whatever side is taken, there is increasing agreement that the strategy of standardization is, however, now worn out. Achievement results hit a plateau, primary school parents complained about loss of pleasure in their children's learning because of excessive emphasis on test-prep for the SATs, cheating scandals became increasingly widespread, and difficulties in teacher retention and leadership recruitment pointed to a crisis of professional motivation in the nation's educational system. The curriculum became more lopsided and less creative as all energies were directed towards increasing measured performance. The effects in other countries were similar, as my research documents in *Teaching in the Knowledge Society* (Hargreaves 2003). Scotland had always eschewed the excesses of targets and standardization. Wales determined to abandon them altogether until well into the secondary school years. Northern Ireland proposes to abolish the eleven-plus, the nearest thing to them. If the age of standardization was becoming chronically sick, then the patient was a predominantly English one. The Second Way of standardization and marketization increased coherence, certainty and accountability, but at the price of innovation, motivation and creativity. There had to be a better way.

The Third Way

Something resembling a Third Way has therefore begun to evolve in many English-speaking jurisdictions. The Third Way of Blairism has increased support for and interest in state education. It has restored financial support in many areas of state education and other public services especially within cities and urban renewal, and yet also extended privatized Second Way strategies even further in others such as in the corporate investment in specialist schools and academies, and in private takeovers of failing local authorities.

The Third Way forms the corpus of this book, promoting more lateral energy to increase motivation among students, teachers and leaders through the creation of more personalized learning; increased emphasis on leadership development; promotion of network-driven improvement to increase achievement; connection of schools to other child services; and even small-scale efforts to encourage more innovation in order to develop the learning and capacities required by advanced knowledge economies.

In practice, though, much of what has passed for the Third Way has been the emergence of a new kind of autocratic and all-seeing state that has used technological and data-driven self-surveillance (data-driven or evidence-based improvement) along with some emotional effervescence in lateral professional interactions to deliver unchanging and even more autocratically asserted government goals. Literacy and numeracy remain pre-eminent even when systemic achievement in them is already high by international standards, as in Australia and in Ontario, Canada. This degree of curriculum prescriptiveness and continued testing in literacy has been virulently criticized by children's authors J.K. Rowling and Philip Pullman, pilloried in movie drama by celebrated film director Mike Leigh and caustically challenged by international arts advocate Sir Ken Robinson. Meanwhile, although networks have some success in securing short-term test gains, the political culture of targets and testing undermines longer-term or more innovative efforts. Personalized learning often falls short of lifelong learning that connects students' learning to wider life projects, and instead becomes a customized way to access existing forms of conventional learning – individually or cooperatively, slower or faster, online or offline, within one learning style or another – as young people meet with their academic 'progress managers' every few weeks to subject themselves to the relentless surveillance of their advancement or not in measured achievement towards agreed targets. The Third Way was meant to be a strategy of development, but it has degenerated into a slickly spun system of delivery.

The Third Way has become even more politically autocratic than the Second in its stipulation and micromanagement of goals, performance and targets; it has instituted testing and data collection as an inescapable and anticipatory system of endless surveillance where schools and teachers now monitor themselves in relation to performance goals and targets, adjusting every curriculum emphasis, professional development choice, workshop strategy and student conversation in relation to the next looming deadline of tested achievement; and it has turned potentially productive professional interactions between teachers and schools into so much collective effervescence or light and bubbly energy to increase teacher motivation while retaining a tight grip on the form and focus of these conversations that remain tied to improving measured performance in tested basics. The technocratic rhetoric is to raise the bar and narrow the gap, but while it is certainly true that having the posts that support the bar too far apart so there is no focus at all will lead it to sag as in the First Way, keeping the posts too close together so the goal is only tested achievement, will make the bar unstable and unsustainable and cause it to topple.

An initiative that exemplifies some of the more positive aspects of Third Way thinking while struggling and striving to get beyond its limitations within the context of Blair's Labour has been the more than 300 secondary schools in the Raising Achievement/Transforming Learning (RATL) project of the Specialist Schools and Academies Trust (SSAT). My evaluation of this project with Dennis Shirley and other colleagues (Shirley and Hargreaves 2006) highlights how two-thirds of the schools improved at double the rate of the national average over two years through the use of a specific design or architecture of improvement which

- emphasized improvement by schools, with schools in peer-driven networks of lateral pressure and support where the peer factor replaces the fear factor as the key driver in raising standards
- combined outside-in knowledge of experts at conferences, with inside-out knowledge of successful and experienced practitioners working openly and inclusively with less successful colleagues in transparent processes (not just outcomes) of assistance and support
- made mentor schools available to lower performing peers in cultures of strong expectation for improvement within transparent lateral systems, but not mandating these mentor relationships in general or in any particular case
- supplied modest amounts of additional resourcing to facilitate these improvements and interactions
- provided clear, practical menus of short-term, medium-term and long-term strategies for improvement and transformation with proven success among experienced administrators.

The evaluation of this network and intervention points to the undoubted success and promise of this professionally peer-driven strategy of the strong helping the weak in cultures of committed and transparent improvement, especially in relation to short-term goals. At the same time, it also highlights the limitations imposed by continuing standardization and data-driven surveillance in the surrounding policy environment – in the unrelenting emphasis on SAT scores in basic subjects, in hit-and-run OfSTED inspections that over-rely on printed achievement data rather than direct observation to assess the satisfactoriness of schools, and on unending waves of short-term government initiatives. As a result, lateral network activity focuses disproportionately on short-term improvements in delivering existing learning rather than long-term transformations towards creating different and better teaching and learning. In effect, lateral professional energy and motivation is being harnessed and even hijacked to deliver unquestioned government purposes and targets in conventionally tested learning more efficiently and even more enthusiastically, rather than contributing to a redefinition of those educational purposes in a more visionary, inclusive and transformational way that is appropriate to life and learning in the twenty-first century. The RATL project and other promising Labour initiatives to develop more innovation illustrate the promise of Third Way strategies but also quickly rub up against their limitations.

The Fourth Way

To get a sense of how lateral professional and public energy might be used not to manipulate the public and profession into conforming with politically determined purposes but to contribute in an active and democratic way to those very purposes themselves, we need to move to a place that achieves outstanding results without and beside standardization. Such places already exist and we have too much to learn from them.

In 2007, with colleagues Beatriz Pont and Gabor Halász, I led a team for OECD to Finland, to examine the relationship between leadership and school improvement in the world's number one performer at age 15 in literacy, maths and science in the influential OECD Programme for International Student Assessment (PISA) rankings (Hargreaves et al. 2007). Finland also ranks top in economic competitiveness and corporate transparency. How does Finland achieve these remarkable results that include some of the narrowest achievement gaps in the world?

- After being one of the most backward economies in Europe in the 1950s, and after an international banking crisis, the loss of its Russian market, and the escalation of unemployment rates to almost 19 per cent in the early 1990s, Finland consciously connected economic transformation towards being a creative and flexible knowledge economy to the development of a significantly more decentralized educational system.
- This effort is coordinated at the highest political level where chief executives from leading companies like Nokia meet regularly with university presidents on a science and technological development committee chaired by the

prime minister. Indeed Anthony Giddens and his Finnish colleagues argue that Finland is already a classic and successful Third Way society, as originally conceived (Giddens 1998).

- The coherence, however, is not merely bureaucratic and governmental, but visionary and inspirational. Finns have a common vision that connects their creative high-tech future to their past as a creative, craft-like people. There are more composers per capita in Finland than any other developed country, and all young people engage in creative and performing arts to the end of their secondary education.

- This vision is shared at every level and accords teaching high status among all Finns since teachers create their country's future as a creative and inclusive nation. Though paid only at the OECD average, teaching in Finland is highly competitive with only a one in ten chance of acceptance. Retention is very high because conditions are good along with feelings of professional trust so training costs remain low. Finns control quality at the most important point – the point of entry.

- Within broad guidelines, or steering by the state, highly qualified teachers then create curriculum together in each municipality for the children they know best. Curriculum and pedagogy are not separated – they are in a common tradition of didactics. The sense of delivering a curriculum devised by others from afar is utterly alien to them.

- The vision and quality bind teachers in every school together in cultures of trust, cooperation and responsibility for every child, not just children in their own classes.

- In small classes rarely larger than 20, and with generous definitions of special educational need, the push for quality is driven largely by quietly lifting all children up from the bottom, one at a time, through knowing them well in small classes, not having to deal with excessive paperwork and endless external initiatives, and having specialist support as needed.

- Principals work across schools, sharing resources where they are needed, and feeling responsible together for all the children and young people in their town and city, not competitively only for the children in their own school.

- Assessment strategies are largely diagnostic forms of assessment for learning and internal to the school. External accountability is confidential and undertaken on a sample basis for monitoring purposes only.

- Principals are seen as being part of a 'society of equals' in their schools, not as line managers. They are often recruited from within their schools and they engage in considerable informal distributed leadership with their colleagues. It is illegal for a principal to be recruited from outside education, and all principals teach for at least two hours per week. They are able to do this, they say, because they are not inundated with requirements to respond to endless imposed initiatives like the Anglo-Saxon countries. Teachers say that if the principal is indisposed or ineffective, they take over the school because the school belongs to all of them, not just to the principal.

Peer-driven reform through trust, cooperation and responsibility is possible among high quality professionals attracted and rewarded by a compelling social vision, not by salary adjustments or status gimmicks. England has no such compelling social vision. Unlike Scotland, Northern Ireland or Wales, it has no distinctive sense of who or what it is. England imagines itself to be imperial and all-encompassing Britain minus the Celtic fringe and can therefore neither advance nor articulate a compelling and inclusive vision and identity. The educational result is a regression to arithmetical achievement gaps or vacuous claims to world-class standards as evasions rather than articulations of any such vision. In the end, therefore, English education comes across as an accumulation of competitive private interest and opportunity rather than an articulation of a compelling, inclusive and inspiring public good.

Until England can find its identity, or redefine it for an inclusive twenty-first century, it will not be able to attract or retain the highest quality people in the profession, as the keepers of that vision for the nation's next generation. It will be able to move neither beside nor beyond the age of standardization, in ways that the Welsh are now pursuing and that many European nations have already proven leads to stronger international success. It will not be able to emulate mainland European neighbours in their quest for innovation and creativity, as evidenced in 2009 being the European Commission's Year of Innovation and Creativity. England will continue to reduce the public good of English education to the accumulated private interests of a population that has too often seemed more interested in the value of its property than in the properties of its values. Only another approach to change, a Fourth Way, can move England ahead. What might such a Fourth Way look like?

Inspired by a commitment to more innovative and inclusive goals for the future, informed by an effort to identify and learn from the best of the past, and enlightened by high-performing exemplars such as Finland in the present, a Fourth Way of educational and social change brings together government policy with professional involvement and public engagement as equal partners in the pursuit and fulfilment of a common, inspiring and inclusive social and educational mission.

The theory-in-action of the Fourth Way consists of five pillars of purpose and partnership, three principles of professionalism and four catalysts of coherence.

Five pillars of purpose and partnership

A viable theory-in-action of educational change must rest on the basic principles of sustainability and the original meaning of the verb to sustain, which means not merely to maintain or endure, but also to hold up or bear the weight of something. What ultimately bears the weight of sustainable educational change is not an overarching set of government policies and interventions, but people working together as partners around shared and compelling purposes. Sustainable educational change therefore rests, first of all, on five pillars of purpose and partnership.

- *An Inspiring and Inclusive Vision* that draws people together in pursuit of an uplifting common purpose that connects them to something bigger than themselves, links an innovative future to the best of a nation's past, and draws the best people into the education profession. What is Britain's inspiring and inclusive vision and how is that expressed in its collective educational aspirations?
- *Deepened Public Engagement* beyond elite representation, focus group consultation or increased consumer choice for parents, that inspires another Great Public Debate about the future of education – in 2020, say – as a public and not merely a private and individual good, city by city, town by town.
- *Achievement Through Investment* where social policy is no longer only about outputs and test-based achievement gaps for which professionals are solely responsible, but also reconnects with the First Way's emphasis on inputs as a shared social responsibility to support and create better opportunities for the poor, through increased investment in educational facilities and other social services. *Building Schools for the Future* and *Excellence in Cities* have been good starts but investment in other social developments, and expectations that parents have responsibilities as well as teachers need to be part of the new narrative of reform.
- *Corporate Educational Responsibility* where the corporations that contribute to public educational and educational reform, at any and every level, are expected and required to practise Corporate Social Responsibility in a relationship where educational and business partners are equally accountable.
- *Students as Partners in Change* rather than merely targets of change efforts and services, so that they become more involved in their own learning and learning choices, are actively consulted about the quality and improvement of teaching, and substantially engaged in the overall governance of the school and its development.

Three principles of professionalism

Teachers are the ultimate arbiters of change. They are also often the initiators of it within their own schools and classrooms. The classroom door is the portal to implementation or the drawbridge that holds it at bay. No theory-in-action of sustainable educational change can ignore or bypass the teacher. As in Finland, it must involve teachers not only in delivering pedagogical details, but also in determining the basic purposes of their work. Three principles of professionalism are indispensable components of any sustainable theory-in-action of educational change.

- *High Quality Teachers* who are attracted by their country's inspiring and inclusive vision that also accords high status to them as builders of their nation's future, who enjoy supportive working conditions as well as sufficient pay and professional autonomy, and who are trained to a rigorous intellectual and practical standard that is the hallmark of any demanding profession.

- *Powerful Professionalism* in which much of the professional quality agenda is driven by a self-regulating professional body in teaching like those in medicine or law, that sets rigorous professional teaching standards for its members as well as the more customary dealing with disciplinary and registration issues or offering of symbolic commentary.
- *Lively Learning Communities* where teachers learn and improve together in lively cultures of collaboration, trust and responsibility that include substantive commitment to curriculum development as well as pedagogical change and intelligent conversation between evidence and experience, rather than cooperation being mainly focused on short-term, contrived and bolted-on efforts to analyse performance data in order to raise test scores or narrow numerical achievement gaps in time for the upcoming standardized assessment.

Four catalysts of coherence

The hardest part of any theory-in-action in educational change is not how to start it, but how to make it spread. Detailed prescription and alignment increase consistency but at the cost of depth, breadth and complexity. The challenge of coherence is not to clone or align everything so it looks the same in all schools. Rather, it is how to bring diverse people together to work skillfully and effectively for a common cause that lifts them up and has them moving in the same direction. The Fourth Way has four catalysts that create this coherence.

- *Sustainable Leadership* that is integral to educational change, not its afterthought. Effective leaders pull their communities together to achieve a common purpose. They were the ones that made the difference in previous periods of educational change. The effort has become much more co-ordinated in recent years but mainly around building capacity by increasing leadership supply through emerging, aspiring and accelerated leadership programmes. Change efforts must now also address the excessive demands that deter many potential leaders from stepping up to the number 1 position in the school, and policy strategies must go beyond treating leaders as mere managers and implementers of imposed targets and external initiatives, to become developers of their communities. Singapore now advises 'Teach Less, Learn More'. *We* could say the same systemically: 'Reform Less, Improve More'.
- *Networks of Mutual Learning* with specific architectures where schools support and learn from schools, become collectively responsible for all the children in their city or community, and commit to systems and dispositions where the strong help the weak – but where governments refrain from over-regulating the networks they initiate or support.
- *Responsibility Before Accountability* where collective professional responsibility has a higher and prior priority compared to external accountability and where external accountability is organized by samples that monitor standards

of practice rather than by a politically controlling census, which tends to distort that practice.

- *Building from the Bottom; Steering from the top* – not letting a thousand flowers bloom, or micromanaging everything in detail or even retaining top-down control over narrowly defined goals and targets with the assistance of technocratic surveillance and effervescent interactions. The Fourth Way, rather, is a democratic and sustainable path to improvement that builds from the bottom and steers from the top.

Conclusion

As educationalists, we should be able to learn what to keep and what to throw away from each of the three ways of change. The spirit of innovation and flexibility of the First Way can restore the capacity of teachers to create much of their own curriculum, and to rekindle the inspiration of world-changing social and educational missions that bind teachers together and connect them to ideals beyond themselves. From the interregnum, we can take the guiding power of broadly defined common standards, and the technical advances of portfolio and performance assessments that began to make assessment part of learning. Even the Second Way of standardization has bequeathed a sense of urgency about standards and equity, drawn attention to the needs of all students in every school, improved the quality of some skill-specific training, coaching and teaching, and highlighted the benefits of using achievement data to inform teachers' judgements and interventions. Last, while the educational realization of the Third Way has departed from and distorted some of its highest ideals, it has also purged the discourses of shame that characterized the Second Way, increased resources for and confidence in public education, developed a more sophisticated evidence base for improvement, given more support and recognition to the teaching profession, and stimulated professional learning, improvement and support across schools. These shrewdly selected legacies can lay important foundations for the way ahead.

In the Fourth Way, a robust social democracy builds an inspiring and inclusive vision that draws teachers to the profession and grants them public status within it; it involves parents and the public as highly engaged partners and also draws on as well as making a contribution to the development of corporate educational responsibility. In the Fourth Way, a lot is expected of educators, but the burden of narrowing achievement gaps and achieving social justice does not rest on their shoulders alone. It is shared with a strongly supported health service, housing system and social service sector. In all this, students in the Fourth Way are not merely targets of change but vigorous and active partners in its development.

The Fourth Way achieves coherence by assigning huge priority to the development of sustainable and distributed leadership that is knowledgeable about learning; by placing responsibility before accountability (with account-ability serving as a conscience through sampling); by initiating and supporting but not over-regulating professional networks of improvement; and – most of all – by developing an inspiring and inclusive educational and societal vision that connects the future to the past, and leaves teachers collectively responsible for pedagogical decisions and a lot of curriculum development. The Third Way of Change has already done a great deal to demonstrate the power of increased professional energy, but it has increased central political control at the price of innovation and creativity. It is time for a Fourth Way to harness increased professional learning and energy to more inspiring and inclusive purposes of creativity, sustainability and democracy. It is time for the public to rediscover its collective spirit, for the profession to find its voice again and for the government to learn to let go. Times are changing, new professional generations are emerging, and people are coming out of their consumer cocoons. Our future is not going to be standardized. Why should our schools be?

The chapters in this book take on the ideas and issues such as standardization in depth. A challenge for the reader draws on the evidence and arguments presented in the following chapters to reflect on which elements need to be kept, which need to be developed and what should be ejected from the three ways of change. Furthermore, and perhaps most importantly, how may the Fourth Way of change play out in practice?

3   Accountability for improvement

Rhetoric or reality?

Daniel Muijs and Christopher Chapman

Introduction

This chapter considers the rise of accountability systems as a lever for school improvement within education systems. A number of educational systems around the world have adopted approaches based on high levels of accountability. For example, in the United States 'high-stakes' testing and the No Child Left Behind Act 2002 tend to dominate a culture of performativity and accountability (Meiner and Wood 2004). A number of systems in developing countries have also adopted such approaches; in Malawi systematic inspection has been introduced as a lever for school improvement (West 2003) and several European countries have developed various accountability systems which are underpinned by the elements of inspection combined with use of performance data and target-setting (Zachariou 2008).

For the purposes of this chapter we draw on the English experience as an example of a 'high-stakes accountability system' where league tables and inspection reports are integral to a government orthodoxy attempting to drive up school standards in order to compete within a globalized economy. Most aspects of this system emerged from the Education Acts of 1988 and 1992, products of the neoliberal Conservative government of the time. However, when New Labour took office in 1997 and set its stall out, claiming its inheritance included some positive aspects such as the introduction of regular independent inspection of all schools and the publication of school performance tables, the government intended to build on rather than replace some of the previous administration's attempts to improve the system. When Michael Barber (2001a; Barber and Sebba 1999), one of the New Labour architects of change, argued to move from the relatively underperforming system of the mid 1990s to a world-class system for the twenty-first century, the context for change required attention, not least because the previous administration had attempted to change the system by identifying problems and increasing the level of challenge, neglecting to increase levels of support needed to counter conflict and demoralization within the system. New Labour's belief was that excellent education systems are underpinned by high levels of challenge and support which would lead to, in its terms, 'a framework for continuous improvement' (Barber 2001a). This framework remained sharp with a focus on raising standards, accountability, data and targets but added supporting elements including devolved responsibility and an intention to provide high quality professional development.

This chapter focuses on three key dimensions of accountability that have emerged since the late 1980s. First, we consider the development and impact of standardized inspection, second, the use of performance data, and third, we investigate target-setting as a lever for school improvement. In conclusion, we reflect on these developments and speculate how such policies may need to evolve if they are to retain or improve their relevance within a changing educational context.

Improvement through inspection

Recent developments in school inspection in England

The history of school inspection in England can be traced back to the 1800s but the current regime emerged from the Education (Schools) Act 1992, which provided the legal framework for the launch of the Office for Standards in Education (OfSTED). This policy, implemented by the Conservative government of the time, set out to inspect and report on the performance of every school in England and to drive up standards; the underpinning rationale was that if schools had to attract students, standards would automatically rise in the face of local competition (Learmonth 2000).

OfSTED's early years were not without controversy. Some commentators claimed the Conservative government had legitimately pitted public interests against the self-interest of the educational establishment in an attempt to demystify the closed world of schools and classrooms (Phillips 1996). Others from within the educational establishment argued the process was demoralizing and de-professionalizing (Gray and Wilcox 1995). A number of studies challenged the value of the OfSTED system of inspection (Office for Standards in Inspection (OfSTIN) 1997) but OfSTED has developed its own research and publications arm to support the claim of 'improvement through inspection' (OfSTED 1994, 1995, 1997, 2000). The Conservative government launched a new framework in 1996, but for the most part implementation would be left to its successors, New Labour. The new framework marked a number of changes to the system including the stretching of the cycle from four to six years for most schools, a reduction in the notice of inspection to between six and ten weeks and an entitlement of individual feedback to teachers on their lesson performance. The new framework moved OfSTED further in to the terrain of school improvement by promoting '*school improvement by identifying priorities for action*' (OfSTED 1996: 2), as well as assessing the school's capacity to manage change and review its internal systems (Earley et al. 1996). However, in many cases the key elements of trust and mutual respect between the inspecting and the inspected remained limited and curtailed OfSTED's contribution to school improvement, therefore the improvements made because of inspection continued to be challenged (Cullingford 1999).

Despite calls for change from within the educational establishment, the election of New Labour heralded more of the same. *Intervention in inverse proportion to success* continued as an overt policy, with schools being identified as failing or *at risk of failing*, being subjected to compressed inspection cycles and public exposure through extravagant local and occasionally national media headlines. However, many teachers and schools were becoming tired of the treadmill of inspection cycles and process seemed to be losing some of its potency. Teachers began to realize that for the most part inspections came and went, policies and plans were prepared, reports were published, but unless there was a crisis not much changed.

A government response to this situation was to create a cycle for continuous improvement through a 'New Relationship' with schools. The Minister for School Standards (Miliband 2004a) outlined the three key aspects of the relationship as being rigorous ongoing self-evaluation combined with focused external inspection, linked into the improvement cycle of the school. Miliband argued that this simplified improvement process underpinned by a 'single conversation' with a School Improvement Partner (SIP) to discuss and negotiate appropriate targets, priorities for development and strategies for support provides the high challenge and high support environment necessary to deliver the progress and performance necessary to become a world-class education system (MacBeath 2006). The new relationship with schools led to significant changes in the inspection system including an increased focus on self-evaluation. The Self-Evaluation Form (SEF) has become the driver of a streamlined inspection that now lasts no more than two days, focuses on the core systems and senior managers, and is informed by statistical data and lesson observations, rather than being led by them. The size of the inspection team is also likely to be smaller than in the past, and probably led by an experienced Her Majesty's Inspector (HMI). Notice of an inspection was also reduced to between two and five days and schools can expect to be inspected once every three years. Inspection reports have also been streamlined from over thirty pages in length to five or six pages and they are presented to the governing body (in at least draft form) the same week of the inspection. Rather than preparing a response to the 'key issues' raised, schools now incorporate their response into the school development plan. The most recent changes to the inspection system have been structural. In April 2007 the four separate inspectorates were merged to form the Office for Standards in Education, Children's Services and Skills (OfSTED). This body is responsible for the inspection and regulation of care for children and young people and the inspection of education and training for learners of all ages including further education (FE) provision and teacher training. This new body aims to raise aspirations and contribute to long-term improvement of standards and life chances of service users (OfSTED 2008).

Inspection and school improvement

Since its introduction in the early 1990s OfSTED has undergone a number of developments, reflecting the changing demands of the political and educational landscapes; in terms of experience and tone current school inspections bear little resemblance to those conducted in the early 1990s. However, despite structural and cultural shifts and the evolution of a more streamlined process, the budget needed to sustain inspection in England remains considerable, totalling £238 million in 2007–08 of which £90 million has been allocated to education (schools, teacher training and joint area reviews of children's services) (OfSTED 2008).

During the early years of OfSTED there was little independent research investigating the contribution of inspections to school improvement (Earley et al. 1996). However, the agency itself produced and continues to produce a plethora of literature to support its claim of 'improvement through inspection' (OfSTED 1995, 1997, 1999a, 2000), the extent to which (or not) OfSTED inspection contributes to school improvement remains contested at a number of levels. One issue is that of reliability of judgement. Fitz-Gibbon (1998) argues that inspectors make inaccurate guesses about progress and the effectiveness of schools. If this is the case, this suggests government may have based national educational policy on inaccurate data (Fitz-Gibbon 1996) obtained through potentially unreliable methodologies (Wilcox and Gray 1996). In turn this may lead to inappropriate priorities for improvement being identified and subsequently, important opportunities for improvement overlooked. Some researchers have considered the impact of inspection prior to the inspection period, arguing notice of inspection can trigger improvements during the run-up period. Improvement efforts include smartening up school buildings (Matthews and Smith 1995) and the preparation of new interactive displays of the pupils' work mounted on walls, high quality of lesson preparation and marking by teachers but that these improvements are likely to be short lived with 'normality returning when the inspection is over' (Gray and Wilcox 1995: 82). It would seem the reduction in notice time is likely to have further eroded any potential for improvement during the build-up period. However, the publication of a three-year cycle allows school leaders to predict when they should be inspected and to prepare accordingly; interestingly we have some evidence to suggest this practice is operating (gleaned from informal con-versations with school leaders after their schools had been inspected during February–March 2008). Other researchers have explored post-inspection impact. Lowe (1998) focuses on the implementation of recommendations one year after inspection. This research highlights a wide variation in how schools respond to inspection and the extent to which recommendations related to teaching and learning are tackled. Other research takes an alternative perspective on classroom change. Brimblecombe et al. (1996) and Chapman (2001) report that approximately one-third of teachers intend to change their practice as a result of inspection and of those, most report they intend to do so as a result of the direct feedback they receive from inspectors (Chapman 2002). However, despite an entitlement to feedback, considerable variations in quality and in quantity to feedback persist (Ferguson et al. 2000). It would seem that lesson observation and quality feedback are potentially important levers for improvement.

One area where we may expect to see inspection making considerable contributions to school improvement is in the weakest schools. Here inspection and performance data suggest that schools identified as *failing* within the system are more likely to sustain the improvement they make after inspection than those that are relatively more effective but still causing concern (Matthews and Sammons 2005) but we see a number of schools being removed from special measures, only to find themselves being placed back in the category after subsequent inspections (Gray 2000). Since 1998 there has been one English secondary school that illustrates the limitations of New Labour's attempt to 'radically reform' schools. During New Labour's reign the Ridings School in Halifax has attracted much media attention, often appearing on the front pages of local and national newspapers. There have been a number of highly resourced, government-backed interventions aimed at improving the educational standards achieved by the school, yet the school never managed to break the cycle of low attainment and underachievement before its recent closure. In 1998 Peter Clark (now a senior government adviser), former headteacher at the school, reflected on the school's future but highlighted the difficulty the school was experiencing prior to New Labour taking office:

> For a few weeks in the autumn of 1996 it was hell for the staff and many of the pupils, but over the next few months together they made the difference, building a secure foundation for its future success.
>
> (Clark 1998: 208)

By 2003 the picture looked brighter and the media (BBC 2003) were reporting the progress made by the school in positive terms, highlighting the fact that the school had achieved targets set by central government:

> future now looks assured after the number of pupils achieving five GCSE grade A★ to C reached 25 per cent – up from 7 per cent last year . . . The results, published on Thursday, show the Ridings has reached exam targets set by government and is even above national average for pupils achieving at least one GCSE A★ to G grade.

Clark's former deputy and successor Anna White and the Schools Standards Minister appeared to share a sense of optimism about the school's future:

> We are absolutely delighted for the students. An awful lot of hard work has gone in to getting to this point and it is a great moment for the school. Hopefully, this is the long awaited turning point.
>
> (Anna White, headteacher, quoted in BBC 2003)

It has been a huge challenge but the commitment from staff has been inspiring. I am delighted the results are moving in the right direction.
(David Milliband, Schools Standards Minister, quoted in BBC 2003)

However, by 2005 it was clear another false dawn had passed and by November, despite the recent appointment of a new headteacher and senior leadership team, the school was judged as inadequate and in March 2007 it was returned to Special Measures. During 2008 it was decided there would be no new intake in September 2008 and the school would be closed in July 2009 within a local reorganization.

This example illustrates the weight of focused inspections, within a compressed inspection cycle and additional HMI monitoring combined with increased resources and targeted school improvement interventions (see for example MacBeath et al. 2007) could not secure continuous improvement. It may be the local context was so important, and the odds staked so highly against the school, that no amount of external intervention would have secured 'improvement through inspection'. However, what is particularly depressing is that inspection was not the only method implemented to improve the situation. The framework for improvement had failed. Increased resources, continuous professional development focusing on teaching and learning, target-setting and use of data were all features of school improvement initiatives. So the lessons would seem to suggest that however one quantifies inspection's contribution to improvement, inspection alone is an insufficient ingredient for success, and in this case the framework for continuous improvement drawing on inspection combined with a raft of additional resources and school improvement initiatives are also insufficiently powerful to overcome the challenging circumstances faced by the school and its community.

Performance data and school improvement

National Tests and Performance tables are another key element of the accountability system implemented in England. These evolutions predate the Labour government and up until the 1980s these tests were seen as a way of sorting students rather than being used as part of an accountability framework for schools. The Education Reform Act 1988 and the Citizens Charter of 1992 led to the publication of exam results by school, in order to provide information parents could use to make rational choice decisions alongside the OfSTED inspection reports (West and Pennell 1997). This information was to be made available in local education authority (LEA) and school prospectuses, and more recently has been published on the central government's website. It is not accurate to say that the government publishes, or has ever published, school league tables. This is done by media outlets such as national and local papers on the basis of the published results, but it is clear that this is an inevitable consequence of the open publication of the school-level data. As well as providing information to parents, this publication of results provided a powerful spur to the desired creation of quasi-markets in education, and an additional lever of accountability and school improvement as competing schools had a powerful incentive to improve their position in local 'league tables' to attract parents.

Prior to the 1997 general election there had been a number of studies critical of the performance tables (e.g. Fitz et al. 1993) and there had been evidence of increasing problems with admissions. However, in their manifesto, while making a commitment to fairer admission procedures and the set-up of adjudication, the Labour Party made clear that national tests and school performance tables would remain. In parallel with inspection this was very much the position taken during the early years of New Labour rule, though, as in other aspects of government education policy, the initial hard line taken was gradually softened, with criticisms of the raw league tables leading to the introduction of value added performance measures, not instead of but alongside the existing raw data. Increasingly feedback on performance to schools was provided in value added form, with schools compared to those statistically similar in Performance and Assessment (PANDA) reports, RAISEonline (Reporting and Analysis for Improvement through School Self-Evaluation website) and in regional initiatives such as the 'Families of Schools' in the London Challenge. Most recently, Contextual Value Added scores, which are a further refinement of value added measures, were introduced in 2007.

Whether published performance data has had the positive impacts on school improvement predicted by its supporters remains unclear. First, it has long been clear that socio-economic status (SES) is related to the ability to access the necessary information and to navigate the vagaries of the school choice system, meaning that parental choice tends to lead to middle-class parents having greater opportunities to select the school of their choice for their children (Ball and Gewirtz 1999). There is an irony here, in that school effectiveness research has shown that the impact of schools is up to three times stronger for pupils from lower than those from higher SES backgrounds (Muijs and Reynolds 2002). The fact that schools compete in the quasi-market, with the 'prize' being more middle-class pupils (leading to better performance in the league tables), has led to an inevitable polarization of schools, with a minority of schools left with those pupils hardest to teach. The other negative impacts of the testing regime are also well known. Teaching to the test is a phenomenon that has been observed wherever high-stakes testing systems have been introduced (e.g. Amerein and Berliner 2002), and England is no exception to this rule. The extent to which such teaching to the test seriously harms learning is less clear, though obviously time spent on one area (in this case test preparation) will go at a cost to effort expended on others; while we know that opportunity to learn is one of the main predictors of outcomes in learning, so inevitably some damage to learning will result (Creemers 1994). This is connected to a frequent complaint about the standardized tests, in particular in the primary sector, in that they lead to a narrower curriculum, with more focus on those subject that are part of national assessments and therefore league tables, or, in other words, an increase in the time spent on literacy, numeracy and to a lesser extent science at the expense of other subjects. While this is likely to be the case, it has to be pointed out that there is a paradox here, in that while there are constant complaints about narrowing the curriculum, these are mirrored by equally persistent calls for primary schools to make sure all pupils have the necessary literacy and numeracy skills to access the secondary curriculum. It is clear that in a school day of necessarily limited length not all of these desires can be fulfilled, and that if one sees the acquisition of firm basic literacy and numeracy skills as an absolute prerequisite to accessing a broader curriculum, a strong focus on these skills in the primary years is justified, particularly for those pupils from disadvantaged backgrounds least likely to acquire them outside of school.

A key issue with league tables is their inherent unfairness. Educational research has long shown that pupils' social background is a key determinant of their performance, with the school affecting no more than 30 per cent of the variance in outcomes. Therefore, in any league table, positions will be very largely determined by the intake of the school, with schools in the most socio-economically advantaged areas achieving the best results. Not only does this appear unfair to the efforts of schools working in disadvantaged areas, but also it provides an incorrect picture of the effectiveness of the school. This is why, in school effectiveness research for a long time, and in policy somewhat more recently, there has been a lot of attention to so-called value added models. Such models attempt to measure the impact of the school on performance, or the value added by the school, once other factors have been taken into account. Statistically value added models therefore attempt to create a like-for-like comparison by taking into account the fact that schools differ in intake. Variables such as free school meal eligibility or ethnicity, and in many cases prior achievement, are entered as predictors of achievement, and the impact of the school is then calculated as the difference the school makes once the effect of these variables has been statistically taken into account. This obviously leads to fairer comparisons between schools, as schools serving different catchment areas can be judged on what they can do, rather than on their pupil intake. It also allows schools to compare themselves with schools with a similar intake, to see whether they are adding more or less value, and then to learn from each other. This is facilitated where data are presented in groups according to intake, such as in the 'London Families of Schools' outputs. In the English system, simple value added models based on prior performance have been superseded by more complex and accurate models of Contextual Value Added, that take other (socio-demographic) intake variables into account.

However, value added is too often seen as the panacea for all that is wrong with raw score league tables, and we therefore need to supply a number of caveats. Value added tables are the results of statistical modelling, which implies a number of things. First, as in any statistical model, we have a choice as to what variables to enter into the model. For example, what measures of pupil background do we use, for example free school meal eligibility or postcode? Do we enter gender, as there are established differences between boys and girls in performance, or do we leave this out as these differences appear to be susceptible to change (not being consistent over educational history or between schools) and adding the variable may reinforce culturally defined rather than actual differences? There are a whole number of decisions to be made, and what decisions are made will affect the outcome, leading to schools changing position in whatever table results. There is no single value added indicator. A second consequence of value added results from statistical modelling is that the value added score that is the outcome is, unlike a raw exam score, an estimate. This is because however good the predictor variables in our model (and in education they are not actually very good at all) they are always inaccurate measures (thinking of prior achievement, for example, we know that various factors may influence performance on a test). This means that the value added score will typically have a 'confidence interval'. Thus, rather than being able to say with confidence that the value added score is, say 1002, all we can really say is that the 'true' score is likely to lie somewhere between, for example, 999 and 1005. The actual size of the confidence interval will vary depending on a number of factors, but what is clear is that most schools' confidence interval will overlap with that of other schools, making the idea of a value added league table de facto impossible. Figure 3.1 shows the output from a value added model calculated using multilevel modelling. The triangle is the value added estimate, but the vertical lines signify the confidence intervals. In this case, most overlap. This is not always the case to the same extent; in this case the sample sizes in each school were small, so uncertainty was great. Where we have larger sample sizes our confidence intervals will be shorter, and schools therefore are more strongly distinguished.

Furthermore, the more statistically sophisticated value added models show clearly that many schools don't add any value, but that performance is as could

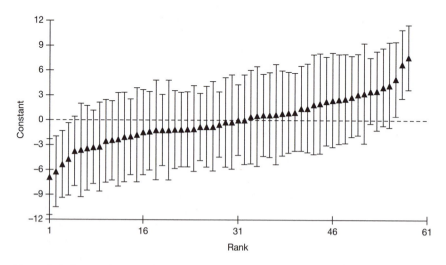

Figure 3.1 Output from a value added model using multilevel modelling

be expected based on intake. A final issue with value added measures is that they are balanced, in that value added by one school needs statistically to be balanced by value 'subtracted' by another. This means that in any value added model you will only have a minority of schools at any one time adding value, and there will always be schools below the value added line, however much improvement the system as a whole makes.

Value added scores then are definitely an advance over raw score measures, and can be highly useful for schools, policy-makers and parents in comparing themselves to other schools on a like-by-like basis, and can thus aid under-standing of school effectiveness and school improvement initiatives. The introduction of value added measures therefore represents one of the key innovations of New Labour to the accountability regime. They can help local authorities and governments to make informed decisions about which schools need support or pressure. However, the publication of these data needs to include confidence intervals as well as an explanation of the limitations of these models, and the variables included, if they are not to be badly misinterpreted.

The high-stakes testing regime has also come under attack as leading to overly high levels of stress among pupils, especially in primary school. Though not much research exists on this aspect of the high-stakes testing, there is a wealth of research that points to the relationship between academic achievement and self-concept (e.g. Marsh et al. 1988; Muijs 1997), and the more stress is put on the outcome of a particular test, the stronger this relationship is likely to be.

Targets and standards for improvement

There is a developing evidence base concerning the effectiveness of target-setting strategies for improvement, though it is also quite inconclusive. Looking at quantitative evidence, it is clear that in the years following the percentage of pupils reaching target levels increased, from 63 per cent in 1997 to 75 per cent in 2003 in literacy and from 61 per cent to 73 per cent in mathematics. However, a lot of the improvement had already occurred before the roll-out of the strategies in 1998 and 1999 respectively, and the target of 80 per cent of pupils reaching expected levels in literacy and 75 per cent in numeracy by 2002 was not reached. OfSTED inspections suggested that between the introduction of the strategies in 1997 and 2003 teaching quality had improved, however, with the percentage of lessons judged to be good or better increasing from just over half to two-thirds. Qualitative research paints a more subtle picture. First, somewhat unusually for such large-scale reform, the majority of teachers appeared to be using the strategies in their teaching, in part prompted by the threat of OfSTED inspection, but in part as a result of strong programmes of professional devel-opment, with almost every school having received some training. Literacy and numeracy had become more central in schools than before, and more elements of literacy and numeracy were included in teaching (Earl et al. 2003). However, change in teaching methods in many cases seems to have represented a refinement rather than radical reform to teachers' traditional practices (Smith et al. 2004). As improvements in performance tailed off, government has sought new approaches, which has led to an emphasis on personalization, allowing more flexibility for schools and eroding the fixed approach advocated in the earlier national strategies. It is too early to state whether or not this approach is more effective, but, especially in literacy, there are still strong voices for a centralized approach, based on the use of phonics, found to be the most effective way of teaching literacy skills to, in particular, disadvantaged pupils (Ehri 2003).

A further method of ensuring accountability and improving performance that has been particularly popular under New Labour, not just in the education sector but in the public sector more generally, has been the setting of performance targets. These operate at the national level, in the form, for example, of the at the time much publicized targets for the percentage of pupils to reach level 4 at Key Stage 2 Literacy and Numeracy mentioned above. England has a uniquely comprehensive target-setting policy in the public sector, with, for example, Local Area Agreements (LAAs) specifying that each local authority (LA) will have up to 35 targets drawn from the new Local Government National Indicator Set (NIS) covering the key priorities that LAs deliver for central government either by themselves or in partnership with others. The statutory education performance targets, also drawn from the NIS, will sit alongside the improvement targets in the LAA. For 2008 LAs had to set 18 statutory education performance targets and also report targets to narrow achievement gaps for black and minority ethnic pupils (DCSF 2008a). Schools have responsibility for setting their own targets, but the LA is supposed to ensure that these targets are sufficiently ambitious, the School Improvement Partner in practice often fulfilling this role. Therefore, targets operate across the system, at school, local authority and national levels, and within schools are usually translated into individual target-setting for pupils.

An obvious question is whether or not target-setting in this way is an effective form of accountability. On the plus side, proponents argue that targets allow organizations to focus on what is important, provide clear, ambitious, measurable and attainable goals to work towards (making them far more useful than general exhortations or vision statements), and that this provides a powerful vehicle for school improvement and the evaluation of current practice. On the negative side, targets are likely to lead to distortions and unintended consequences due to neglect of factors not included or measured as part of the targets, as schools focus on the targets to the exclusion on anything else. The government's tendency to try to solve this problem by setting ever more targets (see above) tends to render them overly bureaucratic, and lead to micro-management and box-ticking exercises. Furthermore, a small number of clear goals has generally been found to be more effective than a large number of targets (Reynolds 1999). At the school level, target-setting, which should always be based on data in order for it to be realistic and useful, has been found to be a spur to school improvement in many schools (Muijs et al. 2005; Reynolds et al. 1996), and there is some evidence that setting targets for individual students can aid performance (Rubie-Davies et al. 2008). Flecknoe (2001) suggests that target-setting can be effective, provided it is underpinned by a consensus about them and their usefulness. This can be problematic in the way target-setting operates in the English system, with the approach seen as controversial, and the overuse of targets making it increasingly hard for organizations to be able to reach all simultaneously (Fielding 2004a). Overall, there is actually remarkably little evidence of the effectiveness of different approaches to target-setting, not least as most studies that do exist originate from authors touting their own target-setting systems.

Conclusion: reflections and speculations

Considering the importance of accountability mechanisms in education, an importance that has clearly increased under New Labour, there is in fact a remarkable paucity of evidence around the impact of these measures. The debate around accountability tends to be couched in an emotional tone with the emphasis firmly on advocacy rather than research (see the US debates around testing, for example Amrein and Berliner 2002). Clearly, more extensive research, especially in an English context, on the range of accountability measures in existence would be beneficial to the creation of a more research-based and effective system.

Nevertheless, some lessons can be taken from the current evidence on accountability, and some suggestions can be made for improvements to the accountability system as it exists (we are not here going to discuss the possibility of not having an accountability system, which we do not believe either to be desirable or politically realistic).

First, it is clear that the use of school league tables in raw form may have had its place when the policy was introduced, serving as a wake-up call for many schools, but that the inherent unfairness and distortion it causes contains more negative than functional aspects in the present system. The emphasis in publication should be on Contextual Value Added (CVA) results, which provide a more accurate assessment of the effectiveness of schools in those areas that they can actually affect. However, the publication of CVA figures must be accompanied with the necessary caveats around model imperfection and confidence intervals, and better information is needed to educate the general public in terms of creating an understanding of why CVA is the better measure, what it means and what its limitations are. Of course, once the genie of league tables is out of the box it is hard to put it back in, and freedom of information means that whatever is officially published it would be possible for interested parties to access the data necessary to construct league tables. However, the publication and publicizing of CVA as the main event, the publication of performance data in formats that makes constructing simple league tables more complex, and time-delaying mechanisms could help entrench a greater attention to CVA. Certainly, official accountability mechanisms need to make judgements based solely on value added rather than raw score measures.

A further recommendation with regards to accountability relates to the current tension between competition and collaboration in the system. While the policy of the previous Conservative governments, and initially that of New Labour, was premised on encouraging competition between schools as a mechanism for improvement, it has become increasingly clear that this approach is not in the best interests of all children, as while competition may lead to the improvement of some schools, and greater popularity of these schools among parents, it also leads to lower performance among neighbouring schools as the best pupils are creamed off, rather than to better performance through competition as its advocates claim. This is potentially a key issue that supporters of more competition in education tend to lose sight of. Competition in the economy in part works through a survival of the fittest mechanism, which incorporates failure as an important element. In business competition does not merely lead to all becoming more effective and efficient and providing those products and services most desired by consumers. In fact, part of the competitive mechanism is that businesses fail, either abruptly or by slowly fading over time. In fact, in the UK in 2005 more than 12,000 companies were liquidated. This failure is unproblematic, in the sense that the market will be able to source products and services elsewhere, while, in economic theory at least, in flexible labour markets workers are able to get jobs in more successful firms (that of course there are many inherent inflexibilities that this oversimplistic reading of economic theory doesn't account for is a discussion for a different volume). For a school to fail due to the competitive pressures from, say, a newly built trust school in the area is highly problematic, however. Children will still have received their education from this school, have been taught by demoralized teachers, in a class full of demoralized pupils where peer support for education is not available, and in most cases will not have a second chance at gaining an academic education. Furthermore, collaborative pressure works as a disincentive to the sharing of best practice between schools, thus hindering school improvement. Realization of these weaknesses has led the government to increasingly promote collaborative approaches in schools, through programmes such as the Federations initiative and the 14–19 initiative, which has led to the setting up of joint programmes. However, a paradox exists in that while collaboration is encouraged through financial and other incentives, the accountability system, be it inspection or testing, is still premised entirely on the individual school. This has limited the extent to which some schools feel able to collaborate with each other, especially where they are geographically close and thus competing for the same pupils (Lindsay et al. 2007). It is therefore imperative, if the needs of all pupils in an area are to be served, that accountability mechanisms operate at the right level, and that where schools collaborate closely they are able to be jointly accountable. This will become an increasingly pressing issue, as current curricular developments are leading to increased joint provision, where school boundaries become increasingly blurred and teachers' and students' endeavour become located across rather than situated within institutions. It is likely it will become increasingly difficult to distinguish clearly whether a qualification has been the results of work of an individual school.

A final issue that is coming to the fore in accountability is that of the disjunction between the current aims of education in England and its accountability system. *Every Child Matters* (ECM) states that schools should aim to ensure that every child has the support they need to be healthy, stay safe, enjoy and achieve, make a positive contribution and achieve economic well-being. All are stated in DCSF publications as being equally important aims. However, in accountability practice this is certainly not the case. While OfSTED does look at all aspects of ECM, this is certainly not the case for the outcome measures that are such a key part of the accountability system. In fact, it can be said that outcome measures as they currently exist measure only one-half of one ECM target, 'achieve'. This is problematic to say the least, as it is a well-known phenomenon that organizations will concentrate their efforts on those things they are judged on. As such, the other aims of ECM are always likely to be seen as of lesser importance than achievement as long as this situation persists. It would therefore, if the government is serious about ECM, be desirable to create more multidimensional measures of school outcomes, focusing on all aspects of ECM. Local authorities and schools are currently engaged in a variety of initiatives, but if accountability is going to be fostered this needs to be extended to all schools and LAs in England, and included in official performance output alongside CVA achievement measures. This would focus the efforts of schools on all outcomes they are supposed to meet, and would have the added advantage that multidimensional outcome data would again make the construction of simple league tables more complex, as differential effectiveness in the achievement of different goals is likely.

4 Control and response in primary school teachers' work

Rosemary Webb

Introduction

In addition to its impact on national economies globalization also has major political, demographic, cultural and environmental consequences (Bottery 2001). While nation states have always felt the need to make changes in their education systems in response to international trends and modernizing ideas, for Dale (2000: 90) globalization represents a 'new and distinct shift in the relationship between state and supranational forces, and it has affected education profoundly and in a range of ways'. A powerful global influence is exerted through the publication of international surveys of pupil achievement – most notably the Programme for International Student Assessment (PISA) and the International Association for the Evaluation of Educational Achievement (IEA) studies – together with notions of the knowledge, values and skills that should be taught to tomorrow's citizens to make them economically competitive and methods of delivering these. As international and national pressures to improve educational performance intensify, governments look for direction in the education policies of their more successful rivals or from explicit policy guidance offered by international agencies such as the OECD. Across the western industrialized world, in the drive to make education systems more effective, a multiplicity of accountability mechanisms (such as accreditation, standards, high-stakes testing, external evaluation and career profiles) have been introduced by many governments in order to bring about change, enforce 'best practice' and control teachers' work. For example, a large-scale education reform to improve performance driven by faith in such mechanisms is the controversial No Child Left Behind Act 2002 in the USA, which links high-stakes testing with strict accountability measures to ensure that no child is left behind (Smith 2005).

The primary aim of this chapter is to examine how, as a result of New Labour's Standards and Workforce Remodelling agendas, Key Stage 2 teachers' work was informed and changed and the implications of this for their professional self-identity. Through drawing on data from the *Fifty Schools Revisited* (FSR) project it will document teachers' perspectives on, and experiences of, changes in their classroom practice and whole-school roles. The FSR project involved research in a national sample of 50 primary schools in England from 2003 to

2007 that were first researched by Webb and Vulliamy between 1992 and 1994 in order to investigate the impact of the Education Reform Act (ERA) 1988. However, in addition this chapter has a secondary aim to consider what lessons can be learned from comparing the FSR project findings with data on the impact on primary teachers' work of national reforms in Finland. Finnish schools and teachers have become the focus of international attention because of the high performance of Finnish pupils in PISA (Välijärvi et al. 2002). Finland is particularly interesting because its education system is very different from that of England and since the late 1990s in many ways the thrust of its education policy has been in the opposite direction (Sahlberg 2007). As argued elsewhere (Webb et al. 2004, 2006), it is important to supplement policy analysis with research into the reception of these policies by teachers because 'glocalized' (Robertson 1995) mediations of such global reforms occur both at national and local levels.

Informed by Smyth et al.'s (2000) developing critical theory of teachers' work, which has the purposes and forms of control at its core, explanations for the nature and extent of these changes are explored through examining how teachers in the FSR project schools were being controlled and the effect of those controls on their work and self-perception. Three different control systems derived from the literature on teachers' work, which although overlapping and interrelated, for purposes of analysis are considered in turn in order to identify the ways in which pressures to make these changes were experienced and responded to at school level. First, ideological control which is exerted through beliefs, ideas and values concerning official versions of 'good practice' and teacher professionalism (for discussion of teacher professionalism as a social construction and the current debates surrounding it, see Vulliamy 2006; Webb et al. 2004). Second, disciplinary control (Ball 1994) whereby teacher compliance with government policy is achieved through punitive regimes of testing, record keeping, performance management, inspections and marketization. Third, technical control (Apple 1986) that is embedded in prescribed objectives-led curricula and supporting materials and texts in order to determine what is taught and how, the sequence and pace of lessons and when and what will be assessed. While teachers can ignore or modify such materials, as will be demonstrated, the freedom to do so is severely constrained when they are augmented by ideological and disciplinary controls.

National policy contexts

The ERA 1988 initiated a series of major reforms in England, Wales and Northern Ireland (but not Scotland). As argued by Ball (1990) these reforms had their ideological underpinnings in different, and sometimes conflicting, aspects of 'new right' ideology. On the one hand, moves towards the local management of schools (LMS) and open enrolment reflected a neoliberal ideology, and on the other, the implementation of a national curriculum and national assessment reflected a neo-conservative ideology. The education policies of the New Labour government in office from 1997 maintained the thrust of these changes. However, concern that English primary school pupils were falling behind in the global competition for basic skills (Reynolds and Farrell 1996) led to a raft of reforms intended to raise standards, such as the National Literary Strategy (NLS) in 1998 and the National Numeracy Strategy (NNS) in 1999. Mechanisms by which individual teachers and schools were held accountable for pupil attainment were increasingly tightened through targets, testing and league tables, the introduction of performance management and OfSTED inspections. Since the late 1990s in the name of public accountability the controls over the work of schools and their teachers have escalated and strengthened challenging teachers' integrity and promoting 'a low trust relationship' between society and its teachers (Whitty 2002).

In the early 1990s the Finnish economy was badly shaken by the economic and political changes in Eastern Europe and the collapse of the previous lucrative Soviet market. Finland suffered severe economic decline, rising unemployment and soaring public debt. Economic recovery was achieved through encouraging business innovation particularly the new knowledge-based industries (Sahlberg 2007). Cost cutting was achieved through the streamlining of the administrative structure justified as necessary to reduce inefficient bureaucracy and achieve participative democracy by moving decision-making powers closer to the consumer. In education the state grants to the municipalities were delegated to schools, which became self-managing but without the accompanying external accountability mechanisms experienced in England. In order to meet the needs of a rapidly changing society requiring a more flexible approach to teaching and learning, curriculum reform in 1994 dismantled the longstanding national curriculum and gave responsibility to schools to develop their own curricula through teacher collaboration and parental involvement. As argued by Sahlberg (2007) the Finnish education system has been remarkably resistant to global education reform particularly in relation to the three common strategies employed by nation states – an emphasis on standards, an increased focus on literacy and numeracy and accountability systems, which reward and punish schools and teachers according to school performance.

Research methodology

The FSR project incorporates a longitudinal dimension through the replication of a previous Association of Teachers and Lecturers-funded research project (Webb and Vulliamy 1996). The same qualitative research strategy based on condensed fieldwork was used as in the earlier research. In its first phase (2003–2005), the FSR project involved day-long visits to 50 schools in 16 local authorities (LAs) – which replaced local education authorities (LEAs) – throughout England and comprised 188 tape-recorded in-depth interviews with primary teachers in these schools, supplemented by school documentation and classroom observations of 51 lessons. In its second phase it incorporated further fieldwork visits and 43 interviews in a 50 per cent sample of the 50 schools.

The primary concern in selecting the original 1992 sample of 50 schools had been to ensure that it reflected the full diversity of Key Stage 2 provision in terms of size and type of school giving, for example, a mix of inner-city, suburban and rural schools, a multicultural mix (from all-white schools through to one school with 98 per cent ethnic minority pupils) and a mix of religious denominations (including Church of England, Roman Catholic and Methodist). For a full discussion of the criteria for the selection of the 50 schools in the 1992–1994 study together with details of the composition of the teacher interview sample see Webb and Vulliamy (2006: ch. 1).

The findings reported here in relation to the work of teachers in Finland are derived from two interrelated research projects. The York-Finnish project (YFP) examined teachers' responses to national policy changes in primary schooling during the 1990s at a time when in many respects the educational systems of England and Finland were moving in opposite directions (see, Webb and Vulliamy 1999a, 1999b). The YFP involved fieldwork and teacher interviews in six English schools spread across four LEAs, and six Finnish schools across four municipalities. The follow-up York-Jyväskylä project (YJP) (see Webb et al. 2004) involved reinterviewing in 2001 those teachers still teaching in their original schools and some from the original sample who had moved schools or left teaching (24 English teachers and 13 Finnish teachers).

Ideological control

Prior to the ERA 1988, schools and teachers in England were not subject to any government prescription concerning curricula or pedagogy; teaching methods, in particular, were viewed as the product of professional judgement. However, before the ERA primary teachers were subject to considerable ideological control as to what constitutes 'best' practice and a 'good' teacher. In the post Second World War period, although primary education was heavily constrained by its elementary school legacy, particularly its emphasis on the 3Rs (reading, writing and arithmetic) and the effects of selection at age 11, it was a period of curricular and pedagogical experimentation characterized by the work of charismatic advocates of progressive ideals in positions of influence and authority as chief education officers, inspectors and advisers (Alexander 1994). Their work led to and developed from the Plowden Report (Central Advisory Council for Education (CACE) 1967) which endorsed and promoted a form of 'informal', 'progressive' education that emphasized child-centredness, individualization, learning through discovery and experience, curriculum integration, creativity and the importance of play in learning. Such practices offered a vision of primary education to teachers that contrasted with the utilitarianism of the elementary system and celebrated the freedom and potential of children thus appealing to the majority of teachers who entered the profession because of their love of children. However, both research (e.g. Galton et al. 1980) and HMI inspections (Department of Education and Science (DES) 1978) demonstrated that while such progressive ideas had a profound impact on the practice of certain schools, their implementation was geographically extremely patchy. In the majority of schools they merely provided rhetoric to describe and justify a diverse range of practices, such as topic work, the integrated day, individualized work and the organizational device of grouping. As is illustrated by the 1986–1991 evaluation of the Leeds LEA Primary Needs Project (PNP), through this rhetoric primary teachers were subjected to ideological control through notions of best practice:

> the 1944 had passed the power to determine the 'secular' curriculum to LEAs; the progressive movement operated as a network of gurus who inspired unquestioning discipleship, and would-be gurus who insisted on it. Primary teachers, as an historically underpowered and dependent profession, were vulnerable to pressure from all of them.
>
> (Alexander 2000: 141)

However, unlike current all-pervasive notions of good practice emanating from central government which impact on whole schools, external control through LEA patronage was exerted on those individual teachers who needed to conform to advance in their careers. Individuals had the option to reduce this control by moving schools or LEAs.

When the ERA 1988 introduced, for the first time in English schools, government prescription over curriculum content, it was made explicit that:

> The Education Reform Act does not prescribe how pupils should be taught. It is the birthright of the teaching profession, and must always remain so, to decide on the best and most appropriate means of imparting education to pupils.
>
> (National Curriculum Council (NCC) 1990: 7)

However, criticisms of progressive classroom organization and teaching methods in primary education, begun by the publication of the Black Papers shortly after the Plowden Report, escalated and intensified. Following the findings of the evaluation of the Leeds PNP, political and media attention was characterized by what Ball (1990) calls the 'discourse of derision' with simplistic caricatured notions of 'informal' 'progressive' education being the subject of attack. A government-initiated review of evidence on the delivery of primary education was described as providing a basis for debate (Alexander et al. 1992: 5). However, at national level there was no debate:

> Progressive child-centred methods and the Plowden report were subjected to a public deconstruction, progressive teachers were disciplined and the groundwork was laid for a thoroughgoing reintroduction of traditional teaching methods.
>
> (Ball 1994: 44)

While the government changed in 1997, the messages about best practice remained essentially the same and were specified for teaching the daily literacy and numeracy hours introduced by the NLS and the NNS. The justification for this was that 'the time has long gone when isolated unaccountable professionals made curriculum and pedagogical decisions alone without reference to the outside world' (Department for Education and Employment (DfEE) 1998a, 14). Shifting government discourses on the theme of pedagogy provide a striking insight into the changing nature of policy-makers' definitions of 'teacher professionalism' (Vulliamy 2006). Professional teachers were no longer to make decisions based on their knowledge and expertise but instead unquestioningly follow government diktat. The 'new professionalism' embodied in, and resulting from, New Labour's policy reforms offers different and often conflicting interpretations of the professional teacher from that held by primary teachers. For example, a holistic child-centred concern to benefit children's lives shifts in the 'new professionalism' discourse to a 'making a difference', that is viewed in terms of raising standards, measured by test results, of all children and closing the gap between high and low achievers (see, for example, Hopkins 2003: 60). This narrow conception of the 'moral purpose' of education contrasts with that of teachers in the FSR project who stressed the importance of primary schooling in 'developing the whole child' and enabling children to discover and develop a wide range of potential abilities and aptitudes:

> What I hang onto more than anything and what I have always believed in is that we are here to develop the whole child – not only attainment in literacy and numeracy but the qualities of independence, articulation, self esteem, organizational skills – there is a myriad of qualities you need to develop as a human being.
>
> (Headteacher, February 2004)

In Finland the 1994 curriculum reforms represent in theory at least a very radical departure from previous practice. They suggest a transition from teachers teaching a nationally prescribed subject-based curriculum to school-based community-orientated curricula emphasizing thematic work and active learning pedagogies. While in part the reforms were the result of decentralization and a continuation of an increasing recognition of the problems of an overloaded, centrally prescribed curriculum with its origins in the 1970s, discussion with educationalists and policy-makers in Finland also suggests that such reforms were to a considerable extent 'ideas-driven' by progressive educators who had gained prominence at a national level in organizations such as the National Board of Education. This new generation of educational policy-makers had been influenced by constructivist theories of learning and progressive practice in countries such as England. The Finnish teachers in our research sample, who were already experimenting with the kinds of curriculum and pedagogical change promoted by the reforms, experienced enhanced self-worth as their work became at the forefront of valued practice. However, the majority could not understand the rationale for the reforms that undermined their beliefs and challenged established practices and felt deskilled and devalued. Consequently, they began to experience the same kinds of work intensification and stress reported by the English teachers (Webb and Vulliamy 1999b). Six years later the intensification of Finnish teachers' work and its negative effects on morale had increased, leading to widespread support for Curriculum 2004 with its specified content and lesson hours for subjects in each grade (Webb et al. 2004).

Disciplinary control

In common with other studies (Jeffrey and Woods 1998; Osborn et al. 2000), the FSR project findings strongly reflect the 'performativity discourse of assessment' dominating current educational policy-making (Broadfoot 2001). In the *Five Year Strategy for Children and Learners* (Department for Education and Skills (DfES) 2004d) the government predicted that by 2008:

> we will have reached and sustained our literacy and numeracy targets of 85 per cent of children reaching the expected level at the age of eleven; and the proportion of schools in which fewer than 65 per cent of children reach this level reduced by 40 per cent.
>
> (DfES 2004d: 43)

Teachers described the unremitting pressure on heads, themselves and pupils exerted by the government's standards agenda. It had intensified their work through generating escalating paperwork in the form of school policies, lesson plans, written responses to national and LA initiatives, pupil records and reports to parents and governors. Moreover a culture had been created whereby: 'The head is constantly under pressure to perform, she puts the pressure on us, we put the pressure on the children and then everyone is just under immense pressure and stress'. However many hours teachers committed to school, they never seemed adequate to meet expectations.

The introduction of the NLS and the NNS were central to the achievement of government targets. Consequently, although not mandatory, their implementation was forcefully recommended. As the DfEE (1997b) stated:

> Our presumption will be that the approach to teaching we set out, based on the NLP [National Literacy Project], will be adopted by every school unless a school can demonstrate through its literacy action plan and schemes of work and its performance in NC [National Curriculum] Key Stage tests, that the approach it has adopted is at least as effective.
>
> (DfEE 1997b: 19)

Looking back on the early years of the national strategies teachers in the 50 schools, irrespective of their opinion of the advantages and disadvantages of the strategies for them, their pupils and their schools, were highly critical of the government for their imposition in a such a way that 'You don't have to do it, it is an option, but woe betide anybody who doesn't!' The national strategies were viewed as a further expression of the government's lack of trust in the teaching profession and a public declaration that teachers lacked the required expertise. As one deputy head put it: 'When the Strategies were introduced there was this huge implication that things were terrible and that teachers were not teaching correctly. I think that everybody felt threatened by that.' There were very few teachers who claimed to have been sufficiently confident and non-threatened to evaluate the prescribed changes and make decisions on how to respond to them in the light of their own values and experiences. Only schools with excellent Standard Attainment Test (SAT) results and OfSTED inspection reports were considered to be in a position to resist implementing the national strategies in order to maintain existing preferred practice. The control exerted on schools through OfSTED inspections and the LAs to achieve compliance was also greatly resented.

The strategies have been criticized for not being adequately research based (e.g. Brown et al. 2003) and for failing to achieve the intended fundamental changes in teacher-pupil interaction (e.g. Hargreaves et al. 2003). Also, the government's claim that the strategies have been responsible for a dramatic increase in primary school literacy and numeracy standards has been convincingly challenged (Richards 2005; Tymms 2004). However, the FSR data show that the imposition of the strategies has led to widespread changes in primary classroom practice, not only in literacy and numeracy but also across the curriculum (Webb and Vulliamy 2006). These include:

- a move from an activity-based topic-centred curriculum to an objectives-led subject-centred one
- a dramatic increase in whole-class teaching at the beginning and end or throughout lessons
- lessons with instructional introductory and plenary sessions
- teachers maintaining much tighter control over the pace and direction of lessons than previously
- an increase in the use of setting in literacy and numeracy
- changes in classroom seating patterns with very much more use of pupils seated in rows rather than grouped around tables
- a virtual eradication in our sample of certain practices – such as the integrated day and open-plan classrooms – often associated with the Plowden 'progressive' era.

These changes have incurred strong criticism from academic educationalists (e.g. Wyse et al. 2008). However, generally they were regarded positively by teachers in the FSR project, who believed that they were a considerable improvement on aspects of their previous practice.

In relation to assessment, there was much evidence that teachers had developed more confidence and increased skills in the ways in which they assessed pupils, which contributed to better planning and helped children's learning. However, test preparation narrowed the curriculum throughout Key Stage 2 and completely distorted provision for year 6 (see also Galton and MacBeath 2002). As documented in earlier research (see, for example, Osborn et al. 2000), teachers continued to hold an overwhelmingly negative view of the Key Stage 2 national tests and would like to see them abolished. For them 'testing has gone far too far', resulting in primary schools being 'over tested, scrutinized and squeezed' with 'no allowance for your professional judgement'. Teachers tried to achieve a balance between getting pupils to realize the importance of doing their best but without making them over anxious. However, they found, as concluded by Pollard et al. (2000: 238), that 'overall, the children seemed only too aware that while "trying" was worthy, "achieving" was actually the required outcome'. Such high-stakes testing, which holds schools and teachers accountable for pupil attainment in literacy and numeracy, diminished opportunities for teachers to develop the whole child, caused considerable stress for many children and changed the basis of teacher–pupil relationships.

Although all the headteachers were highly critical of league tables and of the technical problems associated with the value added version of these (criticisms substantiated by Easen and Bolden 2005), they attached considerable importance to moving up the league tables in order to maintain parental support and pupil numbers. This meant that setting and meeting pupil attainment targets were increasingly becoming a crucial component of the performance review of individual teachers. From 2000, owing to the introduction of 'one of the most ambitious and far-reaching schemes of performance related pay ever conceived' (Wragg et al. 2004: 7), schools were required to introduce a system of performance management which was envisaged as the cornerstone of the pay policy. Data from the first phase of the FSR project revealed considerable variation between schools in the attention given to performance management. In a few schools it scarcely existed and in many schools teachers were unable to remember their improvement targets. However, towards the end of the research, teachers were much more likely to be able to recall their targets and to describe the progress that they were making towards achieving them. Performance management was also more often acknowledged to have positive outcomes as several teachers considered that it 'helps to get things done that might have been put off', 'keeps you on your toes' and creates some space to consider career opportunities and professional development.

OfSTED inspections cause teachers to feel anxious and stressed, lose self-confidence and can have an extremely negative impact on their work, health and professional identity (Jeffrey and Woods 1998). According to the FSR project teachers, even when the outcome was positive the process proved exhausting and demoralizing, sometimes leading to temporary or long-term ill-health. As demonstrated by the experience of some of the 50 schools, the effects of a less than wholly positive outcome from an OfSTED inspection can seriously damage a school's ethos and its relationships with parents and the community. However, the introduction of shorter 'light touch' OfSTED inspections that were conducted at short notice were generally welcomed by headteachers and teachers. Also, there were encouraging signs that the inspection system introduced in 2005 with its strong emphasis on school self-evaluation will come to be perceived and experienced differently. While all the headteachers found the initial completion of the lengthy and detailed OfSTED Self-Evaluation Form (SEF) onerous, and a stressful process if an inspection was perceived as likely to be imminent, the SEF was regarded as changing the inspection process for the better by enabling schools to feel more in control of inspection outcomes.

Finnish teachers have long enjoyed a high level of trust at government, municipality and school level in their proficiency and capacity to fulfil curricular aims (Sahlberg 2007; Webb and Vulliamy 1999a). The status of teachers is very high and primary teaching is one of the most popular professions for young people (Ministry of Education (Finland) 2007). In Finland the only national testing is the matriculation examination that concludes upper secondary school. National standards are monitored by the National Board of Education, which administers tests to pupils in the sixth and ninth grade in a sample of schools each spring. In the YJP school pupils received reports twice during the year and the assessments given on these were derived from achievement in class, homework and tests organized by teachers. However, teachers felt that although the purpose of such assessment was purported to be to promote pupil learning, it was increasingly being used for school accountability to the municipalities (Webb et al. 2004). Teachers' performance was reviewed in annual interviews with principals but the latter had no responsibility to observe lessons. Consequently, they experienced difficulty in identifying and addressing any weaknesses in classroom practice (Webb et al. 2006). New standards for schools and teachers were anticipated and have since been introduced through the 2005–2009 Productivity Program, which suggests that Finnish schools and teachers could become increasingly subject to outcomes-based rewards and sanctions (Sahlberg 2007).

The national system of inspections was transferred to a province-based system in the 1970s and this was discontinued in 1991. In the context of decentralization and deregulation, one of the central objectives of curriculum reform was to develop school self-evaluation to ensure continuous review and development at school level. While school self-evaluation appeared to have considerable limitations, 'schools had ownership over their methods of data collection and analysis and commitment to respond to evaluation findings which led to direct and immediate changes to practice' (Webb et al. 1998: 554). In 1999 school self-evaluation became statutory and the YJP research found the initial enthusiasm for it had dissipated. Self-evaluation was regarded as having 'become like a merry-go-round that has to be run beside everything else' with no time to address the issues raised (Webb et al. 2004).

Technical control

Primary teachers are expected to teach a wide range of subjects and research indicates that, especially after the introduction of a broad-based national curriculum, they lacked confidence in their knowledge of, and ability to teach, many of the subjects embodied within it (Bennett et al. 1994). Moreover, prior to the curriculum and pedagogy reforms, there was little attempt in teacher training to give specific guidance on primary teaching pedagogy. A consequence of this is that many older teachers' reflections on changes in their teaching resonate with the experience of J. Strong, whom Earl et al. (2003) quote as an illustration of what has been called an era of 'uninformed professionalism':

> I started teaching [in England] in 1972. There was no curriculum. You could do what you liked . . . I hadn't the faintest idea of what I was doing but I went out there and did what I could . . . Nobody should have been expected to do what I was expected to do.
>
> (Earl et al. 2003: 26)

> I mean when I first started teaching there wasn't a great lot of direction. It was very much up to the headteacher, so as an inexperienced teacher you were left more or less to your own devices in all sorts of ways and I think it's good now that there's certainly direction and help for new teachers coming into schools.
>
> (Deputy head, March 2004)

Galton et al. (1999) speculate that little or no guidance on National Curriculum implementation could be largely responsible for the lack of change in classroom practice following the ERA 1988. In contrast to the implementation of the National Curriculum, the NLS and the NNS prescribed both content and teaching methods. Given this context, most of the FSR interviewees thought that the curriculum and pedagogic guidance that they had received had made them better teachers and had improved their children's learning. For example, previously some teachers who did not have particular expertise in literacy or numeracy 'were scratching around sometimes for activities' whereas post-NLS 'Those days are gone because you're more structured about what you're teaching and it's more like little bite-sized chunks that you put into it'.

Whether or not the changes in classroom practice resulting from government policy met with teachers' approval was determined by their perceived beneficial or detrimental impact on children's learning and well-being. Consequently, those changes introduced by the national strategies, which through experience and critical reflection became viewed as improving pupil learning, were adopted even when doing so involved revising previously held beliefs:

> At first I thought no way is this going to work because with the poorer children . . . I said a week visiting multiplication and division is no good and then going back a term later and doing it. And I was totally wrong

because it, it is absolutely fantastic and it does keep some rolling . . . instead of doing like two, three or four weeks on one topic they can switch and move on and our standards have definitely risen.

(Headteacher, June 2004)

The government's Primary National Strategy (PNS), set out in *Excellence and Enjoyment* (DfES 2003d), states its intention 'to encourage schools to take control of their curriculum, and to be innovative' (para 2.4). As outlined by Brehony (2005), pressure on the government for a new policy direction was coming from a broad coalition that was against the emphasis on testing and qualifications, seeing this as detrimental to the development of the creativity and innovation required of a globalized knowledge-based economy. However, much of the text of *Excellence and Enjoyment* (DfES 2003d) is devoted to reiterating the familiar messages of the standards agenda because 'testing, tables and targets are here to stay' (DfES 2003d: 20). As a consequence, headteachers in the FSR project were reluctant to reduce time spent on literacy and numeracy in order to devote more time to the rest of the curriculum. Nevertheless, the PNS was interpreted by teachers as 'giving them permission' to exercise some professional judgement about ways of teaching that supported the children's 'best interests' and reintroduce elements – such as cross-curricular work and creative arts subjects – that had been lost in the focus on the 'effective' at the expense of the 'affective' (McNess et al. 2003). Schools already involved in their own or LA-wide curriculum and/or teaching and learning initiatives – such as visual, auditory and kinaesthetic learning as a way of personalizing learning, or accelerated learning and thinking skills programmes – saw these as encouraged by the recommendations of the PNS.

In Finland, while the goals of education were identified, decisions about how these might be realized were vested in schools. Within schools the legacy of teacher autonomy, flatter hierarchical management structures and democratic decision-making encouraged diversity and experimentation (Webb et al. 2006). However, lack of in-service training and resources to increase teacher capacity constrained the opportunities available to teachers to develop their pedagogical skills and knowledge. Consequently some teachers felt unprepared and resistant to a move from whole-class teaching and individual work towards the more progressive teaching methods advocated involving thematic project work, group work, independent learning and pupil self-evaluation. Traditionally teachers made considerable use of textbooks and many publishers prior to 1994 produced materials in all subjects including teachers' guides, textbooks, pupil workbooks, tapes and tests. Where teachers had become heavily reliant on these, they were reluctant to devise plans to teach without them.

Conclusion

This chapter has documented the impact of ideological, disciplinary and technical controls on Key Stage 2 teachers' work and revealed how in combination these controls exert immense pressures on teachers to conform to government directives and recommendations. Although, as argued elsewhere (Vulliamy and Webb, 2006), there have been some distinctive aspects of New Labour's education policies (such as a commitment to social justice and inclusion), the controls discussed here are generally a continuation of policies initiated by the former Conservative governments. They can be viewed as reflecting the dominant neoliberal ideology that has characterized many western countries' approaches, led by the United States, to the economic pressures of globalization.

Not surprisingly the FSR project visits to schools revealed a predictable uniformity of concerns reflecting government policies. However, they also illustrated a myriad of minor and major alternative approaches to policy implementation derived by the interaction of different personalities in diverse school environments thus emphasizing the sensitivity of macro-level reform to micro-level contexts. As acknowledged by Bottery (2007a: 167): 'most headteachers felt that they could manage some manoeuvrability within the given policy architecture, such that their preferred direction was not totally lost'.

In the late 1980s Nias (1989) found the personal and occupational self of teachers in England had become so closely related that they fused to form one self-identity. At that time the ideals and values based on holistic child-centred principles and vocationalism espoused in the Plowden Report (CACE 1967) were strongly endorsed by the government of the day, informed the rhetoric if not the practice of primary schools, and generated a uniform, coherent, relatively stable self-identity for the majority of primary teachers. Increasingly since the ERA 1988 teachers have been expected to relinquish the Plowden self-identity and adopt a new assigned social identity emphasizing teacher competences rather than personal qualities, consumerism to replace care, and accountability instead of autonomy (Woods and Jeffrey 2002). As recognized by Hargreaves (1994: 71) in response to the need to change, 'The fragile self becomes a continuous reflexive project. It has to be constantly and continuously remade and reaffirmed'. Teaching in a different way from previously – for example, as a result of the national strategies – when perceived to be beneficial to children was viewed positively and teachers' self-identity reconstructed to accommodate the alternative practices.

However, teachers in the FSR project were exceedingly constrained by the standards agenda, which had very adverse effects on the affective curriculum, the pastoral dimension of their work and their relationships with children. The unremitting stream of policy initiatives, the speed with which these were introduced and then subjected to change before they had become bedded down and evaluated, engendered fatigue, frustration, cynicism and disillusionment, all of which were counterproductive. In response teachers developed multiple and situational identities – that were not there before in the integrated personal and professional self-identity described by Nias (1989) – in order to cope with different situations and purposes in which often they felt they were unable to invest their full selves (see also Day et al. 2006; Woods and Jeffrey 2002). For example, as revealed in the FSR data, teachers putting on a performance for accountability purposes during classroom observations for performance management, visits by LA inspectors or advisers and OfSTED inspectors is now routine, although it continues to be stressful. Emphasizing fragmentation, adaptation and change in the role of professionals in the public services, Stronach et al.'s (2002: 117) research with nurses and teachers also found them 'mobilizing a complex of occasional identities in response to shifting contexts'.

In Finland in the 1990s the thrust of global reform and the drive to increase economic prosperity led to curriculum reform moving in the opposite direction to that of England. In contrast to the compliance expected of teachers in England, the intention was to empower Finnish teachers and enable them to influence the direction of education reform. However, the break with the past and the removal of established disciplinary and technical controls also produced insecurity, stress and work intensification. Above all the presence or absence of national testing as an accountability mechanism constituted a major difference in the working lives of teachers in the two countries. In England it dominated classroom practice and teachers' work consuming the time, energy and effort of teachers and pupils and stifling creativity and innovation. In Finland throughout the 1990s and into the millennium, teachers enjoyed considerable freedom to develop and teach the curriculum in ways appropriate for their pupils and the local community. However, the pressures of performativity are growing resulting in this freedom very slowly being relinquished. The pace of this change and the degree to which it occurs seems likely to be largely determined by the future performance of Finnish pupils in international surveys of pupil performance. Should Finland slide down the international rankings, then government trust in teachers might be questioned and additional controls imposed on schools.

Changes in practice brought about by national policies on curriculum and pedagogy and the restructuring of teachers' work have impacted most strongly on teacher identity in England but teachers in Finland have also had to continuously recreate their identities in response to increased control. However, teacher identities are shaped not only by global trends and government policies but also by national contexts and educational traditions, institutional values and personal biographies. While increasingly teachers in different countries are likely to experience similar pressures on, and controls imposed over, their work, the process of glocalization seems likely to ensure that there will never be a global 'ideal' teacher.

5 Raising standards

What is the evidence?

Joanna Bragg and Bill Boyle

Introduction

The setting and comparison of educational standards of pupil attainment, the routes by which those standards are attained and their relative comparability are research issues of national and international concern. Studies such as the Programme for International Student Asssessment (PISA) and Trend in International Mathematics and Science Study (TIMSS) have stimulated debate about the relative merits of policy choices that are made in education systems. These international studies provide a natural complement to in-depth system level analyses by systematically examining educational outcomes, practices and relationships across educational settings. In England the Education Reform Act 1988 introduced an outcomes-based accountability system of measuring and monitoring pupil performance in national tests and assessments.

Since 1996 the Qualifications and Curriculum Authority (QCA) has funded the Centre For Assessment Studies (CFAS) at the University of Manchester to devise, manage and sustain representative national samples of primary and secondary schools; these schools annually supply their end of key stage test scripts for analysis. These analyses are supplied to the QCA to inform on pupil performance over time and to support evaluation by the national test development agencies of their test instruments and are also supplied in accessible format as performance profile feedback reports to the schools which have provided the test scripts, to support their self-evaluation processes. Over the period from 1996 we have also designed and conducted a mixed methods (quantitative, qualitative and longitudinal) survey of curriculum provision, for example subject timetabling, planning for teaching of subjects as discrete or in combination, with the sample schools as part of the curriculum monitoring research programme funded by the QCA. The findings suggest that the 'fixation' on measuring 'standards' in the narrowest definition of the term. Fixed percentage performance thresholds on population scores on narrowly domained end of key stage tests has resulted in a situation in which quick-fix strategies to produce short-term gains in 'test scores' overrule the learning agenda.

In this chapter we summarize the analyses of end of Key Stages 1, 2 and 3 national test data from the sample schools against the variables that might explain or predict the results. Our findings indicate not only that the variables associated with disadvantage were highly significant predictors of test performance but also that there was a lack of significance of the government improvement strategies.

Context

Since the introduction of national end of key stage testing for pupils aged 7, 11 and 14 in the early 1990s under a Conservative government, educational policy in England has concentrated on raising levels of achievement measured through annual pupil cohort performance in these tests. 'New Labour' in a policy intervention based on a populist rhetoric of 'raising standards' determined that these pupil performances aggregated to school level would be judged against government-decreed percentage targets. This crude accountability measure has in turn created a focus on 'underachievement' and has led to much academic and public domain debate focusing on the link between underachievement and schools in disadvantaged circumstances (Bell 2003; Lupton 2004a).[1] However much policy-makers and the academic research community argue the semantics of 'underachievement' (Smith 2003; see also Gorard and Smith 2004) it is generally accepted that unless social and economic inequities are addressed and a dramatic turnaround of social circumstances achieved (OfSTED 2003c, 2006; Rainwater and Smeeding 2003), schools in disadvantaged circumstances are unlikely to improve in the context of the current measures used to report pupil performance (Lupton 2004b; Thrupp 2005; Whitty 2002).

The prospects of a reversal of the 'accountancy' mentality in the near future seem somewhat bleak, despite former Prime Minister Blair's hollow-sounding assertion that 'our ideology is based on a notion of equality that is not about outcomes' (Blair 2001). Lupton (2004a) using OfSTED inspection data posits that five out of six schools with high free school meal (FSM) percentages do not need to make substantial improvement in their 'quality of education' (i.e. teaching and the curriculum) to meet inspection criteria but unfortunately it is in the aspects of 'standards' (i.e. performance data used to judge attainment and progress) that the 'disadvantaged' schools are viewed and labelled as deficits. The more socially disadvantaged the community served by a school, the very much more likely it is that the school will appear to underachieve. Improving against the odds is now the 'name of the game' as those odds are 'stacked against schools in poorer areas' (Gray 2004: 296).

In 2003, David Bell, then Her Majesty's Chief Inspector of Schools (HMCI), acknowledged the attainment gap between advantaged and disadvantaged pupils: 'we must look urgently at how to close the gap in achievement between youngsters in the most deprived areas and elsewhere' (Bell 2003: 2). In 2007 Christine Gilbert, the current HMCI, in her annual report concluded that 'poorer children still had the odds stacked against them achieving' and added that despite a series of government initiatives to tackle social inequality in schools, 'the relationship between poverty and outcomes for young people is stark' (OfSTED 2006: 6). In addressing the issue of attainment related to disadvantage from our data, we have also concentrated on evidenced statements made by members of the academic research community that 'levels of disadvantage still account, in part, for poor attainment and this relationship is stubbornly resistant to policy intervention' (Harris and Ranson 2005: 575) .

The research

The primary school sample

Data from a sample of 300 primary schools representative of regional geographical distribution, school type and size are used for our analysis of school performance in national statutory tests at Key Stages 1 and 2. Those schools' pupil performance data are analysed against the range of variables that might contribute to or explain their results, e.g. FSM, Special Educational Need (SEN) and English as an Additional Language (EAL) (see box).

Performance indicators

- End of Key Stage 1: percentage of pupils achieving level 2 or above in reading, writing and mathematics and the teacher assessment score for science
- End of Key Stage 2: the percentage of pupils achieving level 4 or above in English, mathematics and science.

Variables to define 'disadvantage'

- Percentage of pupils eligible for free school meals (FSM)
- Percentage of pupils with special educational needs (SEN)
- Percentage of pupils whose mother tongue is not English (EAL).

School background variables

- Size of school
- School type (infant, first, junior, primary)
- Religious status (Church of England, Roman Catholic, Jewish etc.)
- Nursery provider (does the school have a nursery?)

Performance-enhancing strategies

- Teaching time allocation – percentage of time allocated to each subject by key stage
- Improvement initiatives – Optional Tests (years 3, 4 and 5), Performance Indicators in Primary Schools, practice tests (published and/or in-house), revision classes, assessment for learning principles.

All variables were explored to ensure 'normal' distributions and were compared with the national profile (DfES 2004c) for representativeness. In general the sample was slightly biased towards the more 'successful' schools, due to the voluntary nature of the survey and the issue of self-selection. As school leadership literature suggests (Leithwood et al. 2006a; Plewis 2007), the more successful schools are more likely to promote themselves at every opportunity compared with those who are struggling with difficult circumstances.

Summary of primary school sample findings

While the variables that describe disadvantage (FSM, SEN and EAL) proved to be statistically related to test performance at Key Stage 1, none of the other variables proved significant. At Key Stage 2, FSM and SEN as descriptors of disadvantage were significant predictors of performance, but EAL was not. Interestingly, not having English as a first language adversely affected performance at Key Stage 1, but by Key Stage 2 the problem seems to have disappeared. Research has shown that a child's English language proficiency improves during his or her time at school so that if a child with EAL has attended throughout the primary phase, by the end of Key Stage 2 it does not inhibit the child's progress (Burgess and Wilson 2005: 24).

None of the tested-for school background variables (i.e. school size, type, religious status or being a nursery provider) featured in the statistical models, and showed no impact on test performance at Key Stage 1 or 2.

We had expected that test preparation in the form of practice tests and revision classes would have a positive impact on test performance, but as the statistics revealed, the only measure to exert any impact on test results was a borderline effect of revision classes on Key Stage 2 results. The percentage of time allocated to teaching the core subjects also did not statistically relate to test outcomes at either Key Stage.

The more disadvantaged school cohorts don't perform as well as those in more affluent areas; this is a well-established fact in both the research literature (Plewis 2007; Lupton 2004a) and external reports of school inspections and evaluations (OfSTED 2006).

Time allocated to teaching the core subjects is not related to test results at either Key Stage 1 or 2. This finding links to evidence-based concerns raised by the authors (Boyle and Bragg 2006) that the primary curriculum has become increasingly dominated by core subject teaching to the detriment of the remaining non-tested foundation subjects. If teachers are supported at school senior management level to diversify the school curriculum from its current narrow English and mathematics 'testable content' menu, perhaps some of those children who struggle to perform in 'testing' situations can be supported (through having an opportunity for richer and deeper experience of the 'foundation' subjects) to excel in other areas, e.g. art, music, modern foreign languages, sport.

Our data show that performance-boosting strategies, with the exception of revision classes at Key Stage 2, do not correspond to improved test outcomes.

The considerable time that pupils spend completing practice tests could perhaps be better used on other aspects of teaching and learning, e.g. curriculum breadth and diversity, teaching for deeper learning of subject content in the core subjects, i.e. sub-domains that are ignored because they are not tested.

A national sample survey of 465 primary school teachers undertaken by ourselves on the impact of national testing on the curriculum (Bragg and Pearson 2007) revealed a negative attitude towards the statutory tests. More than four out of five schools reported the use of practice tests (year 3 86 per cent; year 6 82 per cent) at Key Stage 2. Test preparation in year 6 in the second half of the spring term accounted for three or more hours per week in two-thirds of schools (66 per cent) and two hours per week in 22 per cent of the sample. Over three-quarters of the sample (77 per cent) indicated that the amount of time devoted to test preparation had increased over the previous ten years. Three out of five schools (62 per cent) felt that teacher assessments were more accurate than testing and 27 per cent felt that teacher assessment was as accurate as testing. A large majority (93 per cent) stated that if national testing was to be reduced and replaced by teacher assessment, then less time would be spent by teachers on test preparation, 91 per cent felt that pupil stress would be reduced and 87 per cent reported that there would be a reduction in teacher stress. The majority of the sample (89 per cent) also felt that national testing has narrowed the curriculum (40 per cent a lot; 49 per cent a little).

Resources are also prioritized and there are cost implications attached to the use of optional tests and published practice tests. This finding could be of particular importance to the schools in more deprived areas, where resources at present consumed on 'raising test standards' could be more productively utilized in resourcing support for social and cultural issues within school. It may be worth considering that whatever strategy is adopted to boost the performance of pupils from the most deprived cohorts, 'drilling' them to pass tests is not really working and perhaps an alternative approach is necessary. It is also regrettable that the many schools which make real differences to the life chances of pupils in difficult circumstances, despite not achieving the required percentage of pupils at level 4 at Key Stage 2, are not acknowledged in the current educational climate.

Many of the schools in the sample are utilizing strategies in order to improve their results but there is no evidence to suggest that any particular type of school, i.e. more disadvantaged or less disadvantaged, is more likely to employ these measures. This could be because the children at primary school age haven't been identified as falling behind significantly yet, as their first 'high-stakes' measure of ability is at the end of Key Stage 1. However, as the children progress through their primary schooling, those who have not achieved the required level at the end of Key Stage 1, due to the effect of the range of cultural and social factors related to a definition of disadvantage, are probably less likely to 'catch up' and achieve the government expectation of level 4 at the end of Key Stage 2. This group of pupils (labelled as 'underperforming') will have been 'set' for their Key Stage 2 levels of work based on their end of Key Stage 1 levels and it might be expected that schools 'target' them with improvement measures. The data cannot distinguish whether a school has targeted a particularly 'in need of support' group in their use of improvement strategies; analysis at the pupil level would be necessary to gain such detailed insight. The evidence does show that at the school level, the improvement strategies have had no actual impact on results.

The secondary school sample

We investigated the impact of the range of government initiatives (aimed at increasing pupil and school performance) on the end of key stage national test outcomes at Key Stage 3, while controlling for other factors (school background variables and involvement in national initiatives) that might affect performance.

It is widely accepted that since the late 1990s schools have been and still are allocating more teaching time to the tested subjects, are 'teaching to the test' and devoting more and more time to test preparation (Boyle and Bragg 2006):

> Under pressure from bureaucrats to achieve, schools which desperately need to cater to their pupils' diverse requirements are having to tailor teaching to the tests. This distortion matters because of the gaps it leaves in understanding and learning.
>
> (de Waal 2006: 19)

The government performance targets have necessitated the production by schools of quantifiable performance measures which in turn require an emphasis on external testing to generate nationally standardized performance data on the basis of which the government can self-congratulate on the success of its interventions in education:

> The result has been an obsession with target-chasing . . . instead of being a useful tool to measure pupils' achievements, standardized tests have become the 'raison d'etre' of teaching, the benchmark of whether a school lives or falls.
>
> (de Waal 2006: 19)

To achieve these targets or at least achieve accounting parity with their neighbours, statistical and geographical, and therefore the anonymity of parity within the mass, many schools pay a substantial percentage of their resource budget to purchase, implement and mark Optional Tests (which are available in English and mathematics for every non-end of key stage tested school year group, i.e. year 3, year 4, year 5, year 7 and year 8). Schools widely use government promoted catch-up programmes and 'booster classes' as more cost-free methods of improving test outcomes.

The government, in acknowledgement of the link between schools in disadvantaged circumstances and poor test performance, and concerned at the failure by many of these schools labelled as socially 'disadvantaged' to achieve the government set targets for external test performance (Gorard and Smith 2004; Gray 2001, 2004; Lupton 2004a; Smith 2003), has supplied a range of centre–periphery initiatives designed to address the issue of raising school performance. However, Leithwood et al. (2006c: 460) contest that 'actually improving achievement has proven to be an extraordinarily difficult and badly underestimated challenge, even when vastly greater resources are devoted to it'. We therefore tested the possibility that a school's participation in one or more of the various government schemes could have an effect on its performance.

Performance indicators

- The only nationally standardized measurement of achievement available for Key Stage 3 (aged 14 years) is the percentage of pupils achieving level 5 or above in English, mathematics and science (DfES 2006).

Variables to define 'disadvantage'

- Percentage of pupils eligible for FSM
- Percentage of pupils with SEN
- Percentages of pupils with EAL.

School background variables

- Size of school
- Gender
- Religious status.

Performance-enhancing strategies

- Percentage of teaching time allocated to each tested subject in year 8
- Use of initiatives such as catch-up programmes, booster classes, summer schools and optional tests.

Government initiatives

Each school supplied information about which of the national initiatives they were involved in: Specialist School status,[2] Excellence in Cities, Key Stage 3 National Strategy,[3] Healthy Schools,[4] Increased Flexibility Programme,[5] 14–19 Enterprise (Pathfinders),[6] Leadership Incentive Grant (LIG), Leading Edge,[7] Federations,[8] Young Apprenticeships,[9] Partnerships for Progression/Aim Higher,[10] Networked Learning Communities.[11]

Summary of secondary school sample findings

All variables were analysed using multiple regression modelling statistics to investigate their significance in predicting or explaining test outcomes at Key Stage 3. We wanted to explore how the percentage of teaching time allocated to English and mathematics in year 8 or the Optional Tests taken in year 8 might relate to the Key Stage 3 English and mathematics test results at the end of year 9, while controlling for as many additional variables that might also impact on the results. There were a lot of variables to consider within this model, but many did not prove significant when considered alongside the other factors. Following a gradual whittling down process, to remove those variables with the least significance, the final models resulted.

The analysis indicates that the composition of a school, i.e. school type and socio-economic status of its cohort, has a significant influence on test performance at Key Stage 3. Schools with fewer pupils disadvantaged by social or cultural circumstances and schools that carefully select their pupils according to ability and religion – which following recent research we can take to mean by social class, i.e. middle class parents migrating to faith schools and faith schools 'selecting' their own intake (Waterman 2006) – will achieve higher test results. As already discussed, the relationship between disadvantage and attainment has been widely researched, e.g. Bracey (2004) shows that

> among 17,000 US schools all sustained success as measured by test scores came in more affluent schools, not one school out of 2,100 with a poverty rate above 75% and hardly any of the 7,000 more with the rate above 25% were able to show consistent improvement over more than two years.
>
> (Bracey 2004: 635)

This has been acknowledged by the UK government, which provided the numerous national initiatives aimed at helping the more disadvantaged schools. It might be expected that these national initiatives have impacted on test outcome, although research (e.g. Harris and Ranson 2005) has alluded to the failure of externally funded improvement programmes raising achievement in the poorest schools. However, the only national initiatives that figured significantly in the multiple regression analysis were specialist school status, which exerted a positive impact, and the LIG, which had a negative effect.

With the immense pressure placed on schools to achieve nationally set targets and the self-imposed pressure on the government to hit its own percentage performance targets, one would expect the wide provision and implementation of performance-enhancing measures that are currently being supplied to schools. It was interesting to note that within the final analyses, the use of Optional Tests in English and mathematics in year 8 did not have any effect on test outcome for that same group of pupils taking their end of Key Stage 3 tests in year 9. Further analysis also revealed that the more disadvantaged schools (i.e. those with higher percentage of FSM) were more likely to use Optional Tests. This is perhaps cause for concern not only due to the prioritization of resource cost of implementing the tests, but also that schools could be wasting valuable 'teaching' time while conducting practice tests. Perhaps those schools who spend most time actually teaching the core subjects achieve higher results? Analysis revealed that the more disadvantaged schools tend to allocate more time to teaching English and mathematics than schools in more affluent areas. However, English teaching time allocation had a detrimental effect on test outcome at Key Stage 3, B = -1.09 indicating that test score decreases by -1.09 as percentage teaching time increases. This suggests that 'drilling' pupils to pass the national tests in English isn't really working for those in more disadvantaged circumstances.

It must be noted that our analysis is at the school level and exploration at pupil level would be necessary before making any evidence-based recommendation to change practice in schools. However, the suggestion from the analysis is that if the high percentage of teaching time allocated to core subjects and in administering practice tests is not directly impacting on test outcome, then perhaps some of that time should be directed elsewhere in curriculum provision to enrich pupils' school-learning experiences. If the use of expensive 'practice' tests does not improve test results, then perhaps this money could be better spent elsewhere: it really could be seen as a 'waste of money'. The government-implemented national initiatives do not create a significant impact on test outcomes either, but this should not be seen as their sole objective (even if it is the government's intention). Those projects which aim to improve social and cultural circumstances in highly deprived areas will impact over a wide range of factors. The impact of such initiatives will be very hard to evaluate and should ultimately improve test performance over a period of time. However, research (Lupton 2004b; Whitty 2001) has shown that cultural and social changes are needed to change the profile of the labelled 'disadvantaged' schools and bring about the transformation required by the government. Worryingly after ten years of New Labour governments, not only is the societal gap between rich and poor wider than when Labour came to office but also in 2007 an OfSTED annual report confirmed that schools were not closing the performance gap between those in affluent and poorer areas (OfSTED 2006).

Conclusion

There has been an international obsession since the late 1980s with measuring and comparing summative outcomes of pupil/school performance. The New Labour government despite its protested espousal of a belief system based on equity and inclusion has simply followed this trend – and carried it to extremes. In the ten years during which we have been carrying out curriculum monitoring for the QCA across a large sample of schools in both primary and secondary settings, we have observed the growth of a 'testing culture'. Schools have increased the teaching time allocated to core subjects (Boyle and Bragg 2006) to the detriment of all other areas of the curriculum. Science in particular has decreased in teaching time and curriculum provision more than any other subject, which is surprising given that this is a core tested subject at Key Stages 2 and 3, but more understandable as the government did not issue percentage target populations at a level for the subject (as it did for mathematics and English) thereby implying to teachers a hierarchy of subject esteem in which science lost out (Boyle and Bragg 2005). This neglect of science has recently been highlighted in the results of the PISA, which studied science ability across 57 countries and reported that school science performance in the UK had slipped from fourth place (OECD and PISA 2000) to twelfth place (BBC 2007c).

The curriculum is not one of 'breadth and balance' as specified in the original conception of the Education Reform Act 1988. Schools are increasingly teaching to the test, with a grudging compliance after ten years of pressure and strategy imposition, employing numerous performance-enhancing strategies in attempts to improve their results. Implementation of the National Literacy and Numeracy Strategies (1998 and 1999) enforced and endorsed the core subject emphasis, instructing primary schools to spend one hour per day on literacy and 45 minutes per day on numeracy. In addition to encouraging an increase of teaching time allocation for the core subjects, these strategies also resulted in primary schools adopting a separate subject approach to teaching rather than the integrated, topic-based cross-curricular approach that was previously commonplace.

Not only is the proportion of time allocated to teaching the core subjects a cause for concern, but also within that time pupils are spending large amounts of time on test preparation. At the lowest level of concern, there is a danger that pupils will become bored and 'switch off' from 'learning'; the deeper danger is that this 'test preparation' is becoming encultured in classrooms and confused with 'learning' (Boyle 2007; Hall et al. 2004). The lower ability pupils in more disadvantaged school circumstances, who are being subjected to more time being taught literacy and numeracy and who are more likely to sit optional tests, do not seem to be benefiting. Drilling pupils to pass the statutory tests is not working; perhaps there are better ways to inspire children to learn, make learning an enjoyable, motivating experience rather than a stressful environment after which they are, in some cases inevitably, set to fail.

In the tenth year of New Labour's tenure, national media headlines were still focused on 'fewer teens achieve maths target' (BBC 2007b) and 'primary test results improving' (BBC 2007a), which puts the assertion that 'our ideology is based on a notion of equality that is not about outcomes' (Blair 2001) to shame. Schools Minister Andrew Adonis publicly welcomed 'the best set of Key Stage 2 results we have ever seen' as 'record results but of course we have got further to go' and stated that with the 85 per cent target missed for two years in a row, discussions were ongoing about where the government 'went next with targets' (BBC News 2007b). Not teaching and learning note, not exposure of a generation of young minds to a broad and balanced entitlement curriculum, but tests and targets, rehearsing for tests and practising tests, reducing the teaching time of all but the tested core (Boyle and Bragg 2006). Is there any more fitting indictment of a decade of government intervention in education than the following supplied by the leader of the biggest teaching union? Steve Sinnott (2007) states: 'we surely must be able to come up with a better system than one which encourages the hot-house pressures of teaching to the test at the expense of the rest of the curriculum'.

6 School leaders

Meeting the challenge of change

Gillian Forrester and Helen M. Gunter

Introduction

The ascendancy of school leadership in England is linked to the UK government's goals of raising educational standards and modernizing the education system. The primacy of leadership is part of a wider agenda of transformation across public services where leaders are the vehicle by which policy reforms can be implemented and change realized (Cabinet Office 1999; Prime Minister's Strategy Unit (PMSU) 2006). School leadership has received greater attention by policy-makers and by academics both nationally and internationally where there has been a proliferation of research and writing (Mullen et al. 2002). Following Gunter (2005) we recognize that while research indicates the field to be pluralistic, New Labour policy-makers have shown a preference for functional organizational leadership with an emphasis on measuring the impact on student outcomes (e.g. Leithwood and Levin 2005). While the intention is for policy to directly impact on the practice of local leaders in the delivery of national reforms (Barber 2007) the issue for this chapter is whether and how headteachers respond and develop their own practice (Gunter 2001). We draw on Bowe and Ball (1992: 22), who argue that 'practitioners do not confront policy texts as naïve readers, they come with histories, with experience, with values and purposes of their own, they have vested interests in the meaning of policy'. A study of practice enables an examination of leader and leadership dispositions, together with how 'policy ensembles' (Ball 1994: 22) such as performance audits and choice work in ways to constrain 'the possibilities we have for thinking "otherwise"; thus it limits our responses to change, and leads us to misunderstand what policy is by misunderstanding what it does' (Ball 1994: 23). In this chapter we explore these matters, and we present data from headteacher respondents in the *Knowledge Production in Educational Leadership* (KPEL) project (ESRC RES-000–23–1192) to show how headteachers as school leaders in England understand their role and the approaches they take to leadership.

The ascendancy of school leadership

Leadership has emerged in policy-making as a 'lever' for promoting change, particularly supporting neoliberal attacks on the state and the public provision of education around the world (see Caldwell and Spinks 1992; Leithwood et al. 1999). From the 1980s the focus on 'management' underpinned much of the Conservative government's policies (see Coopers and Lybrand 1988). The idea that the right to manage, as favoured in business (and by New Right reformers of trade union rights), would improve the quality and efficiency of public services led to managerialist activities and greater control (Clarke and Newman 1997). The emergence of a New Public Management (Ferlie et al. 1996; Hood 1991) was a driving force behind government policies worldwide and connected to concerns about quality, performance and measurable outcomes (Chubb and Moe 1990). By the 1990s the discourse of leadership superseded that of management and was constructed as the means by which organizational culture could be transformed (Gunter 2004). Leadership, often defined as a process of influence (Yukl 2002), is associated with being visionary, motivational, inspirational and innovative. Leadership came to be regarded as the label for professional practice in order to secure change in education, and this discourse of the leadership of schools was embraced by New Labour (Gunter and Forrester 2008).

New Labour's aim was to improve standards, modernize education and develop a 'world-class' system (Barber 2001b). *Excellence in Schools* (Department for Education and Employment (DfEE) 1997a) was published within weeks of New Labour taking office. It provided insight into the direction of policy and drew attention to the importance and quality of leadership from headteachers. Subsequently, in *teachers: meeting the challenge of change* (DfEE 1998a), a whole chapter was devoted to school leadership. The development of a national training framework for headship was pronounced (see also Hopkins 2001) along with extended pay scales and performance-related pay (DfEE 1998a). Headteachers were fundamental to the government's overarching strategy for education:

> All schools need a leader who creates a sense of purpose and direction, sets high expectations of staff and pupils, focuses on teaching and learning, monitors performance and motivates staff to give of their best. The best heads are as good as the best leaders in any sector; including business.
>
> (DfEE 1998a: 22)

It is evident from policy texts that leadership in schools clearly resided with the headteacher who was entrusted with the task of implementing reforms (Department for Education and Skills (DfES) 2004a). However, the quality and effectiveness of some heads, and their ability to achieve results, was doubted by policy-makers who perceived the need to ensure that heads were equipped with the necessary skills and competence to respond to the challenges of change (House of Commons 1998). The existing training of heads was regarded as inadequate and so the discourse was around an urgent need for a coherent training programme. Policy-makers were also aware of a looming headteacher shortage. Government intervention was thus required to ensure a succession of school leaders as the local implementers of reform.

Policy-makers' interest in school leadership follows evidence from the fields of school improvement and school effectiveness, where educational researchers identified a link between the quality of leadership and effective schooling (Hopkins 2001; Sammons et al. 1995; Stoll and Fink 1996; Teddlie and Reynolds 2000). Policy-makers have contracted 'experts' from these fields to construct school leadership and accepted the configuration as a model that is 'transformational'. In New Labour's first term, this took the form of the 'hero head' whereby strong leadership was invested in a sole individual who would, to use New Labour speak, 'turn a school around'. In order to ensure this model was propagated among headteachers, New Labour made two major interventions: first, it instructed the then Teacher Training Agency (TTA) to produce *National Standards for Headteachers* (TTA 1998). The professional competence and conduct of headteachers has therefore been made explicit and this has structured the content of formal national preparation and professional development programmes, and framed constructions of 'good practice'. Second, a National College for School Leadership (NCSL) was created for 'cutting edge leadership training' (DfEE 1998a).

Training transformational leadership

The idea of a national college had been developing prior to New Labour coming into government (Wood 1982). Bolam (2004: 256) argues that a college became 'feasible from 1997 for three main reasons: first, it was ideally suited to New Labour's plans for enhancing the status of the teaching profession as part of its core strategy of raising standards in education; second, ICT developments opened up a range of communication possibilities previously not available; and third, the government was prepared to invest substantial sums of pubic money in both a national college and ICT.'

Plans to establish a national college for headteachers were announced by Prime Minister Tony Blair at the first New Heads Conference organized by the DfEE in October 1998 (DfEE 1998b). The Prime Minister declared that £10 million would be available for setting-up costs and investment in the training of new and serving heads would be increased to £25 million for 1999–2000 (more than double for the previous year). The Prime Minister called for better recognition of heads and higher salaries for good heads, while those who were not effective would be weeded out (Passmore 1998). The NCSL was subsequently launched in November 2000, housed initially in temporary premises on the University of Nottingham campus, prior to moving into its own purpose-built premises there in 2002.

The NCSL has three core areas of activity: national training programmes (such as the National Professional Qualification for Headship) (NPQH), research and development, and online learning, networks and information. It is a non-departmental public body (NDPB) with a remit from the Secretary of State for Education. The first remit letter stated that the college 'develop and oversee a coherent national training and development framework for heads, deputies and others in leadership positions' (Blunkett 2000: 2) and 'develop its role as a powerhouse for high quality research on leadership issues directly related to actual practice in schools' (Blunkett 2000: 3). A linear training framework was developed: from aspiring and serving middle leaders and heads through to experienced heads. In terms of research, Riley and Mulford (2007: 84) assert 'as a recipient of government funding for educational leadership research, the NCSL can exert an unprecedented influence on the direction and scope of research within England'. The NSCL epitomizes a centralized monopoly and branding for the configuration of the leadership of schools as a practical and research field in England.

Headteacher experiences of transformational leadership

The pressures of unrelenting government policies has inevitably impacted upon the lives of those leading (and working in) schools (Sellgren 2007). There are too many initiatives to list here, but we draw attention to some in order to illustrate the inherent tensions within policy, which headteachers have to try to reconcile at the local level. First, the narrow standards agenda versus personalized learning and creativity; second, the production of evidence as individual high-performing learning organizations versus the inter-agency collaboration demanded by the *Every Child Matters* (DfES 2004e) agenda; third, the promotion of a new professionalism for teachers (higher status and higher rewards) versus Workforce Remodelling including Teaching Assistants (not teacher-trained), who increasingly have teaching roles and responsibilities (Butt and Gunter 2007).

Headteachers have been required to implement New Labour's reforms and manage change and are held accountable for their school's performance. What has transpired is a situation where the nature of the headship role is too much for one single person; demographically headteacher numbers are declining; and there are too few people in schools willing to become a headteacher. To address this situation government has gradually reworked the 'hero-head', top-down model of school leadership towards one whereby leadership is distributed throughout the organization (Harris 2005; Leithwood 2001). Others in schools are thus charged with taking on responsibilities and the head's role involves building a strong and effective leadership team, reflecting trends in leadership more generally elsewhere. The government is also seeking new forms of leadership and commissioned PricewaterhouseCoopers (PwC) to examine a range of 'existing, emerging and potential models' (DfES/PwC 2007: 3). Federations of schools with an executive at the top of the hierarchy and co-headship are being given consideration along with whether the person leading a school needs to have Qualified Teacher Status (QTS) (DfES/PwC 2007). The government is also actively pushing for more collaborative ways where schools work together in partnerships (Gunter et al. 2007).

Concerns are being raised about the heroic and distributed leadership models promoted by New Labour and its NDPBs (Barker 2005; Gunter 2001; Gunter and Rayner 2007). However, the state monopoly over knowledge production through the control of preparation, development and research means that there is a marginalization of studies of experiences (e.g. Hall 1996; Ribbins 1997; Southworth 1995) in favour of impact studies (e.g. Leithwood and Levin 2005; Leithwood et al. 2006b). Consequently, little is currently known about how headteachers actually do the job and how they position themselves at this time of permanent revolution.

Researching headteachers

The *Knowledge Production in Educational Leadership* project investigated the rise of school leadership in public policy-making and as a policy strategy under New Labour. Knowledge about school leadership and how that knowledge is produced and used was central to this project, and the investigation focused on the relationship between the state, public policy and knowledge production (Gunter and Forrester 2008). This chapter focuses specially on the data generated through interviews with 25 headteachers.

Table 6.1 presents the full sample, and like Ribbins and Marland (1994: 7), 'we have tried to select people who we believed would be interesting' and were 'different in terms of their life experiences and their views'. The heads are at diverse stages in their careers and we adopted Sugrue's (2005) categorization as 'recent' appointees, 'experienced' or 'veterans'. The heads are individuals with different career trajectories, life experiences, ages and the number of years spent in the teaching profession. They have their own perspectives and philosophies about education and learning. Their training, both as teachers and as leaders, has been undertaken in different periods of time and is underpinned by different educational ideologies and philosophies. Different generations of headteachers have known different levels of professional autonomy and managerial control. There have been different expectations of headteachers over time and so leading a school has had different meanings for them. Their experience of working in the context of different school settings varies as does the types of schools in which they are currently headteachers. Some are heads in rural locations, others are in urban areas; the surrounding communities may be described as deprived and disadvantaged, affluent and prosperous or somewhere in-between. The performance of each school, as defined by its league table positioning, encompasses the full range from low to high performing. The schools may be faith schools, non-denominational, community schools or specialist schools.

Fieldwork (September 2006 to March 2007) focused on the relationship between school leadership as a form of national public policy and school leadership as lived practice. A biographical approach was adopted whereby the

Table 6.1 Sample of headteachers

Headteachers	Primary	Secondary	Special	Total heads
Recent (1–5 years)	3 males 2 females	1 male 3 females		9
Experienced (6 –15 years)	3 females	3 males 1 female	1 male	8
Experienced (retired) (6–15 years, now retired)	1 female			1
Veteran (over 16 years)	1 female	2 males	1 female	4
Veteran (retired) (over 16 years, now retired)		3 males		3
Total schools	10	13	2	25

headteachers were invited to talk about their professional experiences. Each headteacher responded to a series of questions on aspects of their reasons for becoming a headteacher, the nature of their training and professional development, and their likes and concerns about headship. Their views of New Labour's policies were sought as was their understanding of official model(s) of school leadership. Particular attention was given to how each headteacher perceived their leadership approach, to reflect upon how this had been learned and how effective they believed their approach was. Limited space does not permit a full presentation of each of the 25 individual approaches to leadership and so we provide a focus on 5 headteachers who illustrate themes from the whole dataset (see Table 6.2).

Of the 25 headteachers interviewed some articulated their leadership approach in terms of different phases. These were 'experienced' heads or 'veterans' who could reflect on a number of years of headship. They perceived that at first they were 'directive' and later moved towards 'collaboration' whereby they devolved leadership to others. Susan described her leadership approach in three distinct phases. In the first phase ('this has got to change' phase) it was necessary to instigate change quickly to achieve what she believed the governors had appointed her to do. There was a sense of urgency during this phase and she was authoritarian; leading from the front, directing change and was 'reactive'. Subsequently, she attended the Leadership Programme for Serving Heads (LPSH) and her staff were required to complete a questionnaire relating to her leadership. She was 'quite shocked' to find staff regarded her as 'didactic'. This prompted her to review her practice, which she perceived as 'harsh' and she was determined to 'soften'. She vowed to make time to talk and listen to people, though she found this time-consuming. In the second phase (described as 'giving responsibility') she gave staff members specific responsibilities in order to give them a sense of ownership within the school (in terms of its mission, decision-making etc.). However, she did not make staff accountable and found that

Table 6.2 Summary of five heads

Headteacher	Sex	Status	School type	School location
Susan	Female	Experienced	Primary	Small town/urban
Mary	Female	Recent	Primary	Village/rural
John	Male	Recent	Primary	City/urban
Linda	Female	Experienced	Secondary	City/urban
Bill	Male	Veteran (retired)	Secondary	City/urban

accountability remained with herself. In the third phase ('giving responsibility and accountability' phase) she was 'better organized'. Staff have responsibility but now with accountability. She sets time limits on these responsibilities (e.g. developing policies, initiatives etc.); they are undertaken within specified timeframes which she monitors and this enables her to have some control. She operates an open-door policy for staff to talk to her about any issues or concerns and she places great importance on being able to see people when they need to see her. Leadership in the school is described as 'distributed' though Susan is adamant that distributed leadership as a specific approach is not new, but rather 'trendy jargon' for an approach that has always existed in schools.

Some headteachers articulated the importance of the 'team', of 'sharing' leadership and 'working together'. We draw on data from Mary to exemplify this approach. Mary states that she 'shares' leadership of the school 'as much as possible'. She considers she has 'a very open style' where 'everything that goes on [is] discussed in a very open way'. She regards herself as the 'ideas person' whereby she makes suggestions to staff which they then deliberate together. When she first came to the school she devised the school development plan herself. Now she provides the structures and time for staff to 'fulfil their roles', contribute to the school development plan and 'take responsibility so they have much more autonomy over their own subjects'. She 'coaches' staff and gives them responsibility 'so that they can develop themselves'. She actively encourages staff to engage in continuing professional development (CPD) and 'sends them out as much as possible'. She believes however that she is 'too friendly' with staff and so possibly there are times when she is 'taken advantage of' because she is 'not as assertive as [she] should be'. This she attributes partly to the 'context of this school' and partly as her 'own fault'. She considers that staff 'know me very well' and so it would be difficult 'to suddenly change' her leadership approach. She has contemplated the nature of her approach though doubts whether she would actually have been able to achieve as much if she had been 'harder-nosed'. She is however shortly moving to a new school where she plans to be 'more assertive' stating, 'Fundamentally you are what you are but you can try and incorporate, you can develop some [leadership] styles, which I have tried to do. And when I move I intend to be different.'

For some headteachers 'networking' is an important component of their leadership approach. John typifies this approach. He enjoys 'professional contact with other heads and sharing ideas' and meets formally with a network of local heads. He talked at length about the nature of the network and the federation of schools to which his own school belonged. He is 'constantly engaged' in his own professional development and is 'always out on courses' or at the NCSL. He describes his leadership approach as 'quite open', 'quite democratic' and as being 'totally approachable'. As a leader he believes crucially in 'empowering' his staff and giving them 'independence'. He relies a great deal on his 'personality as a manager' and believes in presenting to staff 'a model of stability'. John strives to be 'the calming influence in the storm', where he says, 'I'd like to think I give that stability, I give that kind of control when things are tough and I know that's what they look for and that's what they look for from me'. John is 'committed to maximizing development in other human beings' and has thus sought to develop the teaching staff and teaching assistants. He states:

> if we were to produce a fertile environment in which children should grow, all the adults in charge of that environment have got to have a meaningful and active role in that process. And that I hope is what goes on, in fact I know that's what goes on in this school.

John has concerns about the pace of government change and new initiatives in education. He favours approximately '80 per cent' of these though considers some need to be 'given more time to be looked at and thought out in a more contextually based way'. Nevertheless he claims that courses he has attended have been particularly influential so that he approaches 'change in a totally different way' whereby he 'goes out and seeks and demands change'.

Some headteachers identified with transformational leadership. We draw on data from Linda to illustrate this approach. She perceives herself as a 'charismatic leader' and indeed has been identified by the Department for Children, Schools and Families (DCSF) as a 'transformational leader'. Her approach to school leadership 'is to be creative and passionate about this school' and entails having 'vision for the school', and 'imagination'. She described herself as a 'risk-taker' and her approach is 'collaborative'. The school leadership team (SLT) comprises nine people who devise the school's development plan. The vision for the school is 'drawn down into step changes' and priorities are determined each year. These are printed on posters and placed around the school so that 'everybody can own them and engage them in the whole school'. Linda regards herself as 'a people-orientated person' and an 'ideas person' – she is 'much more fired up about things we can do' rather than what the school has already done. She has the 'vision for the school' and has appointed people to 'embrace the vision of where we are going'. She believes she is intuitive in being able to appoint staff who will fit into the school's particular environment and culture. She believes she draws on a 'fairly eclectic mix' of leadership styles depending on circumstances and situations. She regards herself as 'outgoing' and ensures she has a visible presence in the school by being out on the school corridors, going 'round school twice a day' and conversing with staff and students: 'I am a walk and talk person'. She does not regard herself as 'an interferer', believing 'people should be trusted to get on'. Trust is therefore an important attribute, although she has structures (described as 'antennae') in place to make sure things work in the way they should.

Some headteachers emphasized the importance of having clear sets of values that underpinned their whole leadership approach. Bill typifies this approach. He had 'a values-driven approach to school leadership', which had a child-centred focus. At an 'intellectual level' his leadership was bound up with a conceptual map (in the form of a detailed chart) which enabled him to understand the school and 'all its interrelated complexities'. The conceptual map was underpinned by 'the values of the school' and the aims of the school stemmed from those values. The values were identified by 'the staff, conversations with governors and to some extent by parents through the PTA [Parent Teacher Association] and pupils'. He devised the conceptual map and this was deliberated by staff. This process created: 'a corporate understanding of what the school is about because it's only when we have a corporate understanding of what the school is about that we can work as a team, and teams within that larger team.'

He dealt with administrative matters each morning before the school opened, 'met with the deputies at 8.30am every day' and 'did a lot before school actually began'. During the day he could thus 'channel [his] energies into being around and playing a fairly typical role in things' and was 'not an office bound bureaucrat-administrator'. He 'spent a huge amount of time working on the ethos' and creating a climate where 'pupils can learn and be successful'. He was 'always pushing for improvement in every area'. At the 'practical level' he 'attempted to be omnipresent':

> I did yard duties, I did lunch duties. I consider those to be of huge importance especially lunch duty. I was on the corridors virtually five hours a day, in classrooms, in staff rooms, spending a lot of time with the pupils. Staff actually, they never resented it. I think in one sense they saw it as a kind of 'watch it because he might be coming in any minute now' . . . I would sometimes read the work, sit down with a pupil . . . I would sit in on the discussions . . . So that I felt was a very important aspect of my headship.

He regarded his 'greatest strengths as a head was the art of delegation' meaning:

> where you give to an individual an area of responsibility – giving them in a sense the right to make a mistake, not that you want them to make a mistake or that you will be pleased if they do but you have sufficient trust in them to believe that they will discharge their duties in a way which is commensurate with the corporate view of the way in which the school is led.

The research findings presented above provide a snapshot view of leadership approaches at a particular historical moment. The research focused on headteachers' lived experiences of leadership and how, through their approach, they reconcile the demands of transformation and cultural change.

Approaches to school leadership: towards a dynamic positioning

Making sense of headteachers' individual differences and responses in the context of different working environments is challenging, though at the same time seeking patterns and relationships is essential in understanding approaches to school leadership. One way is to create 'types' and this has been utilized in other studies (for example, Grace 1995; Hoyle and Wallace 2005; Woods et al. 1997). However, our analysis of the data identified the complexity of head-teachers' working lives and their approaches to leadership over time; we found that heads' accounts were sometimes contradictory and inconsistent. Like Bottery (2007a, 2007b) we recognize that headteachers are varied in personality, experience and context, and so they cannot be typed or fixed in time and space. What we have created therefore is a dynamic positioning of approach (see Figure 6.1) which takes into consideration a range of approaches which individual headteachers might embrace or move through at different times and in response to different circumstances. Positions are therefore not necessarily fixed, and arguably more than one might be appropriate simultaneously, with a dialogic process in play (Bradbury and Gunter 2006). Positions are not necessarily exclusive and may be informed by characteristics that are shared across others, such as 'trust' for example. Its purpose is to illustrate rather than offer 'proof' of approaches to school leadership, and so it offers a way of thinking about how headteachers approach their leadership work.

The dynamic positioning of leadership approach (Figure 6.1) can be read as follows. The vertical axis is a continuum from heads as autonomous where they decide, through to participatory approaches with staff, students and parents involved in decision-making, or even undertaking bottom-up involvement. The horizontal axis is a continuum of whether heads understand their pro-fessional purposes as being determined by themselves in main as members of an educational community interplayed with others who may require or expect a particular approach, e.g. the school's governing body or central government.

The *Directive Approach* is a position taken by heads when they have a strong sense of their own purpose as head*teacher* and what they want to do and achieve in the job. The *Directed Approach* is very similar and constitutes leading from the front; however, the direction and the process by which change is taking place may be under the direction of internal (e.g. governors) and/or external (e.g. inspectors, local authority, sponsors, NDPBs) interest groups. There are times when both approaches are overlain with the language and behaviours of the official New Labour model of heroic heads as transformational leaders, where heads present themselves as charismatic, inspirational and visionary. For

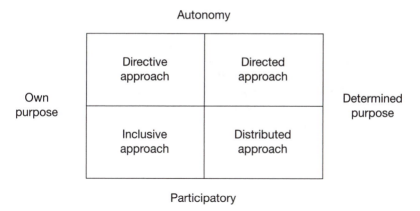

Figure 6.1 Dynamic positioning of approaches

the Directive Approach this can mean when the headteacher adopts the New Labour persona as one congenial to him/herself in driving forward their agenda, while for the Directed Approach this can mean adopting an approved-of identity in order to deliver.

The *Inclusive Approach* incorporates the notion of the school community as a core component, where educational purposes are led on by the headteacher who actively seeks the participation of others through a 'first among equals' position. Relationships at a professional and personal level are fundamental here, as are mutual exchanges, understanding and trust. Here leadership is understood as a communal and relational social practice rather than automatically a product of role. The *Distributed Approach* is a position that follows official good practice where headteachers are directed to create diverse workforce roles and delegate the responsibility and accountability for tasks and projects.

Headteacher approaches to leadership may differ over time and in context, where narratives about what was done and why may not always be clear or coherent. Susan is explicit about how she has positioned her leadership from directed to distributed, and there is a dialogue going on with a more inclusive approach, but she has been directed to move through the LPSH rather than it being based on an explicit model of participation. Mary has not been successful in taking up the inclusive position and intends to be more directive in her next job. Bill has inhabited the directive approach during his long career, with a constant focus on educational values of teaching and learning. Interestingly John and Linda seem to be in dialogue between directive and directed. They have a strong sense of leadership identity and they are determining school purposes, but it is clear that this is in tension with being directed, John by NCSL training and Linda through her links with the DCSF.

Developing explanations of these different positions needs to take into account the interplay between headteacher agency or the sense of determining their work and identity, or the heads' sense of how their work and identity is given to them. Building on Bourdieu's (2000) thinking tool of *habitus*, there is evidence that the headteachers are disposed to the leadership by one person, with individual reflections on what works and does not, and how they think it needs to be done. There is also much evidence that this disposition has been structured by their experiences over time, and is restructured through the ongoing narratives that they construct when talking about it. Hence their agency is shaped and even determined by how headship is understood at that moment in time, and for those who are in post currently, there are often tensions between wanting to set the direction and being directed by others.

There is a predisposition to use the official language and talk about what is regarded as official good practice, and it seems that the child–centred focus of their work can be underplayed as a result. There is some recognition that there is a *doxa* (Bourdieu 2000) or self–evident truths embedded in the New Labour delivery model, though readings of this by the headteachers is highly individual with a range of positions that are not absolute: Susan accepts performance management but is critical of the literacy hour. Interestingly there are dilemmas over the requirement to do distribution, as involving others has traditionally been a part of headteachers and their work, but what is actually going on as distinct from articulating the phrase is unclear with a range of claims and labels being used that would need further on–site research. Central to this analysis is whether the heads recognize that their role is being constructed by others, and that their sense of agency may be a form of what Bourdieu (2000) calls *misrecognition*. Hence heads may talk the language of vision but in reality the space in which they can determine is narrow, and at most it may be a case of interpreting tactically what can be done rather than actual strategizing (Hartley 2007a). While there are claims made about making decisions according to headteacher and school purposes, this is not really resistance as national standards still have to be met and it is heads who are officially successful who position in this way. Indeed a number of heads are involved with the NSCL and the DCSF where they are advising and delivering in a national way, and while some are uneasy about policy strategy, they are prepared to work with it and try to change it from within.

Analysing the narratives remains difficult because the heads talk about how busy they are with no time to think about what they are doing, or read anything other than official texts and approved of writers (e.g. Covey, Fullan). We also experienced that in spite of our attention to appropriate disclosure and interview protocols, many of the heads could not conceive of this research as being independent of the DCSF and the NCSL, and so narrative construction was affected by this. This adds to interpretations of misrecognition, where heads such as John and Linda do not talk about how their positioning, and the tensions within it, is a product of the context in which they are trying to practise. Whereas Susan is more aware of the game in play and how she has accepted direction as a means to an end, and is trying to develop positions that secure her role among the workforce. Interestingly only the veteran head, Bill, has a sense of educational values, whereas the others, even the experienced two, are more likely to position themselves with policy implementation narratives where the emphasis is on making things work locally. In that sense the politics of headship through the exercise of power within and outside the organization, is in need of more development, and the field has intellectual resources from Hoyle (1982) to begin to develop contemporary perspectives. Importantly, none of these five heads talk about their work in ways that show that the inclusive position as one that is the starting point for headship, and as such the continued association of leadership with hierarchical role is enduring. This is how New Labour has been able to rework headship as organizational leadership (directed and distributive) through appealing to the leader-centric nature of education (directive), without engaging productively with professional and collegial ways in which professionals may prefer to work (inclusive).

Conclusion

There is much written about leadership but there is little actual research into headteachers and their work. This is because headteachers have been the objects of radical reform since the late 1980s, with New Labour shifting the emphasis away from heads in a marketplace introduced under Conservative governments to heads in a delivery system. Consequently, headteachers have faced interventions into their professional identities with deliberate strategies to seduce them. In Bourdieu's (2000) terms this has been through, first, the 'symbolic capital' of national recognition by the government (e.g. in speeches, giving honours, higher pay, and, establishing a training college); second, the promotion of headteachers as the linchpin of school improvement as a self-evident truth or 'doxa'. Such positive attention can mean that headteachers misrecognize how this deflects attention away from the coercive force of performance audits (inspections, labelled as failure, league table position, public dismissals). Research is controlled by the government, and so reform priorities dominate, and the main emphasis is on how implementation might be secured better in order to meet targets. The KPEL project has kept alive the tradition of collecting narratives of how heads go about their work (e.g. Hall 1996; Ribbins 1997) and what meanings they attach to it, and consequently there are opportunities through scholarship to 'disrupt totalising technical and managerial strategies of regulation' (Thomson 2001: 19). We have begun to reveal the demanding nature of the job, where words such as style, model and type are inappropriate and damaging. We have presented a much more dynamic framework for enabling headteachers over time and in context to demonstrate that what they do shifts through how leadership is constructed as a social practice. Our data are yielding interesting understandings of how much of the time heads are in dialogue about how they get an increasingly impossible job done, in ways that do no harm to themselves, their colleagues or the students.

7 Remodelling and distributed leadership

The case of the school business manager

Charlotte Woods

Introduction

This chapter examines the current state-funded preparation of school business managers (SBMs) to take on an enhanced leadership role in English schools as a site for exploring some of the tensions inherent in school workforce reform. In so doing, it will focus on a segment of the workforce who have until recently excited little scholarly attention. New Labour school reforms aimed at maximizing value for money, and shaping England's education provision to further international competitiveness, closely resemble market-driven, neoliberal reforms taking place in many other countries (Stevenson 2007). However, it has been argued that in England such reforms have been particularly far-reaching (Gunter and Butt 2007a), and include policies aimed at increasing teacher outputs and developing flexibility within the school workforce through a process of 'remodelling'. A danger inherent in remodelling arises from the fact that it is 'located within a very complex struggle over ideas and territory' (Gunter 2007: 6) and it is such struggles that this chapter seeks to explore.

Stevenson (2007) outlines the tensions inherent in public sector reforms being implemented internationally in response to global economic pressures. He cautions against accepting the official reading of such changes as value-neutral technical fixes. Rather such policies are deeply political and give rise to a questioning of the very purposes of schools and schooling. In England these include the extension of the social services role of schools, which is causing concern among headteachers that the quality of teaching and learning will suffer as a result (Shepherd 2008). Meanwhile, redistribution of labour among the school workforce, via workforce remodelling, implies a significant shift in what characterizes the professional practice of teachers (Hammersley-Fletcher 2007; Stevenson 2007). This mirrors changes in other branches of the public sector, such as the health service and police, where less well-qualified workers are recruited to meet demand at a much reduced cost. Further, the provision of higher level SBM training in England, coupled with the widening social services remit of schools, paves the way for the management of schools by people who are not qualified teachers, thus raising concerns that the focus on the core activities of teaching and learning in schools might be further compromised.

Conceptually, the chapter draws on the notion of 'distributed leadership'. Empirically, it is informed by research conducted for the National College for School Leadership (NCSL)[1] conducted over a number of years in connection with its Bursar Development Programme (BDP), designed to build leadership capacity among staff with business management roles in English schools (Brown et al. 2002; C. Woods et al. 2003, 2007). The chapter begins with a brief overview of New Labour's workforce remodelling strategy and the current position of school business management in schools in England. One perspective on 'distributed leadership' is then offered and used to shape analysis in the remainder of the chapter (Gronn 2002). Then the chapter will consider findings in relation to the division of labour between teaching and administrative colleagues in an increasingly complex task environment in schools. It concludes by outlining implications for the professional development of the school workforce and for further research.

Reforming school business management

Within the context of New Labour's wider public sector reforms, and parallel reforms internationally, the school workforce in England is undergoing transformation (Gunter and Butt 2007b). The process was initiated by the introduction of site-based management from 1988, but has been given a boost through the New Labour solution to a predicted crisis in the recruitment and retention of teachers and future headteachers. New Labour's remodelling strategy was a response to the identification by government consultants of workload as a factor in qualified teachers leaving the profession (Gunter et al. 2005; PricewaterhouseCoopers 2001). From September 2003, schools have been taken through a phased process of developing the role and activities of the part of the workforce usually known as support staff. Significantly, teaching assistants, student pastoral services, site managers and technicians have increased in number and have taken on work that traditionally teachers may have done.[2] Through strategies such as transferring administrative tasks from teachers to support staff, reducing the amount of teaching cover and providing guaranteed time for planning and leadership activities, remodelling was designed to reduce the workload of teaching staff.

As responsibility for financial management has increasingly been devolved to school level since 1998, and complexity in the way schools are funded and structured has grown, so has the need for expertise in the business management aspects of the school become more pressing. PricewaterhouseCoopers (2001) identified significant gaps within administrative and bursarial support for headteachers and teachers, and the NCSL has since been taking the lead in developing leadership capacity among business management staff in schools via its BDP. At present the BDP includes two programmes accredited by the Institute of Administrative Management (Certificate of School Business Management (CSBM) and Diploma of School Business Management (DSBM)), though at the time of writing, plans for piloting two higher-level courses are well advanced.

Through the systematic development of expertise among SBMs, the BDP is designed to alleviate the workload of headteachers and other teaching colleagues grappling with structural and financial complexity. A serious shortfall in headteacher numbers is predicted in English schools, with 58 per cent due to retire between 2008 and 2018, and few younger teachers willing to take on the responsibility and administrative burden, despite increases in pay. Building leadership capacity among SBMs is viewed as having potential to impact favourably on the recruitment and retention of headteachers by making headship more attractive. The fact that SBMs themselves are in an ageing profession (Wood et al. 2007), makes the need to strengthen this capacity still more pressing.

Though it is too early to ascertain the impact of the BDP in this respect, there is evidence that NCSL's training programme is producing notable benefits for the SBM community in England (NCSL 2007). A baseline study mapping developments in school business management between 2004 and 2007 indicates that, while England lags behind some countries (e.g. USA and Australia), it is now being placed on a more professional footing (Wood et al. 2007). There is wide variability in the status and functions of school business management practitioners and the part that they play in New Labour's workforce remodelling reforms. There is also a notable lack of consistency in the way business management functions are organized and labelled in English schools and a marked degree of uncertainty among individuals about whether or not, regardless of job title, they consider themselves to fulfil the SBM function. Wood et al. (2007) have found that this is particularly marked for staff with 'administrator' or 'finance' in their titles, or with multiple titles, perhaps reflecting an increasing understanding that the SBM role suggests a wider and more managerial remit. Relevant job titles include 'School Business Manager', 'Bursar', 'Administrator', 'Finance Manager', 'Office Manager' and 'School Secretary'. Among the most widespread are 'Bursar', historically a high-status role with financial responsibilities, and that of the SBM, which is 'equally high status but implies a far wider role and a level of operation that is managerial' (Wood et al. 2007: 5). For the purposes of this chapter, the latter label is used to denote any non-teaching colleagues with business management responsibilities.

Investment in the BDP is clear evidence of the belief among policy-makers that SBMs have a role to play in sharing in the leadership of schools at a senior level in England. It is this notion of shared or 'distributed' leadership, and its place in remodelling, which will be explored in the remainder of the chapter.

Competing leadership models

Underpinning the argument for workforce remodelling is the idea of sharing, or *redistributing*, the administrative and management work of teaching staff more widely using appropriately skilled and knowledgeable support staff. It is assumed that, by reducing the time spent on administration, workload will be diminished and qualified teachers and teacher leaders will be able to devote more time to the core business of teaching and learning. In turn, so the thinking goes, this should have a positive impact on teacher recruitment and retention and on educational outcomes.[3] Hartley (2007a) argues that despite a lack of evidence of a causal link between distributed leadership and pupil attainment, the idea is one whose 'time has come' in the field of education leadership, and it has received 'official endorsement' in England and in other national contexts (Hartley 2007a: 202). An exploration of NCSL's website reveals evidence that distributed leadership has been a major thrust in New Labour education policy, including its BDP (NCSL 2008).

The term 'distributed leadership' is not unproblematic, however. It has considerable 'conceptual elasticity' with authors defining and applying the idea in quite different ways (Hartley 2007a: 202). A comprehensive exploration of the term is beyond the scope of this chapter, though more thorough discussions of the concept are provided elsewhere (e.g. Bennett et al. 2003; Gronn 2002; Spillane et al. 2001). Hartley attributes the recent emergence of the concept of distributed leadership in education to both political and social factors. From the social perspective, it sits well with a 'general weakening of classifications' in contemporary culture and a trend away from organized social structure and towards networks (Hartley 2007a: 209). In political terms, Hartley links the rise of distributed leadership to disenchantment with transformational models of leadership. These two political influences resonate with an influential article mapping the conceptual territory of distributed leadership, and which will be used to shape analysis in the remainder of this chapter (Gronn 2002).

Gronn (2002) locates the origins of 'transformational leadership' in the work of Bernard Bass. In this analysis, this 'apogee of individualism' can be characterized as a belief that the effective performance of a group or organization depends on the ability of a single leader (Gronn 2000: 317). With its 'exaggerated sense of agency', transformational leadership assumes 'a crudely abstracted leader–follower(s) dualism, in which, inter alia, leaders are superior to followers, followers depend on leaders and leadership consists in doing something to, for and on behalf of others' (Gronn 2000: 319). Though it has been criticized in academic circles (e.g. Gunter 2006), this transformational view of leadership is one whose appeal endures both in the popular imagination and in a substantial proportion of organizational scholarship. It is also the view that is evident in early New Labour education policy, which saw headteachers as change agents with the power to deliver reform by framing vision and motivating and inspiring staff. The government's assumption that headteachers would be pivotal in their change agenda can further be inferred from the concerted efforts to focus on increasing the status and leadership capacity of this section of the workforce. This can be seen, for example, in the foundation of the NCSL and in increased remuneration and prestigious events to reward headteacher achievement (Gunter and Forrester 2008).

As bureaucratic and administrative requirements on schools have increased, so have the range and complexity of school management tasks, and the diversity of school structures and their interactions with other agencies. In England, in addition to the impact of educational reforms on schools, the global economic impacts on national social policy more widely have given rise to a collection of welfare reforms under the label of *Every Child Matters* (www.everychild matters.gov.uk). These require schools to liaise with bodies such as social services, local authorities, the police and drug teams and to provide extended services outside normal hours. Recognition of the unsustainability of the position of one individual shouldering this increasing burden, coupled with concerns over the recruitment and retention of teachers and future headteachers, subsequently contributed to the promotion of a more distributed view of leadership in New Labour education policy. This shift in emphasis is visible, for example, from the greater prominence being given to developing leadership capacity *throughout the school system* and increasing reference to 'senior managers' and 'leadership teams' (Gunter and Forrester 2008).

Although the idea of distributed leadership has now firmly taken hold in espoused education policy, a number of inconsistencies can be identified between the stated commitment to distributed leadership and the ways in which policy is enacted in relation to the professional development of school leaders, including business managers. A number of these tensions arise from the adoption of normative standards of leadership practice. Gronn (2002: 666) sees the use of standards 'framed as a set of normative leadership expectations for *individual* management jobholders' as being fundamentally at odds with the notion of leadership that is *shared*. Building on work by Stewart, he proposes an 'indeterminate role space' as a more appropriate interpretation of a managerial job than that of a 'slot to be filled by an individual incumbent carrying out a prescribed set of duties' (Gronn 2002: 666). Nonetheless, normative standards that delineate the expectations on an individual postholder often act as a template for shaping leadership training. This is the case in leadership training offered by the Interstate School Leaders Licensure Consortium in the USA and the NCSL in England.

Further, Gronn (2002) argues that normative leadership standards tend to conflate the role of headship (i.e. having legal authority) and leadership (to which any organizational member can contribute). As the chief incumbent, the common public perception is that headteachers are the best person to consult on all matters of importance, even if they are not the member of staff who is the leader in the relevant aspect of the school. By tending to vest in the headteacher both the role as legal authority and as leader in all aspects of the school, normative standards tend to reinforce and perpetuate the heroic leader paradigm. Both headteacher and SBM informants have referred to the reluctance on the part of parents, or other members of the school community, to deal with members of the workforce other than the headteacher (C. Woods et al. 2007). Conservatism among stakeholder groups (headteachers themselves, other teaching colleagues, teaching unions, school governors, the general public, local authorities) was the most commonly cited barrier to SBMs being able to contribute effectively to school leadership in areas where they have expertise, a finding consistent with those of (PricewaterhouseCoopers 2007). These perceptions suggest that though policy-makers may no longer be in thrall to the notion of the 'hero head', public attitudes, and those of teachers and head-teachers in some cases, may have remained largely fixed within this perspective, a tendency that the use of normative standards may unwittingly help perpetuate.

Gronn (2002) identifies further tensions arising from the use of normative standards in leadership training in England which are relevant to the professional development of SBMs in England. First, the normative standards that underpin the training of school leaders are not based in practice but are an ideal to be aspired to, designed to elevate the profession. Gronn notes the irony that by itemizing in detail the high expectations placed on *individual* school leaders, such standards may have increased perceptions of work overload and discouraged future recruitment among an already diminishing talent pool. Gronn (2002) is referring to headteachers, but given the ageing profile of SBMs in England, the relative lack of professional development that many have received to date and perceptions that workload is growing, an unfortunate inadvertent consequence of setting out standards for SBMs could also be one of discouraging recruitment and retention. Second, Gronn notes that the way innovators codify information, via such standards in the early stages of the diffusion process, tends to influence their development by subsequent adopters. Gunter (2006: 210) warns against allowing the trading of leadership models to become 'a form of economic, social and political colonialization'. This is significant in light of the fact that an adapted form of NCSL's BDP was being piloted in South Africa at the time of writing.

Articulation of school leadership tasks

A second strand in Gronn's (2002) discussion of distributed leadership that resonates with the findings from the research on which this chapter draws is that concerning the articulation of workflow. This section employs this notion in presenting and discussing instances and implications of the way labour is divided between teaching and non-classroom-based support staff in informants' accounts. Demands on schools, both in terms of the information required and of foreshortened timescales for its production, have increased simultaneously. Meanwhile, capability in ICT has grown in tandem with accountability and public expectation. The intensification of administrative work implied by these trends, Gronn argues, has impacted on workflow articulation in two interrelated ways, both of which tend to favour the emergence of distributed forms of leadership. Intensification has led to a growth not only in *interdependence* between work roles but also in new types of work *coordination*.

The first of these, *interdependence* between work roles in the accomplishment of tasks, is deemed to have a number of organizational benefits, including reduced likelihood of decision error; effective utilization of individual competences as groups engaged in tasks establish the most appropriate division of labour; opportunities for developing new expertise through the 'huddle effect' (Gronn 2002: 671); higher levels of trust and increased mutual support through the closer bond that sharing the success or failure of task outcomes brings.

However, BDP research data suggest that the benefits of interdependence between teaching and support roles could be more effectively realized in some schools (C. Woods et al. 2007). For example, there was evidence of remodelling resulting in the routine delegation of administrative tasks in their entirety to support staff, regardless of whether or not input by teaching colleagues was required for their successful completion (e.g. preparing risk assessments for field trips). In other cases, repercussions were more far reaching. In one such case, the facilities management expertise of the SBM was not drawn on in creating a link between a primary and a special school. In consequence, the lack of disabled facilities was not spotted within the project proposal and children had to be transported between the schools during the course of the day in order to use the toilet. Greater work role interdependence between teaching and support staff in such cases offers potential organizational benefits of the type proposed above, such as error reduction and the development of new expertise.

Differing mental models of distributed leadership might contribute to an understanding of why interdependence of support and teaching roles may be limited in some contexts. In a school where an *additive* version of distributed leadership is the predominant model in the minds of staff, work roles in different domains of operation would remain largely distinct in the minds of members. For example, in this context, leadership on any matters perceived to be directly relevant to teaching and learning would tend to be focused on the headteacher, and their qualified teacher delegates, with little contribution from support staff. The SBM, or their support staff delegates, meanwhile, would take charge of matters that most obviously fall within their remit, such as finance and risk. This mental model would be at odds with a more holistic view of leadership distribution, in which teaching and support staff work in concert, contributing to decision-making according to their particular expertise. In a school where a *holistic* model of leadership is widely ascribed to, this more collaborative way of working would tend to be adopted for all decisions of potential significance for pupil learning and welfare, regardless of whether it is most closely associated with teaching or non-teaching aspects of operation.

In NCSL's preparation of SBMs, it is the latter, holistic, model of distributed leadership that is promulgated where teaching and support staff work in concert, as evidenced in candidate handbooks for the certificate and diploma qualifications they offer. These are replete with phrases indicative of this version of distributive leadership ('making a broader contribution to the leadership of the school as a whole'; 'multi-professional teams'; 'a contribution to the development of the whole school as learning community'; 'interface between school business management and teaching and learning'). The study findings indicate that where the model predominating in their school is the additive one, confusion or frustration may result for the SBM in training whose own perspective has embraced a more holistic one through continuing professional development (CPD). They also indicate that this was most likely to be the case where senior teaching colleagues have not themselves undergone recent CPD. The number and type of professional networks that headteachers, and other members of the school's Senior Leadership Team (SLT), belonged to were felt to have a major impact on teaching colleagues' attitudes. For example, headteacher or middle leader participation on the National Professional Qualification for Headship (NPQH), or acting as one of the NCSL's virtual support network for head-teachers, were perceived to make a real difference to how readily SBMs and other support staff are able to contribute effectively to leadership in a particular school.

Closely linked to the notion of interdependence is the second aspect of workflow articulation identified by Gronn (2002): *coordination*. This concerns 'the design, elaboration, allocation, oversight and monitoring of those activities comprising an organization's technical core' and encompasses the necessary 'personnel, resources, materials, trajectories, tasks and output requirements' (Gronn 2002: 672). The dynamics of coordination may be explicit, such as in roles and responsibilities set out in job descriptions, or *implicit*. The fact that a large proportion of work coordination is implicit can lead to the impression that it gets done automatically. Gronn cites Lucy Suchman's ironic observation that, in the case of staff with a supporting role, 'the better the work is done, the less visible it is to those who benefit from it' (Suchman 1995: 58 cited in Gronn 2002: 673).

There is evidence in the BDP data that SBMs suffer a lack of visibility in some contexts. That increases in workload in schools since 1998 have been mainly in terms of administration can be in little doubt. In the study there was broad agreement between teaching staff and SBMs that business management tasks had increased both in number and in difficulty since 2005. However, there were marked differences in perceptions of the extent of these changes between the two staff categories. Among non-teaching staff, agreement that SBM tasks had increased in number and in complexity was almost universal (93 per cent), with a small proportion (5 per cent) believing they had stayed the same and 2 per cent being uncertain. Among teaching staff, on the other hand, the picture was more mixed, with 78 per cent and 75 per cent respectively believing that SBM tasks had grown in number and complexity and 7 per cent being uncertain (C. Woods et al. 2007). These differences in perception might suggest that the true extent of the workload increases among SBMs implied by workforce reforms is not visible to teaching colleagues. Indeed, there were strong indications in interview data that SBMs perceived themselves to be exposed to very considerable work pressure, working 'at full stretch and beyond', with a proportion having 'fallen off their perches' as a result. Work pressures for SBMs are unlikely to decrease in the short to medium term. An explicit aim of work-force remodelling is to 'enhance the status and work/life balance of all adults who work in our schools' (TeacherNet 2007). It would be regrettable if, in lightening the administrative burden on teaching staff, undue strain were unwittingly placed on support staff

Another danger associated with the lack of visibility of SBM and support staff more generally in workforce reform, is that of the inequities that it may disguise. Wood et al. (2007) provide evidence that colleagues with SBM functions in schools in England are on average better qualified and better remunerated in 2007 than in 2004, with some reduction in pay differentials between males and females. However, gender imbalances still exist. Males typically earn more than their female counterparts and are almost universally assigned high-status titles (Bursar, SBM, Business Director, or titles including the word 'manager'), while lower status titles are generally reserved for women, with some being labelled '"School Secretary" despite having adopted a wider business management role' (Wood et al. 2007: 24).

Discussion of inequities in the distribution of work underscores the social dimension of the division of labour. In some schools, SBMs were keen to join the SLT, or at least to participate in discussion of agenda items where they have a significant contribution to make, but were not being given this opportunity. One SBM, though her offer to sit in on relevant discussions was declined, still received regular phone calls during team meetings to ask her for advice or information. The perception that support staff were often consulted too little and too late was common to both teaching and non-teaching staff. Although involvement in leadership was perceived to be increasing, only 16 per cent of informants believed that their leadership potential had been fully realized. These data indicate that SBMs have untapped potential for improving the quality of decision-making.

Interviewee accounts indicate that SBMs and other support staff in some schools in England are functioning at levels that would have been unthinkable just a few years ago. They have become indispensable to the effective functioning of schools and in some contexts their contribution is both welcome and fully recognized. However, elsewhere the reported reluctance of teacher leaders to accept support staff as partners in relevant areas of decision-making, might suggest a lack of understanding of SBM expertise and how it relates to pupil education and welfare. Some SBMs interviewed believed that a proportion of their teaching colleagues viewed the SBM role in very narrow terms (e.g. as 'completing paperwork' or 'anything with a pound sign on it'). One SBM referred to the manner in which administrative work was often delegated to support staff by teachers as 'smacking of "this is paperwork and is beneath us"'. Interviewees emphasized that, while support staff fully recognize that theirs is a service role, what seemed to be lacking in some schools was the mutual respect required for support and teaching staff to develop the synergies necessary to capitalize on their complementary talents and knowledge.

It is important to note that lack of understanding and respect was not unidirectional, however. SBM interviewees used phrases such as 'cosseted', 'spoilt' or 'not on this planet' to describe how some support staff viewed teachers, though none of them admitted to harbouring such sentiments themselves. Some also lacked confidence in the ability of teaching staff to make decisions in areas of SBM expertise. One, for example, suggested that teachers did not understand the implications for teaching and learning of their financial decisions and that the power to make such decisions should therefore be taken from them. Especially where SBMs have entered education from a business context, such mutual incomprehension between teaching and business management colleagues may be in part attributable to differences in professional discourse, and the values that underpin it.

Half of the SBM respondents in the study had business management experience not in a school setting, of whom 78 per cent had experience in private sector organizations. Many bring with them qualifications specifically related to management and, while their potential to bring practices from more business-oriented environments might be viewed as a benefit by some involved in shaping policy (Pricewaterhouse Coopers 2007), difficulties may arise through what might be conceptualized as a form 'intercultural communication' in which the way people think and express themselves and leads to lack of understanding between different cultural groups (Gudykunst 2005).

Differences in values and in styles of communication between colleagues socialized into the teaching profession and those from a business culture may account for the somewhat polarized 'them and us' views in the BDP data between teaching and support staff in some contexts. A number of teaching colleagues suggested that the style of communication of some SBMs made it difficult for their voices to be heard on the SLT. One referred to their SBM as being 'a bit bulldoggish and rather frightening', and excellent communication skills were felt to be essential for SBMs to realize their leadership potential. Others referred to the need for SBMs to have a better understanding of teaching and learning.

Meanwhile, SBMs considered that teaching colleagues often underestimated the ability of support staff to be as pupil-oriented as they were themselves. One SBM, who had left the private sector because of a commitment to education, recognized that colleagues who 'had never worked outside education' would not necessarily appreciate the connection between business management and educational outcomes. Nonetheless, she was sometimes frustrated by questions during SLT meetings couched in terms of 'And what's your view coming from the private sector?'. She attributed the lack of SBM input into decision-making in some schools to this limited understanding of how business management connects with educational outcomes and, in her view, the erroneous belief among some teaching staff that the ultimate goals of school business managers are somehow different from their own.

Conclusion

Current international, market-driven public sector reforms, together with concerns over the recruitment and retention of sufficient numbers of teachers and headteachers, have given rise to radical change in the way work is co-ordinated in English schools. Indeed, it could be argued that the very purpose of schools is beginning to be challenged via the welfare reforms underpinning *Every Child Matters*. The inexorable rise in administrative workload, and the trend towards schools working in partnership with other educational organizations and public sector bodies, imply an increased role for SBMs in assisting their teaching colleagues in managing their schools' complex agendas in future. A number of implications may be drawn from the BDP research findings in terms of the professional development of the school workforce and for further research.

First, the use of normative standards to shape the professional development of school leaders may be counterproductive. Such standards tend to emphasize the roles and responsibilities of individual postholders rather than the value of more interdependent ways of working. Second, a degree of mutual incomprehension between administrative and teaching staff in some schools may be acting as a block to the most effective work coordination. This might indicate the desirability of underlining in the CPD of school staff the contribution of the work of both groups towards the same ultimate goals of achieving the best possible pupil learning and welfare outcomes. Through fostering a shared understanding of how their contributions in this endeavour are *different*, but nonetheless essential given the way schools now operate, potential for greater interdependence between teaching and administrative staff may result over the longer term. Interdependence between the various staff groups may benefit the workforce through alleviating perceived work pressures, building leadership capacity, increasing social support and ultimately enabling schools to meet their challenging goals. In encouraging interdependence, professional development which includes elements where teaching and administrative staff learn together, would seem particularly appropriate.

The perspective of the SBM, and the tensions inherent in the enhanced leadership role of this staff group implied in current reforms, have been little researched or debated. There is work to be done by the research community in illuminating this area and perhaps in combating polarization of debates between the two stereotypical perspectives of teachers 'defending their privileges' versus that of business management as destructive of professional cultures and as 'subjecting practice to the workings of the market' (Gunter 2007: 6). The SBMs interviewed saw themselves as working 'alongside and behind' the headteacher, rather than in front. They were not in favour of schools being taken over by 'pen-pushers', many drawing parallels with the disastrous consequences in some quarters of the National Health Service of the overzealous adoption of leadership models from business. However, in some cases, there was a palpable sense of frustration among SBMs at being unable to contribute to the leadership of their schools in ways that their professional development had prepared them.

8   Initial Teacher Education

A(nother) decade of radical reform

Olwen McNamara

Introduction

The two decades since 1984 have been a period of sustained and radical reform to the structure, content and regulation of teacher preparation and training in England. The centralizing tendencies first apparent during the early Conservative governments, and the accountability culture which grew apace during later Conservative governments, were intensified in New Labour's first period of office; both in terms of the degree of micromanagement of the sector, and the scope and pace of the reform agenda. The Teacher Training Agency (TTA), established two years prior to New Labour taking office, was the key driver of change in England; and it was from this point that policy with respect to Initial Teacher Education (ITE) across the UK began to diverge markedly. It could be argued that towards the end of New Labour's second term there was a slight plateauing in the rate of systemic change in England and in this chapter I identify a number of contributory factors. I also trace the historical trends that have led to such a positioning of ITE in England and offer a very brief overview of the increasing divergence in policy and practice in the devolved administrations of Northern Ireland, Scotland and Wales. Overall, the key characteristic of the first decade of New Labour is an intrusiveness of policy requirements, micro-management and accountability that has created a compliance culture which has rendered many fundamentally important debates about ITE as peripheral. Further detail on the issues covered can be found in Brown and McNamara (2005) and McNamara et al. (2008).

Politicization

The establishment in 1984 of the Council for Accreditation of Teacher Education (CATE) (Circular 3/84, Department of Education and Science (DES) 1984) was a key watershed for ITE introducing, as it did, the notion of accreditation for the first time. The subsequent two decades were a period of sustained and increasingly radical reform. Successive governments progressively increased control mechanisms and regulatory prescription in respect of process and curriculum, and none more so than in the first term of New Labour (Furlong et al. 2000; Mahony and Hextall 2000).

Some ascribe the move of ITE from relative obscurity to strategic significance to an assumption, on the part of the successive governments, that ITE was an effective mechanism for steering change in the school curriculum and transforming teacher professionalism (Furlong 2001, 2005). Alexander et al. (1984) identify the appointment of Keith Joseph as Secretary of State for Education in 1976, and the availability of increased evidence from Her Majesty's Inspectorate (HMI) surveys of the impact of training on the competence of new teachers, as the catalysts for central government interest in the sector. A corpus of inspection evidence in the early 1980s had indicated that all was not well in the training sector: newly qualified primary teachers emerged as more competent in teaching skills than their secondary counterparts, but less so in curricular areas (HMI 1982, 1983b). CATE's solution was to create more practically based teacher education and prescribe minimum lengths of school-based training for different courses (Circular 24/89, DES 1989a). The targets were met by all and exceeded by some, but HMI (1991), expressing caution about capacity and resourcing, particularly in the primary sector, recommended a 'measured' increase only in the extent and formality of school-based training arrangements. 'School-based training' morphed into 'partnership' and was now the new mantra promoted in 1992 by Kenneth Clarke, Secretary of State for Education, at the North of England Conference. Legislation (Secondary Circular 9/92 and Primary Circular 14/93, Department for Education (DfE) 1992, 1993a) rapidly followed, increasing the school-based component of courses still further and prescribing a competences-based assessment model of subject knowledge and classroom skills. The combined effect of these modifications increased the level of intensification of courses, rendering them over-full and squeezing out what had previously been key aspects of curricular and professional learning (Furlong et al. 2000: 103). The new arrangements were condemned variously as 'political rape' (Gilroy 1992), 'time constrained', 'lacking flexibility', diluting the intellectual and professional foundation of ITE (Wilkin 1996) and 'eroding rigour' – largely against international trends in teacher education (Holyoake 1993; Judge et al. 1994). An additional impact of the changes was the apportioning of funds between higher education institutions (HEIs) and schools in respect of the latter's greatly increased role. This in turn increased financial pressures (Gilroy 1998), caused a marked casualization of the workforce and also, indirectly, increased pressure on the delivery of courses (Taylor 2000).

There was also a drive at this time to diversify routes into teaching through establishing school-based schemes (later to be renamed employment-based routes) (DES 1989b) and School-Centred Initial Teacher Training (SCITT) providers (DfE 1993c). Indications of further drastic reform came with the establishment of the TTA as a successor to CATE (DfE 1993b). The move from 'Council' to 'Agency' signalled a change in governance and the, now formal, redesignation of 'Teacher Education' as 'Teacher Training' augured a profound ideological shift (Wilkin 1999). The proposals attracted much opposition from all quarters (Edwards 1994). The TTA's brief, more wide-ranging than that of CATE, was to include: teacher recruitment, quality control and assurance, and funding and accreditation of training routes. Its remit extended only to England and it is at this point, just before New Labour came into office, that the three devolved administrations began to diverge significantly from England in their teacher training provision.

The relationship between the UK government and the various devolved administrations in relation to legislative, strategic and executive functions in respect of education create an extremely complex and fluid landscape, which Raffe et al. (1999) articulate in great detail. Prior to devolution in 1999 the Welsh Office, Scottish Office and the Department of Education, (DENI) Northern Ireland had for some 25 years administered teacher training in the various territories; although sensitive to local needs they were accountable to the UK Parliament for the implementation of UK policy. A trend toward increasing divergence has, as noted, been apparent since the mid 1990s. The devolution of executive power to Wales, and legislative power to the Scottish Parliament and Northern Ireland Assembly, also meant that responsibility for policy-making no longer sat centrally with the Department for Education and Skills (DfES) and, as a result, a steadily escalating level of divergence emerged across the UK (Raffe et al. 1999).

Regulation in England

Returning to the English context, in its first two years the TTA established what could best be described as a turbulent relationship with the sector. By the coming of New Labour in 1997, TTA had nearly doubled its staffing and expenditure, and had broaden its remit to include management of in-service funds to providers. Feelings of 'alienation' and 'hostility' in the sector towards the TTA came to a head, however, with an impending teacher supply crisis and a national debacle over TTA's ill-conceived in-service education policy (Kane 1998, quoted in Gilroy 1998). At its Quinquennial Review (Department for Education and Employment (DfEE) 1999a) in 1999 TTA's portfolio was refocused on initial training and induction.

The TTA's quality assurance remit extended not only to assessment in ITE but also to curriculum content, which was now for the first time regulated. The most radical and comprehensive change with regard to the practice of training providers was heralded by the publication of the National Curriculum for Initial Teacher Training, commonly know as Circular 4/98 (DfEE 1998c), which prescribed requirements for courses including length, partnership arrangements, selection of trainees and quality assurance and assessment processes. A thorough analysis of the procedures and reporting of the 1997 consultation process left Hextall and Mahony (2000: 323) 'concerned about the state of democracy in England'. Central to Circular 4/98 were the standards for the award of Qualified Teacher Status (QTS), which set down in unimaginable detail around 100 standards relating to: trainees' knowledge and understanding; planning, teaching and classroom management; monitoring, assessment, recording, reporting and accountability in relation to subject knowledge, teaching studies and monitoring and assessment; and other professional requirements. It was subject to much critique (e.g. Richards et al. 1998).

In addition to the QTS standards, Circular 4/98 also specified in detail extensive subject knowledge. For primary schools the impending changes were linked to the introduction of the National Literacy Strategy (Medwell et al. 1998; Wyse 2003) and National Numeracy Strategy (Askew et al. 1997; Brown and McNamara 2005). ITE was being mobilized to support the reform agenda. Subject knowledge demands were further increased in 2001 by the introduction of QTS skills tests in mathematics, English and ICT, controversial not least because they focused on professional knowledge, such as interpretation of data, rather than curricular knowledge; and there was evidence to suggest that certain minority constituencies were disadvantaged (Hextall et al. 2001).

It was at this time also that a formal three-term induction period was reintroduced in England (DfEE 1999b). Newly qualified teachers (NQTs) were entitled to support from a school-based induction mentor and a 10 per cent reduction in contact hours for professional development activities; they were assessed against induction standards. A large-scale DfES-funded evaluation (Totterdell et al. 2002) reported that the vast majority of NQTs, headteachers, induction tutors and local education authority (LEA) representatives considered the process beneficial. Reports of the actuality falling short of intentions were in respect of entitlement for reduction in contact hours, access to professional development activities, mentoring, and funding (Bubb et al. 2005; Heilbronn et al. 2002; Jones et al. 2002; Kyriacou and O'Connor 2003). An HMI survey (2001) noted that large numbers of NQTs on short-term contracts had no entitlement to support and that 60 per cent of primary and 30 per cent of secondary NQTs were appointed on temporary contracts.

In 2002 Circular 4/98 was superseded by the slimline *Qualifying to Teach* (DfES 2002), New Labour having now explicitly abandoned attempts to prescribe pedagogy and detail subject knowledge. The new framework, which contained about 40 QTS standards, was much more positively received by the profession (Simco and Wilson 2002), not least because of its explicit focus on professional values and practice. The next manifestation of the QTS Standards (DfES 2007) were a subtle refinement of the 2002 version foregrounding the new *Every Child Matters* agenda and reducing the number of standards still further (to 33).

The significance of the 2007 version was that for the first time it placed the QTS standards within a coherent framework of National Professional Standards for the whole workforce, first mooted ten years earlier. This was made possible because in 2005, a decade after its inception, the TTA was relaunched as the TDA (Training and Development Agency *for Schools*) with a remit to raise children's standards of achievement and promote their well-being by improving the training and development of the whole school workforce. ITE was, it seemed, set to take a back seat as TDA faced the challenge of its vastly extended remit. Furlong (2005: 132), reflecting on the new positioning of ITE, concluded: 'the end of the era is to be regretted'.

Inspection

If policy had been deployed to refocus the content of ITE to engage with subject knowledge as it was situated in the classroom and to more closely align with and steer changes in the curriculum, then the inspection regime was mobilized to ensure that providers were 'on message' and this it did with fervour. The inspection of the quality of training provision, previously managed by HMI, was brought under the auspices of OfSTED in 1994. The first of these new-style inspections were a considerable cultural shock to the sector, particularly for primary providers, who were all inspected in 1995/96 and reinspected on the teaching of reading and numeracy the following year, despite the fact that they were not found to be areas of weaknesses in the original inspection (Furlong and Kane 1996). Upon taking office New Labour embraced the inspection system wholeheartedly and the subsequent round of primary inspections was planned to coincide with the most extensive curriculum change ever undertaken in England, the introduction of the National Literacy and Numeracy Strategies (1998–2000) and, not surprisingly, the inspection focused on English and mathematics.

A system of grading was used to measure standards and low grades or non-compliance incurred real penalties in terms of reduced allocation of training places, or worse! Judgements were fiercely contested and Campbell and Husbands (2000), in a case study of two primary inspections (1996/97 and 1997/98) at Warwick University, contrasted the 'informed connoisseurship' model, formerly deployed by HMI, to the new 'technicist' model adopted by OfSTED. The move from HMI to OfSTED heralded an era of 'surveillance and control' that professed greater transparency of criteria through the Framework for Assessment of Quality and Standards, and had the potential to lead to greater inter-inspector reliability of assessment, and greater consistency of judgements across contexts. Lack of confidence was, however, expressed in the piloting, evaluation and rigour of the evidence base for the criteria statements (the 1997/98 version contained about 160) (Gilroy and Wilcox 1997) and the validity and reliability of the process (Graham and Nabb 1999).

The accumulated corpus of inspection evidence indicated significant improvement had occurred in traditional training provision, including SCITTs, although on the whole they performed less well than HEI providers (OfSTED, 2003d). Evidence of this improvement is supported by data from inspection reports of NQTs during the years 1997–2001 (HMI 2002). Complaints from the sector about the burden and high-stakes nature of inspection, however, led to the Parliamentary Select Committee on Education and Employment recommending the introduction, as a priority, of a four-year inspection cycle with differentiated light-touch provision (House of Commons 1999). The latter, with a focus on management and quality assurance, was introduced in the 2002–2005 Framework of Inspection; although in a survey of providers by the Universities' Council for the Education of Teachers (UCET 2007) the short inspection was not felt to be markedly less onerous. In 2006–2007 under the 2005–2011 framework half of providers inspected were deemed to be 'outstanding' in management and quality assurance (OfSTED 2006). Data from the annual survey of NQTs provide corroborating evidence of continuous improvement, with some 88 per cent of the NQTs (n=11,000) rating their training good or very good (TDA 2007).

By contrast with the inspection of traditional provision, employment-based routes into teaching have, since their (re)launch in 1998 under New Labour, been subject only to survey inspections. The most recent (2003–2006) concluded that the management of training had improved substantially over the period such that during 2005–2006 half of the lessons observed displayed strengths but one sixth still had significant weaknesses. Mentor expectations were low, particularly in respect of subject-specific learning, and overall secondary training was weaker than primary (OfSTED 2007). Despite these repeatedly less than favourable inspection reports, employment-based provision was allowed to substantially increase its proportion of the sector, while inspection grades were being used systematically to inform the allocation of training places for traditional provision.

The combined weight of the QTS standards and the OfSTED framework functioned as a quality assurance instrument for the assessment of training and trainees and the weight of inspection and evaluation evidence cited above indicates an increase in performance indicators. Mahony and Hextall (2000), however, reported that very few providers thought that the overall quality of their courses had improved and generally felt the whole assessment portfolio was a 'bureaucratic nightmare'. Reports indicate that workload for the new short inspections, rather than lessen significantly, had shifted to fall more intensively onto course leaders (UCET 2007). That inspection is still being strategically planned to focus the sector on particular educational enterprises and nationally defined goals is evidenced by the survey inspection in September 2007 of initial training in early reading on the quality and impact of training in phonic work as reflected in the renewed Primary Framework, subsequent to the publication of the Rose Review (2006).

Partnership

Encouraged by CATE in the late 1980s, providers had voluntarily made considerable strides in the sector towards developing formal models of school-based training. Once such arrangements were mandated in legislation (Circular 14/93, DfE 1993a) many providers challenged what they saw as the government's simplistic depiction of partnership as the trainee developing practical skills in schools and subject knowledge in the university (Edwards 1995). They argued that the changes had reinforced 'hierarchical relations' and the 'demarcation of practice in schools from educational theory' (Dunne et al. 1996: 41). Taylor (2000: 55) not only speculated that 'specification of who does what, is less important than the existence of shared values based as far as possible on a common knowledge base', but also expressed concern at the lack of acknow-ledgement of the additional costs or the equity of the relative distribution of resources and accountability.

Furlong et al. (2000) reported that most commonly, partnership throughout the 1990s was HEI-led with contributions from school-based colleagues, although they identified a continuum of more integrated collaborative models. The introduction of school-led SCITT provision and employment-based routes in the mid to late 1990s, however, opened up the possibility of schools having the central role in training without the collaboration of HEI stakeholders, thus undermining the notion of partnership.

Upon New Labour taking office, partnership had undergone renewed scrutiny with the introduction of Circular 4/98 and the coincident teacher supply crisis. The latter triggered a 40 per cent increase in training allocations, which raised grave concerns about the capacity of the system to deliver the relatively new partnership model of training. A number of interventions were planned to increase capacity and quality in school-based training, including a network of high quality, mainly secondary, Training Schools (DfEE 1998c), which have now been subsumed under the specialist schools network (DfES 2004d). The major national intervention was the high-profile National Partnership Project (2001–2005), which distributed £1.7 million of funds annually to support partnership-building activities. The National Project was terminated one year early in 2005 when a decline in pupil numbers precipitated a contraction in the training sector and a lessening of the placement crisis. The evaluation team concluded that the project, with an overall budget of around £6 million, met many of its objectives but argued that many of the funded projects reduced teacher education to a 'technical-rationalist task' (Furlong et al. 2006a: 41).

Routes into teaching

A number of marked shifts in the patterns of training in the decade since New Labour took office can be seen in the disaggregated data in Table 8.1. First, the sixfold increase in the proportion of the market taken by employment-based routes in the first six years of New Labour. Although the political significance of the proliferation of ITE provision in England in the early 1990s was considerable, the relative uptake of non-traditional provision was still extremely small in the 1997. New Labour repackaged and promoted the QTS only employment-based training even, as argued above, when there was evidence that standards were compromised and concern expressed that it lacked academic rigour. Second, the teacher supply crisis at the turn of the millennium led to an increase of 30 per cent in primary training numbers and 50 per cent in secondary numbers and forced New Labour to introduce postgraduate training bursaries in 2002. It was triggered by rising school rolls, low teacher retention and falling recruitment, and was exacerbated when New Labour introduced higher education (HE) tuition fees in 1998. Currently England is in a period of oversupply of teachers as a result of falling rolls, triggering substantial cuts in allocations, particularly in the secondary sector and concentrated in non-shortage subjects (TDA 2006). This temporary downsizing of the 'client base' should, however, be read against the impending retirement of over 25 per cent

Table 8.1 Training recruitment by route and phase of education

	Year	1998/99	1999/00	2000/01	2001/02	2002/03	2003/04	2004/05
Undergraduate	Primary	7,370	6,580	6,390	6,490	6,600	7,030	6,990
	% All primary	53%	47%	43%	40%	36%	36%	37%
	Secondary	1,960	1,520	1,440	1,300	1,260	1,220	1,240
	% All secondary	13%	10%	8%	7%	6%	5%	6%
	% Total	32%	27%	24%	22%	19%	20%	20%
Postgraduate	Primary	6,000	6,590	6,750	8,030	9,040	9,510	9,270
	% All primary	43%	47%	46%	50%	50%	49%	49%
	Secondary	12,880	13,020	14,610	15,460	17,030	16,750	16,210
	% All secondary	84%	84%	79%	78%	75%	74%	74%
	% Total	65%	66%	64%	65%	64%	63%	62%
EBR	Primary	490	830	1,610	1,690	2,510	2,750	2,690
	% All primary	4%	6%	11%	10%	14%	14%	14%
	Secondary	440	960	2,510	3,120	4,300	4,740	4,530
	% All secondary	3%	6%	14%	16%	19%	21%	21%
	% Total	3%	6%	12%	13%	17%	18%	18%
Total	Primary	13,860	14,000	14,750	16,210	18,150	19,290	18,950
	% Total	48%	47%	44%	45%	45%	46%	46%
	Secondary	15,280	15,500	18,560	19,880	22,590	22,710	21,980
	% Total	52%	53%	56%	55%	55%	54%	54%
	Total	29,140	29,500	33,310	36,090	40,740	42,000	40,930

Source: DfES 2006

of classroom teachers who are currently over 50 (DfES 2006) and a greatly increased population growth estimate announced in 2007 by the Office for National Statistics (ONS 2007). Third, the introduction of the HE tuition fee, which had played its part in triggering the teacher supply crisis, also intensified pressure on the four-year primary undergraduate training route, as did the postgraduate training bursary, and by 2004/05 a shortened three-year training model had captured 40 per cent of the undergraduate market in England (Furlong et al. 2006b). Overall undergraduate training reduced from 53 per cent to 37 per cent of primary provision in the first seven years of New Labour.

Compared to other training routes the traditional Postgraduate Certificate in Education (PGCE) has remained remarkably stable over its long history. In 2007, however, to accord with the Framework for HE Qualifications (Quality Assurance Agency (QAA) 2001), it branched into the M (masters) level Postgraduate Certificate of Education and the H (honours undergraduate) level Professional Graduate Certificate of Education. Recent variants have also included an enhanced Fast Track Programme, which offered a lucrative package of incentives for postgraduate trainees and was launched in 2000 as part of the New Labour school improvement/workforce reform agenda. Its ambition was to attract into teaching able young graduates, identified as potential future leaders, and support them in developing the skills to progress rapidly into senior positions. The programme was rolled out to selected providers in 2003/04, only to be terminated in 2005/06.

More recently Teach First, a hybrid employment based route was developed for high-flying graduates willing to commit to teaching in schools facing challenging circumstances for a minimum of two years. Once qualified, and in their second year of teaching, the participants embark on a leadership training programme to prepare them for pursuing a career in commerce, industry or, if they chose to remain in the profession, in education leadership. Quintessentially for New Labour the programme is sponsored by business and industry and, has since its inception, achieved endorsement from the very highest echelons of the political elite. Introduced in London in 2002 Teach First was rolled out regionally from 2006 and its numbers are set to rise substantially.

Home internationals

Wales

The Welsh Assembly Government has jurisdiction for the management of teacher education which it executes through the Higher Education Funding Council for Wales in respect of funding and accreditation of courses and via HM Inspectorate for Education and Training in Wales in respect of inspection. The General Teaching Council for Wales (GTCW, established in 2000), registers teachers, awards QTS and advises on teacher supply. Currently the DCSF oversees teacher supply in Wales and TDA recruitment. Two marked differences in the pattern of Welsh training are the continued popularity of the primary undergraduate route, which is followed by 60 per cent of trainees, and the fact that it is virtually all three years in duration. Employment-based routes and SCITTs have virtually no presence in Wales (Furlong et al. 2006b). ITE is delivered through formal partnership arrangements, such as were instituted in England in the early 1990s, and has not embraced any New Labour reforms. The Welsh Assembly introduced a one-year induction scheme, which replicated the principles and entitlements of the English model in 2003 and ongoing developments include proposals to link the induction standards into a framework of professional milestones and standards (GTCW 2007). In 2006, a review of ITE in Wales recommended a strategic reduction of 50 per cent in primary training numbers and 25 per cent in secondary training numbers before 2010, a shift to graduate-only entry, and a rationalization of training into three regional schools of education (Furlong et al. 2006b).

Scotland

The General Teaching Council Scotland (GTCS) was established in 1965, decades before its counterparts in the rest of the UK, and became the independent regulatory body which registered and advised on teacher supply, reviewed and accredited ITE programmes and set the standards for teachers at each phase of their career. The GTCS undertakes accreditation reviews of Scottish ITE provision and, once approved, providers have the authority to award the Standard for Initial Teacher Education (SITE) which authorizes entry to the GTCS register of teachers. Despite the apparent autonomy of the seven providers, there is a broad consistency of approach which includes a school-based component, although the training is HE-led and there are no formal partnership arrangements (Brisard et al. 2005). The proportions of students following undergraduate and postgraduate routes are similar to those of England, although virtually all undergraduate degrees are primary and four years in duration. Historically, prior to the devolution of power to the Scottish Parliament in 1999, Scotland, more so than the other UK administrations, had begun to diverge in terms of education policy and strategy. In the mid 1990s, in response to UK legislation increasing the proportion of school-based training, the GTCS established a working group that proposed the schools should be active partners in delivering ITE. Events were overtaken by a national review of teachers' pay and conditions (McCrone 2000) and an Induction Scheme was introduced instead which offered a guaranteed salaried one-year training post (Scottish Executive 2007).

Northern Ireland

During the period 1972–1999 Northern Ireland was under direct rule from the UK Parliament and the training of teachers was administered by the Department of Education, Northern Ireland; much the same criticisms were levelled at it as at the English system. In the early 1990s, DENI undertook a comprehensive review of ITE, induction and early professional development

(DENI 1993), which recommended a formal initial training partnership built upon the existing school and HEI collaboration but schools were reluctant to take on responsibility for training and assessment of students (Caul and McWilliams 2002). Eventually, in 1997 an integrated partnership model was agreed which encompassed the three phases of Initial Teacher Education, Early Professional Development and Continuing Professional Development. Additionally, a General Teaching Council for Northern Ireland (GTCNI) was established to register teachers and oversee standards for the profession, inspection being the remit of the Education and Training Inspectorate.

Teacher educators

The nature of the ITE curriculum and requirements in England has made it virtually essential that teacher educators have QTS. More recently non-managerial career development opportunities and the relatively poor remuneration levels in HE have made a move to teacher education financially unattractive. Additionally, the transition from teacher to teacher educator involves 'boundary-crossing' between two very different cultures and activity systems (Boyd et al. 2006) and can take two or three years to establish 'new' professional identities (Murray and Male 2005). The sheer range of knowledge and skills required in the role is challenging (Boyd et al. 2007) and many new recruits report receiving inadequate induction (Murray 2005). The literature identifies three immediate priorities for new teacher educators: first, 'survival', second, 'the differing pedagogic demands of working with adults', and third, 'laying the foundations for scholarship and research activity'. The latter they identify as an especially challenging (Boyd et al. 2007).

In addition to the pressure on the individual, the drive for increased research selectivity, particularly in research-intensive universities, has made non-research-active recruits from school less attractive to employ and more difficult to assimilate into the academic culture. The profile of staff in education departments who made a submission to the Research Assessment Exercise (RAE) in 2001 shows that while research expertise was spread widely across these institutions the spectre of a growing dislocation between teacher education and research was worrying. Departments with no core research funding designated on average 35 per cent of staff as research active, attracted 22 per cent of the total UK external research grant income, focused their research on schools and directed it to the teacher audience. Those departments with core quality-related (QR) research funding also received nearly 80 per cent of total UK external research grant income, returned on average 70 per cent of staff as research active, researched areas such as curriculum, assessment, organization, policy, management and inclusion and directed more of their research to other researchers and policy-makers (Oancea 2004a, 2004b). Profiling teacher education, Dadds and Kynch (2004) found that 80 per cent of teachers were trained in education departments with no core research funding. No data are available regarding the proportion of dedicated teacher educators among staff designated as research active in education departments but one can surmise that this will be considerably less than the figures quoted above.

Mills et al. (2005) in a Demographic Review of the UK Social Sciences considered the profile of education, the second largest unit in the social sciences, against comparable disciplines and concluded that it was significantly different. In terms of research activity at 42.5 per cent it had the lowest proportion of staff entered in the 2001 RAE and only 25 per cent of staff had PhDs. The age profile of education department staff was also older than that in the social sciences generally: in 2003–2004 nearly 70 per cent of staff were over the age of 46 and 50 per cent were over 50. In a survey of research interested or active British Educational Research Association (BERA) members just over one-third of respondents began their research career aged over 38 years (Taylor 2002). The survey was conducted for the Research Capacity Building Network (2002–2005) funded by the Teaching and Learning Research Programme (TLRP: 2000–2008) the largest programme of research ever funded by the Economic and Social Science Research Council (ESRC). TLRP's capacity building work is aimed at the academic educational community but recent capacity building initiatives aimed specifically at teaching include the Higher Education Funding Council for England (HEFCE) Teaching Quality Enhancement Funding (2006–2009) to support the 'research informed teaching environment' in less research-intensive institutions and ESCalate (2003–2009), an Education Subject Centre of the Higher Education Academy, which produces resources, organizes conferences and funds small scale projects. Other initiatives include the TDA-funded Teacher Training Resource Bank and the Teacher Education Reference Group (funded jointly by UCET/BERA/TLRP) offering an educational research literature training resource and the Teacher Education Resource Network (TERN) funded by the ESRC in the north-west of England.

Succession planning in teacher education is undoubtedly of very significant concern and will become more so. The reasons, as rehearsed above, are complex and include increasing research selectivity. The HEFCE Teaching Quality Enhancement Fund has signalled that research and scholarly activity should be seen as essential to underpin teaching and professional learning for teacher educators in less research-intensive universities. In research-intensive institutions the danger is that teacher education may be less attractive to research-active academics if conditions are not conducive to support them, and if teacher educators are not research active, then teacher education may not be valued sufficiently in such institutions to be sustained as core business.

Conclusion

The period since 1987 has seen sustained and radical reforms of a practical and ideological nature in which New Labour has latterly established a common framework of professional expectations and aligned ITE with wider education reform agendas. The impact, as measured by inspection frameworks, has been to embed partnership as a core principle of provision, improve the management and quality assurance of training and increase the preparedness of newly qualified teachers to engage with subject and pedagogic knowledge as it is situated in the classroom. Although the increase in systemic change has plateaued, punitive monitoring and inspection has not and the level of intensification of programmes is still increasing under New Labour. The academic curriculum has been extended to encompass contribution to society, safety, health, and economic well-being and trainees are also expected to develop an understanding of an extended range of professional contexts, from working with others in the classroom to working in multi-professional teams providing access to integrated and specialist services including childcare, parenting and family support, community facilities and learning and, finally, to promoting community cohesion. This leaves little time for previously key aspects of extended professional learning and reflection, especially on primary postgraduate routes and particularly at a time when New Labour aspirations are to make teaching an M level profession (Balls 2007). Additional threats to this aspiration are that the drive for increased research selectivity means that most teachers are trained in departments with no core research funding and that succession planning for the ITE workforce is generally a key issue.

The politicization of education generally has led to a welcome investment of energy and resources but has left the sector subject to short-termism and the vagaries of political whim resulting in vulnerability for institutions and programmes and developments have at times been subject to contradictory ideological forces with evidence of a lack of coherence and consistency in their educational principles and values. The degree of regulation, bureaucratization and accountability, and the linking of performance indicators to resourcing, has engendered a 'technical rationalist' approach to education outcomes and processes that has tended to restrict the nature of professional engagement and create a 'culture of compliance' in both trainees and educators. Most particularly it has rendered many fundamentally important debates about ITE peripheral because of the sheer weight and intrusiveness of policy accountability, monitoring and inspection.

9 New provisions of schooling

Denis Mongon and Christopher Chapman

> Today's scientists have substituted mathematics for experiments, and they wander off through equation after equation, and eventually build a structure which has no relation to reality.
>
> Nikola Tesla (1934)

Introduction

New Labour education policy can be examined through any number of lenses. Some of the banner headlines for its focus on what happens inside schools and classrooms have included reforms of the curriculum, national teaching initiatives and reforms of the workforce. New Labour's starting position was that its priority would be to raise standards rather than to reform structures. 'What works' was what would be done and the organization and institutional forms of schooling could take a back seat – arguably because the new government did not want to be drawn into a politically debilitating and parliamentary time-consuming battle over the 160 or so remaining grammar schools. Given that starting point, it is remarkable how far New Labour has been drawn into an increasing effort to change the constitutional arrangements for schools and for secondary schools in particular. The central argument in this chapter is that this effort might well be contributing to the gains in educational attainment to which many other initiatives are also adding, but that it still leaves the fundamental problem of the education service untouched – a raft of young people are being left increasingly adrift of the progress and opportunity being created for the majority. This chapter is a reminder of just how much effort has been put into structural reform and raises the question whether the light has been worth the candle.

Part 1: so much effort

The focus on plans and targets was plain to see in New Labour's first Education Act (The School Standards and Framework Act 1998) which picked up from the previous year's White Paper *Excellence in Schools* (Department for Education and Employment (DfEE) 1997a) and maintained the momentum of many of the previous Conservative government's reforms. The 1998 Act required changes to the way schools were inspected and the local implementation of seventeen different 'education plans' including infant class size, the National Literacy and Numeracy Strategies, remodelling the school workforce, changes to the school curriculum and local authority education development plans. Amidst all that focus on process and accountability, it would have been hard to discern then how absorbed the government would become in school organization, still less in something approaching an obsession with 'diversity and choice'. The signals on structure in that first Act, far from promoting what is now called a more diverse system, hinted at a more equitable, collegiate approach than previous Conservative governments had taken. The running argument over the divisive effects of Grant Maintained (GM) Schools was to be resolved by bringing them closer into the local authority fold where there would be three main categories of schools – voluntary schools (to embrace mainly existing 'aided' and 'controlled' schools), foundation schools (to embrace the previously GM schools) and community schools (to embrace the 'county schools' which had continued as local authority maintained schools). This simple arrangement in part dealt with the variations in funding between the different kinds of school, all of which would, with a period of protection for those previously favoured, be subject to the local authority's formula. The matter of admissions and school closures which had also been part of the GM arguments was to be 'depoliticized' by the creation of independent School Organization Committees and the appointment, nationally, of independent adjudicators. The Secretary of State would from time to time issue a Code of Practice on admissions to which the relevant bodies would be required 'to have regard' though not, we all noticed, 'to follow'. It had the drawbacks of a compromise position and the benefits of pragmatism.

The 1998 Act also allowed the Secretary of State, if it was 'expedient to do so with a view to improving standards in the provision of education', to allow a group of schools 'to constitute collectively an education action zone [EAZ]' (Section 10.1). EAZs were trailed by Stephen Byers as a way for schools to break free of local authority control – perhaps as a diversion from the partial return of GM schools to that control. Instead of offering an opportunity to promote collegiality in the mainly socio-economically poorer areas where they were established, EAZs were born in a blizzard of bureaucracy and an icy atmosphere of mistrust from otherwise potential local partners. It was not the last time that a macho approach to legislating, to allow schools to do what on the whole they could already, would cause embarrassment for the government. The initial interest among EAZs in community networks and a wider set of performance measures – which would now be recognizable as the *Every Child Matters* agenda (Department for Children, Schools and Families (DCSF) 2008f) – was squeezed by the political demand for fast improvement in the end of key stage scores, so fast that the Department for Education and Skills (DfES) was claiming an EAZ factor in improved General Certificate of Secondary Education (GCSE) outcomes within months of their establishment. It is hardly surprising that EAZs rarely fulfilled their potential (Gewirtz et al. 2002: 97–120). However,

New Labour was soon to develop a commitment to diversity and competition rather than to community and collegiality, to private sector involvement rather than public sector leadership. Specialist Schools, Academies and, more recently, Trust Schools have been three key strands to this: it is worth recalling how much political, administrative and budgetary effort they have absorbed.

Specialist Schools

Specialist Schools were inherited by New Labour from the previous government and have been promoted vigorously since. Initially, they were regarded by many observers as a potential source for division in the education service simply and obviously because some schools, at first a small minority, acquired this attractive title, additional funding and inevitable local kudos; others did not. Since the bidding process for specialist status required schools to acquire sponsorship including financial commitment, some would find it easier than others; it was clear that in general the greatest struggles to raise the funds would be in the areas of greatest need. Although this distinction and division is diminished now that the large majority of secondary schools have at least one specialist designation, it will reappear later in this chapter.

The trajectory for Specialist Schools had taken off in 1995 when the Conservative government offered maintained secondary schools the opportunity to apply for specialist status. By the middle of 1997 and three months into Labour's first term there were 252 Specialist Schools (including 176 Technology Colleges), closing on 10 per cent of those eligible. The Labour government pursued the policy and in the spring of 2001, David Blunkett outlined proposals, including an acceleration in the number of Specialist Schools, which Alastair Campbell, the Prime Minister's spokesman, notoriously described as signalling the end of the 'bog standard' comprehensive. By early 2008, 88 per cent of all secondary schools in England had gained at least one specialism and 26 of the 150 local authorities had entirely specialist secondary sectors (DCSF 2008g). Many schools hold more than one of the fourteen specialisms available, among which 'leadership' is now a specialism in its own right.

Alongside the expansion in the numbers of Specialist Schools, the Specialist Schools and Academies Trust has also grown in influence. Established in 1987 as the City Technology Colleges Trust to sponsor the CTCs, its influence grew slowly through the first half of the 1990s as the Conservative government introduced first Technology Colleges (for Grant Maintained and Voluntary Aided Schools only) and then Specialist Schools. In 1997, New Labour pledged to expand the then Specialist Schools Trust which has happened as the number of Specialist Schools has increased. In September 2005, it became the Specialist Schools and Academies Trust (SSAT) to reflect its new role supporting the Academies programme. Between March 2001 and March 2007 its accounts as a registered charity showed an increase in expenditure from just under £3 million to very close to £50 million. Its present aim, 'to give practical support to the transformation of secondary education in England by building and enabling a world-class network of innovative, high-performing secondary schools in partnership with business and the wider community' (SSAT 2008) does not easily distinguish it from most local authorities in their ambitions for local schools.

In a succession of annual reports (Jesson and Crossley 2008), SSAT has claimed a 'specialist dividend', arguing that Specialist Schools continually outperform non-Specialist Schools on most outcome indicators, including Contextual Value Added and rates of improvement. This will be returned to later, not to argue whether it is correct or incorrect, but to contest its meaning and importance.

Academies

Three years into the Labour Project, in 2000, and as New Labour's 'Fresh Start' programme stumbled, apparently for want of charismatic school leadership and its effective application, David Blunkett heralded the Academies programme with a speech to the Social Market Foundation. The then Secretary of State said the government would back business or voluntary providers who took over the management of weak and failing schools 'where existing measures were clearly not succeeding and where outright closure would be damaging to children and the community' (DfES 2000).

Academies build on the philosophy introduced by Specialist Schools with one enormous difference: Academies not only secure sponsorship from the private sector, but also are owned by the private sector as publicly funded independent schools, established by sponsors, individuals or groups, from the business, faith or voluntary sectors. A Trust, established and controlled by the sponsor, owns and manages the Academy to a contract agreed with the DCSF. Originally designed to maximize the potential for each Academy to operate independently, these contracts have been modified to make demands, for example, for the delivery of some National Curriculum subjects.

An important role of Academies is to challenge long-term cultures of educational underachievement; therefore, many Academies tend to be located in areas of disadvantage, often replacing schools 'in difficulty'. The DCSF claims that because of their location, Academies are ideally placed to have a key role in the regeneration of communities, offering local solutions to local needs, though that, of course, depends on the inclination of the sponsor and school leaders. The government has pledged to introduce 200 Academies by 2010, and 400 eventually. In March 2008, the DCSF website reported that there were 83 academies open in 49 local authorities, with a further 50 to open in each of the following three years. The target of 200 is well in range.

Trust Schools

By 2005, the government was hooked on the idea that 'schools as independent institutions' were the hammer to break through the emerging plateau of attainment and before the general election, in the House of Commons Standing Committee on 22 March, Derek Twigg, the then Parliamentary Secretary at the DfES said, 'We believe there is a positive relationship between the diversity of secondary provision and higher standards' (House of Commons 2005a). The Education Act 2005, passed in the 'wash up' preceding the election, applied competition only to new secondary schools and allowed local authorities to enter any competition with a proposal for a community school. Six months after the election the New Labour government took another step down the same path and published its White Paper, *Higher Standards, Better Schools for All* containing what would have been for any previous Labour administration the breathtaking assertion that, 'no more community schools (primary or secondary) will be established' (DfES 2005a: 107). Instead, when a new school was required, local authorities would be required to arrange competitions, to work with local groups to find a promoter for the new school either as a Trust School or Voluntary Aided School and if that was not possible, make their own proposal for a self-governing Foundation School – no more community schools! Existing schools which wanted to control their own assets and staffing would be able to 'acquire a self-governing Trust similar to those supporting Academies which will give them freedom to work with new partners to help develop their ethos and to raise standards' (DfES 2005a: 8).

The Education and Inspections Act which followed in 2006 has been understandably described as 'Pythonesque', promising one thing and after some surreal convolutions turning into 'a candidate for the "and now for something completely different" treatment' (Baker 2006: 3). The heavy spin which promoted it as a major expansion of 'parent power' turned out to be counterproductive, not least in the opposition it created from Labour MPs who saw the Trust proposals as a device for handing the public education service over to the private sector. The remarkable feature of that storm was that it happened in a teacup that had already been emptied, washed and dried. The 2006 Act makes no use of the phrase 'Trust School' because 'Trust schools are foundation schools with foundations. Trusts are the foundations of such schools. Foundations are defined in section 21 of the School Standards and Framework Act 1998' (DCSF 2008d: 3). Anyone who had read the tea leaves knew that Trust Schools were little more than a reinvention and promotion of the Foundation Schools to which the Labour majority had signed up eight years earlier. That the government risked this approach and some embarrassment as it backtracked on parts of the original bill is a mark of its determination that schools which were more autonomous and closer allied to external sponsors would drive improvement through the system.

In the spring of 2008, there were 42 Trust Schools up and running and almost 400 working towards that status. They manage their own assets, employ their own staff, set their own admission arrangements – subject to the tightened Code of Practice – and have the same core funding as community schools, follow national employment agreements and adhere to the National Curriculum regulations. They are distinguished by being supported by a Charitable Trust which may appoint the majority of governors and, if it does so, must establish a Parents Council at the school.

Federations

Federations also deserve consideration within these new arrangements. Even though they were not one of the trio of Specialist Schools, Academies and Trusts listed at the start of this section, they are another structural response to pressing educational issues. The Education Act 2002 allowed maintained schools to federate by having a single governing body or collaborate by having one or more joint governance committees with delegated powers. Schools were already able to cooperate by having joint governance committees without delegated powers or to network on an ad hoc informal basis. In any case each of the schools involved retains its own legal identity, budget entitlement and head-teacher even if the last is sometimes more nominal than actual.

As the then Secretary of State, Estelle Morris, revealed to the House of Commons in 2002, the underlying purpose of the legislation in the 2002 Act which allowed federations was not to encourage partnerships of equals but to

> promote our best schools to take over and run weak and failing schools. That is why we will provide incentives for our best schools to federate and improve standards in our weaker and coasting schools. That is why we will reward our best heads for taking on new roles as chief executives of clusters of schools.
>
> (House of Commons 2002)

Inevitably that approach has bred some suspicion of federations even when it has been a welcome solution to problems equally shared by local schools and even when it offers some relief to the national pressure on headteacher numbers as, between 2008 and 2011, a large proportion of current headteachers reach retirement age.

Part 2: implications for this

In broad terms, New Labour's educational effort has become diverted into and absorbed by an effort to restructure the school system, and in particular the secondary school system, which is not dealing with the most fundamental challenge facing the public education service – the chronic underachievement of between one-fifth and one-quarter of the student population, the vast majority of whom come from poor homes and too many of whom will be drawn into individually disappointing and publicly expensive lifestyles.

So what kind of difference are Specialist Schools, Academies and Trusts making: a lot, a bit, or very little? It is simply too early to reach any conclusions about Trusts although they offer an intriguing possibility to explore later in the chapter. For the other two, the question remains highly contested.

Specialist Schools?

In her introduction to the analysis of 2007 results, Elizabeth Reid, Chief Executive of SSAT, notes that over the previous seven years the equivalent publication has 'shown the difference that the challenge of becoming and staying a specialist school has made . . . highlighted the rising stars, the successes against the odds and the consistent high-achievers' (Jesson and Crossley 2008: 3). Now, she writes, there is a move into new territory which in part is reflected in a new emphasis on value added analyses for Specialist Schools. There is less comparison between the Specialist Sector and the now small minority of other schools. The numbers make this comparison increasingly less important though where it occurs it unsurprisingly casts the Specialist Sector in a favourable light.

The greater the proportion of secondary schools which have a specialism, the more difficult it becomes to separate the specialist effect from any of the other initiatives aimed at secondary schools. That is already true in London where anyone assessing the success of the early drive encouraging specialist status would find it inextricably linked with the combination of School Advisers, Key Worker Living Scheme, Teach First Programme, Chartered London Teacher Status, Fellowships at the London Centre for Leadership, £1.3 billion rebuilding schemes, school partnerships, cross-borough planning for admissions and summer universities which, alongside other local and national initiatives, the DfES (2005b) comitted to providing for London schools.

A study commissioned by the SSAT (Mongon and Chapman 2006) which examined the Specialist School effect in London concluded the specialist dividend claimed by the SSAT (Jesson and Crossley 2008) was higher in London than nationally. London's Specialist Schools average 59 per cent 5 A*–Cs compared to 45 per cent in non-Specialist Schools, a dividend of 30 per cent (figures are rounded). The equivalent figures including English and Maths were 45 per cent and 33 per cent giving a Specialist Schools' dividend of 38 per cent. However, this was a more complex matter than the headlines reveal and the conclusions also raised questions about the breadth and depth of the 'dividend' when like for like schools are compared.

In broad terms, the research drew upon the London Challenge 2006 *Families of Schools* (DfES 2006b) database in which London's secondary schools were grouped into twenty-three 'Families' based on an average of three years' attainment data and recent free school meals data. This approach provided groupings of schools which have been faced with some similar challenges in their attempts to improve. Performance was analysed in six of those families evenly spread across the range, comparing first the GCSE results including English and Maths and then the Contextual Added Value scores for Specialist and non-Specialist Schools.

The overall conclusion was that when London secondary schools were placed on a continuum constructed to reflect the challenge to improvement they face by using a combination of their previous GCSE results and eligibility of their pupils for free school meals, the trend for higher performance in Specialist

Schools is strongest and statistically significant at the centre of that continuum. The trend for Specialist Schools to perform better than non-Specialist Schools is less often statistically significant away from the median group of schools, as Table 9.1 illustrates.

Family 12 was the median of the continuum (12/23) and inevitably not far from the average in many characteristics. This doubly significant finding therefore echoes Jesson and Crossley's (2008) conclusion:

> The 'bonus' for pupils in Specialist Schools is at its greatest for pupils with around 'average' attainments on entry. Since these pupils form the great majority of pupils in most schools this finding is of considerable substantive importance in re-affirming one of the benefits of specialist education.
>
> (Jesson and Crossley 2008: 13)

The findings in *Families 5 and 9* might be explained by a range of factors including other characteristics of the schools. The sample numbers were small, especially when divided into Specialist and non-Specialist groups. Across those two families, only ten of the forty-two schools were non-Specialist; of the ten, six were Voluntary Aided schools of a religious nature and of the other four, two were single-sex girls' schools. A tentative hypothesis might be that non-Specialist Schools in these families were, because of their Voluntary Aided or single-sex status, more likely already to have access to the kind of ethos and focus which specialism brings.

Families 16, 20 and 23 included many schools in more challenging circumstances than those in Families 5, 9 and 12 and whose performance at Key Stage 4 was below average. The proportion of Specialist Schools in these

Table 9.1 Statistical significance of trends: comparison of specialist and non-specialist schools

London Challenge Family[a]	N1[b]	N2[c]	Statistical significance of trend	
			GCSE including English & Maths	Key Stages 3–4 Contextual Value Added
23	9	6	Trend only	Trend only
20	5	9	Trend only	Significant (p<0.05)
16	12	9	Trend only	Trend only
12	13	5	Highly significant (p<0.01)	Highly significant
9	15	7	Significant	Trend only
5	18	3	Significant	Trend only

a There is some overlap in pupil attainment across schools in different families in this sample. In general terms, attainment is higher in families with a lower number, e.g. pupil attainment is on average higher in Family 5 than in Family 9.
b Number of Specialist Schools in Family
c Number of non-Specialist Schools in Family

three families was lower than in London overall. In general terms, there was a complex set of factors including the smaller proportion of Specialist Schools in these families, the less time on average that these Specialist Schools had been specialist and the lower impact of specialism, which highlighted the difficulty of creating a specialist dividend in these more demanding circumstances.

There was also a tendency for some specialisms to appear more frequently at either end of the families continuum. For example, Engineering, Science, Language and Maths and Computing Colleges were better represented in the less challenging families than in the more challenging. Sports, Technology and Business and Enterprise Colleges were better represented in the more challenging family groups.

Although schools with poorer results are now being allowed into the Specialist fold in increasing numbers – the performance requirements for Specialist status are not what they were – it is still the case that the 638 nationally targeted underperforming schools (below the 30 per cent GCSE threshold) are found disproportionately more among non-Specialist than Specialist Schools. There is an echo here of the findings reported by Jim Taylor (2007), who concludes:

> scarce educational resources have not been used efficiently, at least as indicated by the impact of specialist status on exam results. The schools with the greatest likelihood of improvement as a consequence of acquiring specialist status (i.e. those with a high proportion of pupils eligible for free school meals) have been the least likely to have become specialist schools. Conversely, the schools with the least likelihood of improvement (i.e. those with a low proportion of pupils eligible for free school meals) have been the most likely to have acquired specialist status.
>
> (J. Taylor 2007: 10)

Furthermore, many of the lowest attaining schools have been identified as potential sites for Academies. Given that each Academy must have at least one specialism we are experiencing 'specialization' through the back door. This policy has increased the proportion of schools with Specialist status and supported those schools least likely to hold a specialism to gain a Specialist status.

Academies?

Academies are a very expensive political commitment and accordingly their value is argued over aggressively. The National Audit Office (NAO 2007) reported that with forty-six Academies open, the capital cost of start-up had ranged from £6.5 million to £40.4 million with an average of £24 million – about 10 per cent above comparable maintained sector schools. Seventeen of the first twenty-six Academies had overrun their capital budget by an average of £3 million. Where average start-up grants had been completed (this in addition to the regular annual per pupil funding runs for a fixed period) the average had totalled (i.e.

not per annum) more than £1.6 million. NAO also reported that GCSE performance was improving faster in Academies than in other types of school, including those in similar circumstances, and the gap between the best and worst performance of individual academies had narrowed. Academies had focused their outside connections on the DCSF and feeder primary schools so there was little collaboration with local secondary schools. Tellingly, this mixed NAO (2007: 9) report concluded, 'For the recently announced doubling in the size of the programme to be a success, the sector will require access to greater numbers of highly effective school leaders.' To which every local authority and school governing body would add 'and us too . . .'.

So is that investment paying dividends in a year when the presence of one-third of the current Academies (28) on the national list identified as underachieving unacceptably (i.e. below the 30 per cent threshold at GCSE) is explained by their inheritance of underachievement? Claiming that 'Academies perform better than their predecessor schools' SSAT reports that between 2001 and 2007, 'the 36 academies with underperforming predecessor schools and Year 11 cohorts saw the proportion of pupils gaining five or more GCSEs at A★–C almost double from 22 per cent in 2001 to 43.7 per cent in 2007'. It adds that 'including English and Maths, academies have increased by 5.1 percentage points since 2001, which is two and a half times greater than the 1.8 percentage points nationally' (Jesson and Crossley 2008: 25–26).

It is good news but expensive news, that the students in those schools are doing well, certainly financially expensive and arguably socially expensive. So could the same be achieved in any other way? A simplistic but helpful comparison can be made by trawling through the DCSF four-year school data (www.dcsf.gov.uk/performancetables/) asking is it possible to identify a similar sized group of schools which are not Academies and that have done comparably well? Checking data for a sample of 60 out of the 150 local authorities across four of the government's nine regions, it is easy to pick out 36 schools whose average trajectory is steeper than that of the 36 Academies – there are more. On average these 36 schools had 22 per cent 5A★–C in 2004 and 50 per cent in 2007: the Academy group had 'almost doubled' over six years, this group had more than doubled over four years. On average these schools had 15 per cent 5A★–C including English and Maths in 2004 and 27 per cent in 2007: the Academy group had increased by 5.1 percentage points over six years, this group had increased by 12 percentage points over two fewer years. The point is crude but simple, there are schools bettering the Academy programme without moving beyond community governance and without the associated costs to the taxpayer.

Conclusion

The public education service remains inequitable and, in particular, young people who suffer the greatest disadvantages outside school tend to have the poorest experience in school. That phenomenon is now the greatest challenge for a service which may be approaching the limits of what can be achieved by technical improvements in teaching and school leadership. Tinkering, even extensively and exhaustively, with structures is not making a significant impact and certainly not a value for money impact on that problem. In 2005 the Education and Skills Committee (House of Commons 2005b) concluded that it was 'difficult to detect a coherent overarching strategy' in the government's policies for secondary education and little has changed since. The University of Manchester, Centre for Equity recently concluded that we have reached a point where 'the source of inequities lies largely beyond the school, in social disadvantage. Somehow, efforts at educational attainment have to be linked into a coherent strategy to address wider social and economic issues' (Ainscow et al. 2008: 3).

The better informed parents know that Diversity and Choice, even with Specialisms and Academies, is not about variation in the nationally prescribed curriculum nor in the nationally prescribed testing regime. Those are fixed for every school and therefore, at the core of their work, the Diversity across the offer from publicly funded schools is largely marginal. There is, however, always a local pecking order which can be as influenced by style as well as substance and in which Choice is played out for staff as well as parents. Being an Academy in fine buildings or one of the early Specialist Schools with an appealing title could play an important part in that game – setting an establishment aside from the 'bog standard comprehensive'. The consequence is that

> national policies to promote choice and diversity are working within and compounding existing patterns of inequity and social division. What diversity there is in school provision owes more to historical factors . . . The ways in which parents exercise choices (or not) reinforce inequities and local authorities are largely powerless.
>
> (Ainscow et al. 2007: 7)

The effort that has gone into structural reform, in part through Specialist Schools but more emphatically through Academies and possibly next through Trust Schools, is adding little value to the outcomes in the national tail of achievement and is on the cusp of obstructing the opportunities for progress. Indeed a range of evidence shows that private interests (e.g. religion, private entrepreneurs) are permeating educational provision, and notably, economic interests are ensuring that the market penetrates public services (P. Woods et al. 2007). On the one hand, the government seems to be building a kaleidoscope for local networks – each shake showing the same pieces in a new configuration. So professionals and others take different seats around the table at local strategic partnerships, community regeneration boards, extended school clusters and the rest. Like any kaleidoscope it is a rich and changing picture which will only settle with time and careful handling. On the other hand, these occasions are usually voluntary for the semi or more than semi-autonomous school leaders who can choose to turn up and to participate and collaborate – or not, as their inclination or their sponsor's inclination takes them. It was notable that schools were not listed in the Children Act 2004 as partners required to cooperate with the children's services authority to improve the well-being of children in the area. Perhaps there was a naive parliamentary assumption that all school leaders would do that or a cynical political calculation that they should not all have to. Encouragingly and in contrast, there is an emerging network of school leaders who know that the creation of Public Value, the local community's commitment to the school, which transcends and enhances the outcomes from teaching and learning is the way forward in challenging localities (Leadbeater and Mongon, 2009).

Academies are the extreme example of this independence but the work of the SSAT can also inhibit local strategic collaboration. There is much that can be recommended in the work that SSAT has done to promote improvements in school leadership and in the quality of teaching and learning. It has recently stepped up a gear in its interest in the role of schools in their communities and locally shared responsibilities. Independently commissioned reports show that it is held in very high regard by the schools which are members of the Trust. It has a creditable track record in offering professional development and peer support at every level of school work. There are great advantages to that performance but the specialisms and SSAT's role give schools an alternative locus for their professional identity beyond their local context. In that relationship, SSAT does not have to carry the ambiguous role that local authorities bear to challenge as well as support schools, to intervene at the extremes and to coordinate the delivery of a wider though associated range of children's services. The extended schools programme, about which many schools feel ambivalent, has been passed to local authorities to pursue and while that makes sense, it also creates tensions. It may be a puzzle to some school leaders why their local authority cannot be more like the SSAT, and this raises issues of how local governance and accountability through elections is being undermined.

Nor is this approach improving the engagement of schools with their communities and their accountability to them. Research at Manchester for the Rowntree Joseph Foundation (Dean et al. 2007) concluded that school governance in areas of socio-economic disadvantage was 'decidedly mixed' although it is in precisely such areas that the model of volunteer citizens supporting and challenging the work of professionals seems most problematic. That is not resolved by removing accountability to an arm's-length Academy or Trust School arrangement.

The government has to decide whether it wants a tranche of its schools to be academic fortresses, each with its own baron (or baroness), high walls around the teaching and learning, guarding who comes in and tipping the unwanted back over the battlements. The cost will be high, not least around the gated communities in which the privileged locals will be living as a result. If that is not what the government wants then three profound changes will be needed:

- *New forms of local accountability will have to be designed.* Unless schools are reconnected with their localities how can localities be connected with their schools? Traditional governing bodies and parent evenings are rarely the best way to do this. Representation and empathy can be created in more innovative ways. Interestingly, Trust Schools offer one route to this end if the narrative around them can be diverted from the ascendancy of 'business partners' and into the value of 'community partners'.

- *Schools will need to be incentivized to work with other services and local people in a spirit of equity and mutual esteem.* Educationalists need to know that the stories they tell about the inaccessibility of other services and of families are exactly the stories those others tell about schools. Then schools need to be helped to overcome those barriers. This is not a matter of money – schools that want to do this find the means – it is about having the collaborative work recognized, valued and celebrated.

- *Central government will need to find a way of moving from nationally specified targets for single services*, instead holding local authorities to account for locally negotiated targets for a community. If a small primary school tips its resources into moving two of its thirty 11 year olds from level 3 to level 4 so it just meets the 65 per cent floor target and, as a result, diverts resources from some aspect of well-being and then hands a less well adjusted cohort over to the local secondary school – who has benefited?

10 Networking a more equitable educational future?

Rhetorics and realities

Andy Howes and Jo Frankham

Introduction

Local and national government policy in England under New Labour has emphasized the value of collaborative networking across many fields, including in relation to the more equitable and effective provision of educational services. This is a particularly interesting case in the context of increasingly global and business-related provision of 'public' services affecting many countries.

We begin by critically examining this policy direction and the considerable rhetoric which accompanies it, drawing on examples from a range of English educational institutions in order to raise questions about what networking should and does entail in the context of education. In the second half of the chapter we examine two networking initiatives aiming to address the issue of inclusion and equity in different ways. We conclude by linking the detail of these empirical cases with the questions raised in the first section – and identifying indications for policy thinking in the future.

The seductive language of networks

The language of the network typically emphasizes partnership, collaboration, community, connection and flow (Frankham 2006: 672). This is a hopeful language, an optimistic expression of the potential gain from movement across the boundaries of an individual or organization. As such, it is very tempting to adopt this language in pursuit of developments in education, that most optimistic of human pursuits. This chapter first explores networking in education at the level of rhetoric. Through several empirical examples, we then explore what is or could be entailed in networking between schools as organizations which goes beyond those words.

As an image and a metaphor, the network suggests the value of flexible and non-hierarchical connection. Networks are flat; they spread out, horizontally. The mobile phone network, for example, comprises interconnected cells, locally dependent on masts fixed to buildings, but through that prosaic infrastructure, linking individuals on potentially equal terms across the face of the earth. Likewise the internet, which weaves wonderfully rich ideas of mass participation, individual expression, equality of access, self-regulation, and lack of central control. However misleading these images of equal and universal access are, they nevertheless carry into the metaphor of the network an emphasis on equality, lack of hierarchy, and openness. As Bowers (1992: 119) describes, 'there is no clear beginning or end to the network, nor can the inside/outside distinction be made with confidence'. New Labour's enthusiasm for networks and partnerships has been well documented (e.g. Glendinning et al. 2002) that was not an entirely new trend, however, but built on Conservative rhetorics and policy moves (Clarence and Painter 1998; Newman, 2002). that constituted part of the 'third spirit of capitalism' that emerged in the 1980s. Now, network culture permeates New Labour policy, a central plank of neoliberal policies and practices (Calder 2003). As Newman (2002: 7) describes: 'Networks and partnerships, public participation and democratic renewal, are all symbols of what has been termed a new form of governance in the UK'.

This discourse is evident right across New Labour's agenda: 'the development of a more consultative process of policy formation, a focus on joined-up government and partnership and the extension of public participation and involvement in decision-making' (Newman 2002: 7). In the organization of local government too, New Labour has encouraged 'flexible local networking (including policy experimentation) as part of its more collaborative ethos' (Painter and Clarence 2000: 479). Specific examples include the policy action teams set up by the Social Exclusion Unit, zonal initiatives on health and education, Sure Start, initiatives on crime and disorder and local regeneration. More recently, education-related initiatives such as *Every Child Matters* (Department for Education and Skills (DfES) 2003b) maintain the emphasis on inter-agency collaboration and information sharing across professional groups.

What is being networked in all these examples? The network metaphor itself emphasizes flexibility of form, and downplays questions as to what precisely flows, and why, as a result of this activity. However, alongside the network discourse is the construction of the 'knowledge economy', with its emphasis on the marketability and movement of knowledge:

> Now we have a new concept of knowledge and of its relation to those who create and use it. This new concept is a truly secular concept. Knowledge should flow like money to wherever it can create advantage and profit. Indeed knowledge is not like money, it is money. Knowledge is divorced from persons, their commitments, their personal dedications. These become impediments, restrictions on the flow of knowledge, and introduce deformations in the working of the symbolic market. Moving knowledge about, or even creating it, should not be more difficult than moving or regulating money.
>
> (Bernstein 1996: 87)

On the face of it, it is tempting to hope that useful knowledge can be divorced from persons and their commitments in this way, and can travel unimpeded through a network. It is easy to see the attractiveness of such knowledge networks to those who have or assume responsibility for engineering greater equity in mass educational systems, if they make the assumption that knowledge relevant to changing educational practice can move more freely like this.

The continuing attractiveness of networks in the current context rests on three crucial features. First, there are massive and often local inequities represented by the startling variation in school contexts for learning, not least in urban areas. This is contributing to hugely different life chances for young people in a dynamic postcode lottery that makes health service disparities look insignificant (Lupton 2006). Second, improvements that may have been due to governmental intervention based on target-setting and other centrally authorized processes are increasingly considered to have been exhausted (Tymms and Merrell 2007). Third, the reinstatement of powerful, locally accountable redistributive structures such as local authorities remains inconceivable. In a situation in which the room for manoeuvre is so limited, the optimistic rhetoric of networking has claimed attention as one of the few possibilities conceived for addressing this impasse. Networking, it is hoped, can lead to greater equity in a system through a relatively decentralized flow of knowledge and other resources, managed through relationships which are themselves constructed through the networking activity.

It is worth noting how this situation has come about, for it is largely the result of a series of systemic changes in policy since the late 1980s. Prior to changes introduced at the end of the 1980s in England, local authorities played a role that was beyond any individual school as organization, acting as the legitimate authority over the system in a particular locality. This did nothing to address the major disparities in provision between different authorities, but at least provided a mechanism for addressing major inequalities within each local system. In this organizational structure, local authorities typically maintained a centre–periphery connection with each school, and there was little encouragement given to links between schools as organizations. Rather, links were based on pragmatics: the value of bringing new science teachers together from all local authority schools, to a training session with the local authority science adviser, for example. But the central position of the Local Authority was fundamentally eroded by the local management of schools (LMS) agenda, coupled with the development of a national accountability apparatus (e.g. OfSTED). Both of these changes shifted accountability and influence away from the local authority, towards schools on the one hand, and towards central government on the other.

Superficially then, the development of networks to address school development makes sense. The language of networking makes it clear that issues constructed only around the organization of a single school ignore potentially significant mutual benefits of schools collaborating together, to the detriment of the educational opportunities to many pupils. The admonition to 'network' counters the view of the individual school as the proper and most effective unit of all educational action and effort.

A relevant distinction here is Waks' (2007) notion of the difference between organizational and institutional change. He claims that fundamental change cannot happen at the level of the individual organization, but is always institutional. Organizational change, in this view, is relatively more like rearranging the deckchairs, while the direction of the ship is unaltered. He utilizes a sociological definition of institutions as:

> social arrangements establishing, ordaining, or authorizing the ideas, norms, organizations, and frameworks that regulate the processes of human interaction in the primary areas of human life . . . They are like water to fish, the transparent milieu within which the objects they authorize claim attention.
>
> (Waks 2007: 285–286)

In these terms, networking can be presented as constituting change to just such social arrangements (through shifting the identities, affiliations and primary purposes of individual leaders and teachers, for example) and therefore being capable of creating fundamental change in schools as organizations. Significant challenges to organizational assumptions often come about across the boundary of that organization.

Networks, learning and interests

The language of networks then is a seductive one for those working for change at the level of the educational system. Seduction does not, of course, necessarily lead to good policy, and it is useful to pause at this point to consider the various interests that are involved when networks between schools are proposed in the current English context. Primarily, the identification of an individual teacher with an individual school is in the interests of both that teacher and the school. The appointment of teachers by individual schools marks the first point of identification between the two. Such identification is clearly to the advantage of the school, which can expect and build on the loyalty of the teacher through the operation of, for example, performance management and social culture, and to reinforce the relationship through internal systems of accountability. LMS has effectively reinforced such a position. Correspondingly, the interests of the individual teacher are largely aligned with that of their school, and possibly the young people who attend it, rather than, say, that of the young people of the city in which they teach. Within the school, there is the potential for confirmatory feedback between the learning of young people and the professional development of their teachers. Beyond the school, any such relationship is tenuous, at best, and teachers are unlikely to discern any impact of their network actions. It is difficult to imagine many teachers maintaining a strong commitment to networking for the sake of greater equity across a locality, in the face of such structures of identity and accountability. This does, of course, depend on what exactly is meant by networking, a question that we return to later when considering examples of practice.

A very similar, perhaps even stronger, alignment of interests applies in the case of headteachers and other school leaders. For individual school leaders faced with public judgement based on limited and often misleading information about their individual organization, we may ask what opportunities are there to respond to networking discourse with anything more meaningful than rhetoric? For most headteachers, the school boundary is far more significant to their practice than the relatively abstract notion of equality for the children and young people across a city. Social worlds theory (Clarke 1997) illustrates across a range of examples how often people operate in self-contained worlds, with a set of more or less comfortable and agreed assumptions. What we strive for within those worlds is judged worthwhile from within, but from a broader perspective, may be counterproductive.

For local authority officers, networking offers the possibility of a brokering position between schools, and therefore a possibly enhanced engagement with decisions to influence equity across the authority. There is some evidence that consistent rhetoric, coupled with effective facilitation of networking, can establish such a brokering position. This raises two issues: what do they or what could they broker, beyond that rhetorical talk of value for all, the aspiration of equality, and the discourse of common standards of probity and trust in the public sphere? And furthermore, what to make of the possibility that a network turns into a challenge to that local authority?

Another consideration of interests involves the informal networks that already exist in educational localities. There is a real temptation when orchestrating formal networking arrangements to ignore the considerable existing networks of affiliations between teachers (and headteachers), which develop through, for example, mobility between school positions, through living as neighbours, or through friendships and other personal relationships. If the substance of networking is dependent on the construction of mutually supportive and challenging relationships across the very substantial boundaries of the school as discussed here, then existing networks would make a valuable starting point.

Networks, learning and equity in practice

Given that networking has been so attractive, it is not surprising that it has been at the heart of the rhetoric around several central interventions in England since 2002. Perhaps the most substantial of these was between 2002 and 2006, when Networked Learning Communities were established by the National College for School Leadership (NCSL) involving 1500 schools. The concept of networking between each individual group of (typically) five to seven schools was employed, in the hope that solutions developed in one group would be made available to other schools, who

> should be able to understand and interpret these solutions and transpose them into their own contexts. In this way, network-based forms of organization are seen to carry the potential to accelerate knowledge creation

and innovation right across the education system – to make learning and the resultant knowledge widely available.

(NCSL 2004: 3)

In a series of publications, the leaders of this initiative clearly outlined the expectations placed on networks, placed within a system that is struggling with both the limits of top-down target-setting and also a distrust of the autonomous development of teachers and schools:

> One familiar response to this difficulty has always been that government should 'trust the professionals'. Many teachers still feel that if they could just be left to get on with the job, they would be able to perform successfully. Unfortunately, this is not the case. Teachers, like any other professional group, are just as likely to resort to self-protection in the face of disruptive change as they are to embrace new and better practices. The challenge is to build professional identities and professional learning communities that are oriented towards adaptation and radical innovation.
>
> (Bentley et al. 2005: 3)

The reported experience of the NCSL initiative clearly illustrates and acknowledges the very real challenges entailed in setting up networks that will lead to more equitable local learning contexts for young people. The advice for success, based on the accumulated experience of the leader of the NCSL project, looks intriguingly unlike suggestions for the development of a loose and freely flowing network, with suggestions about opening rituals, and the need for 'strategic . . . tactical . . . operational . . . interpersonal . . . cultural integration' (Bentley et al. 2005: 10) between the partner schools. These efforts suggest the deliberate construction of something more organizational, and there is considerable acknowledgement that the need for this substantial effort reflect the underlying tensions created by the individual 'institutional' focus of schools in a competitive local market where

> the network will be seen by some to threaten the institutional success of individual organizations (schools). Sharing and giving to other partners can appear high risk. This inevitably creates insecurities, uncertainties and opportunities for sceptics to voice difference.
>
> (Bentley et al. 2005: 9)

These tensions relate to the 'enduring dilemmas' of school organization relating to external influences as identified by Ogawa et al. (1999); these are dilemmas around persistence, boundaries and compliance. When investing time and effort in processes that are not under their control, school leaders are faced with doubts relating to benefit, sustainability, accountability and influence. What evidence is there of how these dilemmas are solved in practice? In order to learn more, we want to draw on some empirical, ethnographic work in two unrelated network contexts, looking at what occurred through different lenses, including that of the network. In so doing, we work with two questions: how far do network concepts help us to understand particular cases? And how far do those cases help us to construe the limits of the network concept?

Case A: Collaborative action, networking and learning

The first account comes from a recent action research initiative (Davies and Howes 2008) and parallels a previously documented example of collaborative action (Frankham and Howes 2006). It can be told in two parts. The story begins with the three teachers in a small history department engaged in a substantial piece of action research, involving ongoing discussion and colla-borative action, critically and productively assisted through the involvement of the school educational psychologist. The teachers began with a puzzle: the perceived underachievement and disengagement of a particular group of year 8 girls, for which they had little ready explanation. As a result of their work, they challenged their own assumptions about the girls' motivations, and altered their practice to engage more directly and positively with them, in a way that contributed to the equity of that practice. As an example of networking, this is a case of teachers working together with a sensitive external educationalist, establishing a more informed and localized educational discourse for more inclusive practice within their department – a discourse which does not ignore but grapples with the external standards agenda and associated targets. Networking here involved a localized exchange of perspectives, honesty in relation to challenges in the classroom, and engagement together in critical questioning.

The second part of this story illuminates networking from a very different angle. Towards the end of the history project, the head of department, Mary, was invited to visit another school to discuss their project with a teacher of design and technology. Mary's school was part of a Leadership Incentive Grant (LIG) cluster and Mary's 'old deputy head' had been seconded to the local authority to lead the LIG cluster, and chaired its meetings: 'so I went along to one of them and told them . . . it was other deputy heads and sort of assistant heads in teaching and learning and things like that, and we just talked to them about [the project]'. Then a deputy head who had been at that meeting returned to her school and mentioned Mary's project to her head of design and technology. This teacher subsequently invited Mary to visit her department. Mary's interpretation of the visit was inconclusive as to its value to the teacher concerned:

> I don't know if anything came out of that, no. 'Cause she said, erm, she said that she thought other heads of department at [her school] would be interested. I offered, you know, I said well I'd be quite happy to come along and talk to anybody if they want. She didn't get back to me so I don't know whether she did do anything or not . . . Certainly, at the time, she

said it linked in with a lot of her problems producing lack of stuff and not actually having any, well, meaning or measure to it, so . . .

This series of connections illustrates the flow of networking, and the desire for effect that new connections often bring with them. Mary wants her visit to have been meaningful, reflecting the optimistic opportunism that networking suggests. Without the network structures in the local authority, and the associated brokering of two deputy heads, there would have been no opportunity to link with a head of department in another school addressing similar issues, and not even the possibility of further professional development. In terms of meetings, exchanges and conversations, this second stage of networking worked (Frankham 2006).

However, Mary's visit led to no continuing dialogue; after a sharing of similar problems, and a mutual concern, she ended up only with doubts about the value of her visit. These doubts stand in stark contrast with the confidence expressed in the development in her own department. There was, in practice, no mutual accountability in the relationship between the two heads of department, and only a hope that the visit might have born some fruit in terms of teacher development. In terms of learning, or transfer of knowledge, there is very little evidence that this stage of networking worked.

Case B: City-wide secondary school networking

It could be argued, in relation to the case just described, that the expectation of robust network relationships developing between teachers in different schools is misguided, and that effective networking is likely to require active account-ability structures. In many senses, this seemed to be the message from the guidance materials emanating from the NCSL project, and our second case study represents a closer look at the implications of such thinking. It draws on ethnographic engagement with another LIG-related project, in a disadvantaged inner city in England (Ainscow and Howes 2007). Four clusters of schools were constructed, according to the recommendations of consultants external to the local authority, so that each cluster contained schools operating at every level of overall pupil attainment, with the explicit intention that equity would be developed through their collaboration. This rational, bureaucratic approach ignored geography, and already existing relationships between schools, and initially also overlooked the state of relationships between headteachers. Fortunately, some regrouping was agreed after the intervention of a trusted former headteacher working for the local authority. Networking is unlikely to succeed where design takes no account of history or other elements of context.

In terms of what occurred in the various clusters, we again address the question, how far does networking help us to understand what went on? The differences between the four clusters provide powerful insights in relation to this question.

Between the schools in *Cluster 1*, a network of loose affiliations developed, impeded initially by the reluctance of one school to engage, but eventually taking shape in terms of a series of joint projects around the coordination of external initiatives. The network contributed to the efficiency of delivery of those services, but there was very little engagement addressing equity in the cluster. A similarly loose network of affiliations developed in *Cluster 2*, but one which included mutual commitments such as the joint appointment and employment of a full-time English adviser. This teacher worked effectively with the individual English departments, utilizing video as a way of sharing and discussing practice.

Comparing these two clusters, it seems apparent that while the form of a network can be imposed, the work of the network cannot. As one Cluster 2 headteacher expressed it:

> It's a funny thing. It was imposed on us, otherwise we certainly would not have seen it as a priority. But it was perceptive. The links, where they've gelled, have been positive. Such as a Geography link we have . . . But you can't make the gelling happen. The head of [another cluster school] has been wonderful. He gave me a drama teacher for two days for master classes.

Cluster 3 became real both in form and in work, with mutual benefits between two schools, and as a third school left the group, to the eventual federation of those two schools, with sharing of teachers between them, and the movement of pupils to achieve a wider range of subjects. In other words, this arrangement developed greater equity. This was networking involving close and developing relationships at many levels between the two organizations, from headteachers to ground staff. The network worked at the symbolic level too, with the lower-performing school now associated with a historic organization through badging and other identity work, raising the possibility of an effect on pupil enrolments in the networks of the quasi-market.

Cluster 4 was different again – a strongly bonded leadership group was created, through the advocacy of two experienced headteachers with a strongly collaborative disposition. This was reinforced through regular meetings and the active facilitation by a coordinator at assistant headteacher level, appointed to that role by the group. This active facilitation involved considerable skill in negotiating with the headteachers, each with their own agendas and distinctive styles. An indication of the equity work in this cluster arose in the context of one school in special measures and experiencing severe budgetary difficulties. The other four schools agreed to pool a large proportion of the additional funds made available through the government's Leadership Incentive Grants (contributing £30,000 each per annum for three years) to fund collaborative processes, and to allow the fifth school to be involved without any financial contribution – an example of a transfer of resources and a shared responsibility for development across the group. The head of humanities in one school explained:

I have been working with the head of history at [name of school in special measures]. The previous head of humanities had gone off with all the stuff. J had needed to work with others in the department more experienced than him, all without any schemes. I began by giving him all my old schemes of work. We worked to develop resources. I taught him to write a scheme of work . . . I had a nice letter from the head after they came out of special measures.

What happened in this cluster went beyond generosity to a neighbour in trouble. There was also a discovery of opportunities for learning from 'tough' schools, by those with relatively more compliant pupils, as described by a school coordinator:

I want some of the best practice from our school put forward. One of my main things for that, is the experience of working with challenging kids. There are talented teachers here. I would like to set up the opportunity for teachers from other schools to follow teachers around, seeing what the best teachers in the difficult schools do, and have to do. That would be a great professional development opportunity. We have heads of faculty here who run faculties as well as anyone else. Just how do you put together a faculty and run it well? There are NQTs here with incredible natural skill in putting learning opportunities together.

Such was the strength of the bonds formed through such collaborative discourse and activity, that the group strongly resisted local authority moves to change the groupings of schools in the clusters. They had built an identity as a cluster, reinforced it with logos and a shared history of collaborative achievement, and began to construct boundaries around the cluster as a new form of organization.

Throughout the first year, the cluster grappled with a fundamental question as to how should the effectiveness and quality of collaborative activity should be established. For the coordinator, mapping good practice across the collaborative was a way of balancing control and encouraging the recognition of broad agency in the process of change, and resulted in the production of a directory of good practice. An audit framework was offered to schools to help them to identify lead departments by looking across the criteria to see that, for example, planning is a real strength in this department. The directory was designed to specify the level of detail that they could share. But frustrations quickly surfaced around the unreadiness of staff in schools to use the directory to pursue their own links with staff in other schools. The lessons about the slow and tentative nature of collaborative development at the level of senior staff were hard for them to accept in terms of the needs of their teaching staff – and they were under pressure to move faster than seemed possible by relying on staff interest.

This city-wide example how the allocation of mutual accountability to groups of schools by a local authority can sometimes lead to the creation of durable relationships that contribute to equity, but also how the current networking rhetoric offers little useful interpretative resource with which to understand the collaborative *work* entailed in effective educational networking.

Conclusion

Networking offers rhetorical possibilities which are a potentially valuable challenge to the dominant discourse of school-focused development. Within the concept of networking is embedded a series of ideas of transfer, communication and expansion of spheres of concern. Since the late 1990s, there have been many serious attempts to explore the value of this form of institutional change in search of more equitable solutions in local areas.

What emerges through scrutiny of some of these explorative attempts is that greater emphasis is required on the *work* that goes on at the heart of effective networking. More equitable educational arrangements can be constructed through networking, but the evidence of our studies is that for this to occur, there is no avoiding the need for generating commitment to joint, purposeful collaborative action which can then create practical challenges to assumptions about the educational value of groups of marginalized pupils. Where such collaborative action develops, there is evidence that equity can be served by substantive, mutual relationships between people at different levels in their institutions. Greater recognition of the work entailed in effective networking suggests the need for the commitment of resources at the level of the system, and the need for forms of practical study through which school leaders can reflect on the implications of a commitment to the work of networking for practice in their locality.

11 Personalized learning

Mel West and Daniel Muijs

Introduction

After a number of years when important aspects of education policies seemed to follow on almost seamlessly from those of the previous government, in its third term New Labour began to acknowledge that the national curriculum and its attendant pedagogic practices did not seem to be serving all learners. The debate about whether and how a single curriculum pattern can serve the needs of all children is not new. Indeed, since the launch of a single, integrated education system for England and Wales under the Education Act 1944, it can be argued that this issue has seen four distinct and, to an extent, contradictory emphases in approach from government.

Between 1944 and the late 1960s, the school system in England and Wales was differentiated, with children allocated to secondary schools on the basis of testing in English and mathematics at age 11. As a consequence of this so-called 11-plus assessment, children were placed in grammar, technical or secondary 'modern' schools, according to their performance. Grammar schools, which followed a traditional, academic curriculum took the most able, though whether this was 20 per cent or 50 per cent of the age cohort depended more on where the child lived than on absolute scores or any standardization of the results. For the rest, secondary modern schools offered a less academic, more work-oriented curriculum. Where available (and the distribution nationally was, like the distribution of the grammar schools, very uneven), children could transfer at 12, on the basis of a further assessment of ability, to a technical school. Technical schools offered curricula much closer to the emerging needs of industry and commerce, which might be described as vocational, rather than simply preparation for the notion of work. Thus, the system made some attempt to ensure that for children 'education and training as may be desirable in view of their different ages, abilities and aptitudes' (Ministry of Education 1944) was available, though through a rather crude and often arbitrary allocation model.

Following concerns about the efficacy of this approach – concerns that were rooted as much in social beliefs as in educational evidence – in 1966 selection was abolished in most parts of the UK and comprehensive schools were introduced. The comprehensive school was to bring together children from different social backgrounds and ability levels within a single institution. The increased size of these schools would allow for a broad and differentiated curriculum, so that individual needs could be met though the availability of optional courses and personal choice would enable a degree of specialization. Inevitably however, comprehensives reflected the broad social composition of the neighbourhoods in which they were located, and accordingly differentiation continued to be apparent between, as well as within schools.

Further, significant numbers of young people continued to leave the school system with no formal qualifications and, worryingly for government, without the skills necessary to find work in a rapidly changing and increasingly competitive and international labour market. Thus, the demise of the comprehensive school as a place where individual interests were identified and indulged – if it ever was such a place – was guaranteed following Prime Minister Callaghan's initiation of the 'Great Debate' in 1976, though it was another ten years before the then Conservative government of Margaret Thatcher transformed the school system. The Education Reform Act 1988 introduced a whole series of changes, not the least of which was the imposition of a National Curriculum from 5 to 16.

A variety of reasons underpinned the introduction of a National Curriculum model. Some felt that the removal of an examination at 11-plus, combined with the relative freedom of the comprehensive school to develop its own curriculum pattern, had resulted in too much unstructured or 'child-centred' teaching (see for example the various *Black Papers on Education* by Cox and Dyson 1969; Cox and Boyson 1975, 1977). There was growing frustration with the imbalance in curricular models, both within schools, where between the ages of 14 and 16 some pupils spent as much as one-third of their time studying science subjects, while others avoided science altogether, and between schools, where models sometimes seemed to reflect the teaching interests and strengths of the staff as much as they did the interests and needs of the pupils. And there was a growing determination within government to increase accountability at school level for student performance. This is difficult to do, unless performance can be 'measured' and compared in some way. An attraction of the National Curriculum is that it brings with it the possibility of national testing, and hence provides a basis for the comparison of individual school performance levels. Riding the tide of such considerations, the curriculum model introduced in England and Wales was a rather full one, not only covering 11 years, but also accounting for the whole of the school timetable for most secondary age pupils.

Despite the 'benefits' referred to above, it became obvious during the 1990s that the National Curriculum, with its 'one size fits all' philosophy, was creating problems for both schools and pupils. This is hardly surprising, as it is hard to imagine a whole curriculum model that suits all children regardless of the range of abilities and interests. In truth, it would perhaps have been sensible to reconceptualize the national model, and replace it with a core curriculum, perhaps occupying half of the pupils' time at school, while allowing a range of alternative study patterns to occupy the remainder. However, this would also require the government to acknowledge that its original decision had been misguided. Such acknowledgements being a rare event, there have instead been a series of measures relaxing the straitjacket imposed by the National Curriculum, while the official line remains that the National Curriculum itself is an unqualified blessing, which has continued to stimulate year-on-year improvements in pupil attainment levels.

This fourth phase of curriculum reform, which dates from the election of the Labour government in 1997 and brings individual needs, abilities and interests back to the fore, had something of a ragged start, originally brought about through the disapplication (for pupils with special needs) of the National Curriculum, then relaxation of some requirements at 14-plus (for disaffected pupils). However, the shift from some scope for schools to vary curriculum according to perceptions of need to active encouragement to do so, and the designation of this approach as 'personalized learning' has been most clearly articulated in a speech by the then School Standards Minister, David Miliband, who declared that:

> Decisive progress in educational standards occurs where every child matters; careful attention is paid to their individual learning styles, motivations and needs; there is rigorous use of pupil target-setting linked to high quality assessment; lessons are well paced and enjoyable; and pupils are supported by partnership with others well beyond the classroom.
>
> (Miliband 2004b)

Personalization

In September 2004 the Department for Education and Skills (DfES 2004d) set out what it saw as the key components of personalized learning. These are:

- *Assessment for learning*: the use of evidence from pupil assessment and dialogue between pupils and teachers to identify every pupil's learning needs.
- *Teaching and learning strategies*: that develop the competence and confidence of every learner by actively engaging them in the learning process and in activities that stretch them.
- *Curriculum entitlement and choice*: that delivers breadth of study, personal relevance and flexible learning pathways through the system.
- *A student-centred approach to school organization*: with school leaders and teachers thinking creatively about how to support high quality teaching and learning.
- *Strong partnerships that extend beyond the school*: to reinforce and drive forward progress in the classroom, to remove barriers to learning and to support pupil well-being.

The principle of personalization is, then, to offer education that is tailored to the learner, within systems responsive to learner needs, rather than expecting the learner to adapt to existing systems within the school. A particular merit of such an approach would be to place the needs of the learner back at the heart of the education process, rather than, as many perceive to have been the case over recent years, the testing regime. Indeed, there is widespread feeling that it is the national testing regime, rather than the National Curriculum *per se*, that has induced 'teaching to the test' (e.g. Goldstein 2001) and thus displaced teaching the pupils. If this is the case, then perhaps there should be concerns that while current policies favour a more relaxed approach to curriculum content, there is no parallel relaxation in the government's determination to measure both individual and school performance.

Personalization is, nevertheless, an approach to learning that will potentially

- increase the scope for pupil choice
- involve pupils more actively in assessment processes
- take greater account of the pupils' own perspectives on schooling
- acknowledge the differing strengths and weaknesses individual pupils bring to their learning.

Several developments are currently taking place in schools around these four main aspects of personalization, though inevitably these vary in scope and emphasis.

With regard to the issue of increasing choice, there has, as noted above, been a progressive loosening of the National Curriculum straitjacket over a number of years now. This greater element of pupil choice is evident in initiatives aimed at increasing the range of subjects available to older pupils. In particular, the greater access to vocational options that has been a clear trend in education over the past few years (and encouraged through initiatives such as 14–19) has accelerated, and several new initiatives, such as the promotion of work-based diplomas, are aimed at increasing this offer. Again, increased collaboration between schools has aided this process, by allowing pupils to follow different curriculum options in different school settings. Not only is there a wider range of choice as pupils can study parts of their curriculum in nearby schools, but also the different facilities in different schools (for example, an industrial kitchen in one school, and an electronics workshop in another) can therefore be optimally employed, and resources utilized more efficiently (West et al. 2007). In this regard it can be seen that personalization has given a new stimulus to cooperative arrangements between schools; this is a most welcome further development away from the shuttered mentality that competition and formula-funding spread through the system following the Education Act 1988.

The greater involvement of students in assessment processes was, likewise, already a growing trend in schools in England, not least as a result of the influential report *Inside the Black Box* (Black and Wiliam 1998), which indicated the beneficial impact of formative assessment and feedback strategies on student learning (and remains one of the most important examples of how educational research can influence practice). Nevertheless, and supported by the growing interest in 'student voice' as a key element in school improvement strategies from both members of the educational research community (Rudduck and Flutter 2003) and by official agencies, the personalization agenda has sharpened both interest in and experimentation with the potential of assessment for learning. Both assessment for learning, and initiatives to capture student voice have received significant support from practitioners, and many schools have begun to develop such approaches as part of their own practice. Formative assessment has become increasingly well used in schools, and has often led to the development of structures for an element of peer assessment, which has been seen as especially likely to lead to learning gains, both for the assessed and the assessor (Black et al. 2004).

Of course, the notion of student voice itself has become increasingly popular over recent years. From relatively contained beginnings, usually involving the setting up of 'student councils' or some other representative framework for pupils, via surveys of pupil views on a range of matters from school facilities to the evaluation of teaching, student voice has come to be seen as a particularly rich source of data on how well the school is functioning. In some schools, the concept has been taken much further and much closer towards making the school a more democratic community with pupils involved in decision-making on issues affecting their learning (see for example Fielding 2004b; Mitra 2006). Personalization implies that all schools will become more responsive to the views and preferences of their pupils, and will seek to modify arrangements and practices – both inside and outside the classroom – to reflect these. One consequence of this, made possible to a large extent by the workforce modernization initiative, has been the rapid development of in-school support systems involving adults other than teachers, to provide support, counselling and even just advice on personal organization to pupils whose home circumstances may not offer such support.

Acknowledging and valuing the different strengths that pupils bring to the classroom can be interpreted in a number of ways. On the one hand, the move towards greater vocational provision can be seen as an acknowledgement that the academic curriculum is not the most appropriate pathway for all students, and signals that the school is keen to engage with learners on whatever fronts it can. On the other hand, an increasing number of schools have been influenced by constructs such as multiple intelligence, and have been mapping 'learning styles' in an attempt to provide more suitable learning environments for students with different characteristics and abilities. Typically, instruments 'measuring' learning styles or intelligence are used to determine the characteristics of the individual pupil, with teaching then, in principle, adapted to coincide with the learning preferences of the pupils (Britzman 2003). Leaving aside the fact that 'adapting' method to suit the various needs of a whole class of children will be no small task, there is also some doubt (see below) about the value of such classification. Nevertheless, it is undeniable that schools have picked up on the notion of learning styles, and encouraged by the urge to personalize, there are now very few schools that have not made some efforts to assess and then respond to the learning styles of their pupils.

It is clear from the above that the call to personalize learning is having an impact on schools. Certainly, it may be true that much of what is brought together under New Labour's definition of personalization is not new, and indeed was beginning to happen in schools before the notion of personalization was coined. But it is equally the case that these developments have been accelerated by and are more likely to have become whole-school or even cross-school initiatives as a result of the personalization policy. The question arises therefore: what reasons do we have to believe that the elements of personalized learning do improve either pupil outcomes or the quality of learning?

Personalization and evidence

Personalization can be seen as one in a long line of initiatives that have attempted to make the processes of education more learner-centred and more closely adapted to the needs of individuals. The introduction of vocational curricular patterns in the late nineteenth century, for example, was initially intended to provide an education better fitted to the individual needs of (working-class) students, as well as meeting the needs of the labour market. Later on, educators such as Dewey stressed the need for all education to be centred on the learner, an emphasis subsequently retained by the progressive education movements of the 1960s and 1970s, which in at least some areas revolved around greater attention to the individual differences and needs of pupils (Ravitch 2000). Typically though, periods when student-centred classroom processes prevailed have given way to a backlash as critics claimed standards were falling and that students were being given too much freedom, or were not being introduced to their social responsibilities. In England, this was clearly the case in the 1980s and 1990s, when, following the initial criticisms of progressive education in the 'Black Papers' in the 1970s (Dadds 1992), the Conservative government introduced for the first time a National Curriculum aimed at providing a single curriculum pattern for all. The subsequent Labour government initially continued this trend towards greater uniformity of provision, and indeed tightened it further. The imposition of the National Literacy and Numeracy Strategies, with their emphasis on common teaching strategies to be employed across all primary schools can be seen as representing the high tide of the move towards uniformity of provision (Harris and Ranson 2005). In that respect, as well as a reaction to the problems outlined above that such uniformity generated in the system, the move towards personalization can therefore be seen as part of a continuous pendulum movement in education. The very fact that movements in one direction are followed by a reaction towards the other suggests that none of the past initiatives aimed at improving education has fully been able to reach that goal for all pupils. Although there is evidence of overall increases in pupil attainments as measured by standardized tests, some of which may be due to improvements in teaching and learning as well as the longer schooling in most societies and improvements in health and welfare (Flynn 1987), it is extremely difficult to compare age cohorts across time. It is also a feature of most systems that increases in average attainment are accompanied by a widening gap between the highest and lowest performers. This suggests that even if we know how to improve education for some, or even most children, we continue to have great difficulty in reaching a substantial minority that lag behind. This notwithstanding, there does exist a body of research into effective teaching and learning which can help us both to understand the differential effectiveness of teaching approaches and can allow us to make some predictions of the impact that personalization approaches may have.

The first set of evidence relates to curriculum patterns. There is some evidence both that a more integrated curriculum may be helpful and that different pupils may benefit from different curricular provision. Students of lower socio-economic status (SES), backgrounds, for example, have been found to benefit from a more integrated curriculum across grades and subjects (Connell 1996). Connecting learning to real-life experience and stressing practical applications have also been found to be particularly important to low–SES students, as has demonstrating the curriculum's relevance to their daily lives. Such an approach may diminish disaffection as well as promoting learning (Guthrie et al. 1989; Hopkins and Reynolds 2001; Montgomery et al. 1993). This would support the argument for the adaptation of the curriculum to allow more vocationally oriented, practical courses for certain students, while others may be better suited to following a more traditional academic route. This view is consistent with the principle that students need to be able to choose programmes of study that are most appropriate to their future lives and most suited to their particular skills. This is supported by findings from studies following the introduction of the National Curriculum, where disaffection and alienation, especially among those from lower SES backgrounds, were common features (Charlton et al. 2004).

Furthermore, a diversified curriculum can be said to better meet the needs of society, in that it prepares students to take on the different functions necessary to the maintenance and development of society (Heiskala 2007). On the other hand, an equally strong argument can be made that differentiating the curriculum inevitably disadvantages students from low SES backgrounds, as they get pushed into vocational programmes and prepared for careers that will see them remain in low SES occupations following their schooling, thus contributing to the reproduction of the social class system (Ainsworth and Roscigno 2005). Certainly, there is evidence that low SES pupils are more likely to end up in vocational programmes, and that the perceived parity of esteem between vocational and academic programmes that UK observers sometimes perceive in continental European countries, such as Germany, is largely a myth. In Germany and other countries with a strong vocational system, a 'waterfall' system typically operates where students who fail in the academic streams tend to end up in the vocational sector. Indeed, research in Germany and in Belgium has shown a strong overrepresentation of students from ethnic minority groups in vocational education, even taking into account the lower levels of prior performance common to such groups (Anderson et al. 2004). In a system where vocational education has traditionally never received parity of esteem, as is the case in England, it would be foolish to expect anything else to happen.

The extent to which this is seen as negating the need for a differentiated curriculum is contested, however. An argument could equally be made that it is better for students to receive some qualifications that will allow them to play a useful and remunerated role in society, rather than suffering feelings of alienation in school, or dropping-out with a lack of useful qualifications from a system where they are forced into a general academic curriculum that neither provides them with experiences of success nor is matched to their personal interests. The issue of whether and how much to differentiate the curriculum is also linked to views on the nature of human intelligence and ability. If one believes that people differ in ability, in the sense of either differing in general intelligence or of having differential intelligences, then a differentiated curriculum would appear to be an essential requirement of schooling. Research evidence does appear to point to some genetic differences in the range of pupil abilities, though it is clear that background and education itself matter greatly as well (Plomin and Spinath 2004). Even if there is a need to reorganize societal and educational structures to attempt to break the link between educational outcomes and social class and ethnicity, the evidence suggests that a common curriculum does not offer the solution. If, on the other hand, one believes that it is the class structure itself that is the only or main cause of difference in performance, then perhaps a differentiated curriculum can be seen as merely a vehicle for reinforcing this class structure and of shutting off opportunities from working-class pupils. Despite these disagreements, there is nevertheless ample research evidence to suggest that a degree of personalization will generally improve pupil achievement, however the particular achievement itself is interpreted within society.

Two areas where evidence is weaker are those of student voice and learning styles. The evidence on student voice, while receiving strong advocacy as a means of school improvement (e.g. Rudduck and Flutter 2003), is limited. There is a lot of anecdotal evidence claiming the usefulness of allowing students to have a greater say over key aspects of school life, and various examples of school improvement projects that used increased student voice as part of their improvement strategy. However, equally, there are plenty of examples of school improvement programmes that have not employed a strong student voice element. Further, even where student voice is tapped into, there appears to be little real evidence that it is student voice that has made the difference in those cases where schools have improved (Creemers and Reezigt 2005). That said, what is clear is that pupils are good judges of the effectiveness of teaching strategies and approaches. Pupils' evaluations of their teachers, for example, are often very close to those of external researchers (Muijs 2006), and much more so than the judgements of teachers themselves. Pupils therefore may provide a crucial source of information for schools. But even if their voices are not articulating important truths about how schools or classrooms should be organized, the fact that they are listened to probably, in itself, has an impact on pupil attitudes and, consequently, behaviour.

The evidence for the existence of different learning styles is even weaker. While strong claims are made for the importance of learning styles, and these have generally been received with enthusiasm by teachers, empirical research is so far lacking. Stahl (1999), reviewing a number of studies on the effects of teaching to different learning styles concluded that:

> These five research reviews, published in well-regarded journals found the same thing. One cannot reliably measure children's learning styles and even if one could, matching children to reading programs by learning styles does not improve their learning.
>
> (Stahl 1999: 23)

Similarly, a review by Coffield et al. (2004) of the thirteen most commonly used learning styles frameworks, found no evidence supporting useful outcomes from the use of any of these instruments. But even if there is evidence that different children learn the same things more effectively in different ways, or that the same children learn different things more effectively in different ways, it is not clear what that implies for teaching. A general problem with the evidence on learning styles concerns the question of whether it is 'better' to adapt teaching to match preferred learning behaviour, or on the contrary, whether the role of the teacher is to try to strengthen less favoured learning methods by focusing on those approaches through which the learner does not learn as effectively. While most educators seem to advocate adapting teacher behaviour to match existing learning styles, this may actually keep students from fully developing a repertoire of styles that they need in life. This raises issues about the balance to be struck between learning, and learning to learn. However, the enthusiasm in some schools for learning styles approaches suggests that in some cases they may have been seen as a useful corrective to the overly prescriptive elements of the National Curriculum.

The area for which evidence for a personalized approach is strongest is that of formative assessment practice. As well as the extensive work of Black and Wiliam (1998) in the UK, which demonstrated strongly positive impacts from formative assessment, researchers in North America, such as Guskey (2001) and Cooper (2006) have likewise found that various combinations of formative assessment and initial diagnostic assessment (the two are combined in most Assessment for Learning approaches) have a positive impact on student learning. It is clear that once diagnostic assessment is undertaken the possibilities for adapting learning to the current knowledge and skills levels of pupils is greater, and many schools are undertaking work to more closely differentiate classroom practice in this way.

One element that has not so far received a lot of attention in discussions of personalization is the extent to which it might be useful to differentiate teaching strategies. Initially, teacher effectiveness research concentrated strongly on finding generic characteristics of effective teaching, and a consistent set of teacher behaviours has been identified that appear to be relatively stable across contexts

(Brophy and Good 1986; Mortimore et al. 1988; Muijs and Reynolds 2001; Teddlie and Stringfield 1993). However, a move away from a generic teacher effectiveness model has begun for two main reasons. First, the generic model is counterintuitive, in that it pays insufficient attention to context; an effective teacher teaching a specialist subject to a fast stream in a selective school sixth form with ten students in the class would not be expected to exhibit the same classroom behaviour (except at such a level of generality – show enthusiasm, say – as to be banal) as an effective pre-school teacher with a class of thirty three year olds. Second, researchers in both England (e.g. Harris 1998; Watkins and Mortimore 1999) and the USA (e.g. Walberg 1986) have drawn attention to the apparent effectiveness of differentiated teaching within the same class or lesson. The extent to which the characteristics of effective teaching need to be adapted to meet different learner characteristics has begun to be explored. One of the most contested areas of differentiation for teacher effectiveness is whether different teacher behaviours are necessary for students from different SES backgrounds or different ability levels.

Generally speaking, the evidence shows that lower ability students are more strongly affected by teaching quality than higher ability students (Brophy 1992; Walberg 1986). However, a study in the UK found that relationships between teacher behaviours and student outcomes differed in strength according to school context. In schools with a low proportion of students eligible for free school meals, or a low proportion of high ability students, or a high proportion of students with special needs, correlations tended to be weaker than in other schools, suggesting that, in general, these teacher behaviours have least influence in especially advantaged or disadvantaged schools. In the advantaged schools this is possibly due to the greater support that children from more privileged backgrounds receive at home (Muijs and Reynolds 2001), though it is more difficult to explain why teacher behaviours had so little influence in the most difficult schools. Some have argued, in contrast, that children from lower SES groups need more structure in the classroom, more positive reinforcement from the teacher and need to receive the curriculum in smaller 'packages', that are followed by rapid feedback (Brophy 1992). Such children, Brophy suggests, will generally need more instruction.

Studies looking at students' perceptions of what makes an effective teacher have found that high-ability students are more likely to mention teachers' subject knowledge, while low-ability students are more likely to mention teachers' ability to connect with students (Lloyd and Lloyd 1986). According to Mortimore (1991) effective teaching in schools with a low SES intake should be teacher led and practically focused, but not low-level or undemanding. Maintaining consistency in teaching approach is more important for students from low SES backgrounds, and has been found to be related to improved outcomes (Connell 1996).

However, as those who work regularly with schools know, practice is not always driven by research evidence. Thus, despite the scant evidence to support it – and indeed the paucity of the instruments that purport to 'measure' it –

the notion of learning style has found resonance with teachers, and strategies involving the 'diagnosis' of individual learning preference have become common in many countries. Meanwhile, and despite the wealth of evidence supporting a more customized approach, assessment practices have proved more difficult to shift. So what might a personalization look like in practice? A typical example of the way a personalized learning approach can be applied is set out below.

Personalization in practice

Currently we are working on a range of projects aimed at improving outcomes among marginalized or difficult to reach pupil groups, many of which are in schools that seem to be working quite well for the majority of the pupils (Centre for Equity in Education Annual Report, Ainscow et al. 2008). One secondary school that we are working with has begun to develop a personalized approach to some of its pupils. The school, which is a relatively successful school in a north of England city, has noted that despite its pupils' attainment levels being generally well above the national average, there seems to be a cohort in each year group who underachieve. These have been identified as pupils whose performance dips in years 8 or 9 (at age 13 or 14) and does not seem to recover in time for the major national assessments that take place at 16-plus.

A systematic review of the performance records of the current year 9 identified some 60 pupils (out of a year group of approximately 200) whose attainment levels on entry had not been sustained during secondary schooling. The group was a mix of pupils whose performance seemed to have fallen off across the whole curriculum, and pupils whose opportunities were likely to be restricted because of a fall-off in performance in particular subject areas. The school has targeted this group with a deliberate series of strategies aimed at 'personalizing' their learning experience. These strategies are rooted in a number of the components of a personalization.

Assessment for learning has been at the heart of this development. The school has begun to review the level and quality of feedback these pupils are given on their work. In particular, it has sought to ensure that feedback routinely acknowledges strengths but nevertheless gives clear guidance regarding how the piece of work might be improved. This has led to a significant increase in the dialogue around the assessment process, and, in many cases, has begun to evolve into individual target-setting, as pupils begin to identify for themselves ways in which they can improve their performance.

The degree of individualization has been reinforced by practices which are overtly *student-centred*. For example, this group of pupils has been allocated learning mentors – members of staff with whom they regularly discuss their work plans (personal organization seems to be a key factor in improving the performance of these pupils), their work, their progress, their targets. The school has also organized 'mock examinations' for the group, to give them experience of examination conditions and to build confidence, as well as to ensure that the pupils have a realistic view of their current performance levels, and to provide a basis for discussion with the mentor about revision plans and priorities. The school is currently exploring whether older pupils may have a role to play in this mentoring system, thus introducing an element of peer coaching.

In an attempt to strengthen home–school *partnerships*, and to increase parents' understanding of why and how this group of pupils has been targeted, their parents have been invited to meetings with teachers who explain to them the analysis of pupil performance the school has carried out, and why their children have been targeted for this additional support, and what they hope to achieve. The initiative has been well received by parents, even those who do not often find their way to the school.

Inevitably, this level of attention to a particular group of learners does not go unnoticed by teachers. All teachers of the year group are aware of who these children are, as they need to be involved in the new assessment practices. Through their discussions with these children, they inevitably receive feedback on their own teaching as well as provide feedback on learning. Thus, while the school has not yet been tempted to conduct a 'learning styles' analysis (some would say hurrah to that!), there has nevertheless been a great deal of attention on and no little conversation about *teaching and learning* in the *classroom*.

There has also been some effort to find out more about these pupils' attitudes to school and schooling, and to themselves as learners. As part of this exploration of pupil voice, a number of pupils from this group have been interviewed by university researchers about what is happening in the school, about the attention they are being given, about the impact that is having on their attitudes towards school, on their personal ambitions, and so on. This process is in the very early stages, though the response of pupils interviewed seems very positive. Unsurprisingly, they find themselves quite interested, and generally welcome the school's efforts to better understand and cater for them. Of course, the degree of individual choice that can be made available to these pupils is still very limited, circumscribed by the rather rigid curriculum and testing pattern that the National Curriculum imposes until the end of year 9. However, both the school and the pupils themselves are becoming clearer about what their strengths and preferences are as a result of this programme, so there is an expectation that when a greater degree of *choice and diversity* becomes possible, in the years 10–11 curriculum, more informed and appropriate options will be selected.

Of course, it is much too early to evaluate any actual impact of this move to personalize the pupils' learning experience. Further, one might observe that many of the measures adopted here are being routinely applied in other schools, without any need to brand them as personalization. This is true, but it misses the point. The issue here is not whether personalization is new, or whether it is simply the bringing together of tried and tested practices that many schools have been using successfully for many years. The issue is whether the 'personal-ization' badge increases the likelihood that schools will adopt a series of strategies that seem, on balance, to be efficacious for some pupils at least. Our feeling is that this is the case, and so experiments in personalized approaches to learning, like the one we describe here, should be encouraged and nurtured, and they will over time increase the life chances of at least some pupils.

Conclusion

Personalization is a relatively recent development in New Labour education policy. The policy emerged only in the third term, as a rather belated response to the accumulating evidence that the National Curriculum was not serving all learners. It can also be seen as a move to bring education into line with other public services (Leadbeater 2004), where the principle of greater responsiveness of service to individual need had already be seen as necessary to maintain satisfaction with public provision in a world where choice and diversity were becoming increasingly important to consumers (Ferguson 2007).

In general, personalization has been well received by an educational community keen to serve the needs of *all* pupils, though as implementation is still in the early stages in most schools, the extent to which it will impact on pupil attitudes and attainment is as yet unclear. We can hope that in pursuing personalization strategies, schools will pay attention to those practices – such as assessment for learning and support outside the classroom for learning goals – for which there is strong research evidence demonstrating efficacy. It would be a pity if this potentially important development loses momentum, or collapses under the weight of yet more instruments purporting to measure 'learning styles'. What is needed is a period of continuing commitment to the strategy, and of continuing encouragement to change the way assessment data is used in schools (and by government) as a summative device, rather than the potent force for development we know it can become.

12 'Swing, swing together'

Multi-agency work in the new children's services

Alan Dyson, Peter Farrell, Kirstin Kerr and Nadine Mearns

Introduction

In 2000, 8-year-old Victoria Climbié died at the hands of her carers – a great-aunt and her partner – after an extended period of horrific mistreatment. What made Victoria's death particularly distressing was that she was known to a range of local authority and other children's agencies – housing departments, social services departments, the police, hospitals and a charity – who between them failed to arrive at coordinated effective action to save her. The subsequent independent statutory inquiry, chaired by Lord Laming, concluded that Victoria's death was the consequence not simply of the actions of her carers, but of 'a gross failure of the system' (Laming 2003: par. 1.18). 'I am in no doubt,' Lord Laming stated,

> that effective support for children and families cannot be achieved by a single agency acting alone. It depends on a number of agencies working well together. It is a multi-disciplinary task.
>
> (Laming 2003: par. 1.30)

The government's response was not simply to strengthen child protection procedures, but to view the Climbié affair in the wider context of the role that children's services might play in combating 'social exclusion'. In the same year as the Laming report, it issued a Green Paper with the title *Every Child Matters* (Department for Education and Skills (DfES) 2003b), proposing sweeping changes to these services:

> We want to put children at the heart of our policies, and to organise services around their needs. Radical reform is needed to break down organisational boundaries. The Government's aim is that there should be one person in charge locally and nationally with the responsibility for improving children's lives. Key services for children should be integrated within a single organisational focus at both levels.
>
> (DfES 2003b: 9)

Every Child Matters went on to propose a framework of desirable outcomes for children which might form the basis of common assessment systems, shared working practices, and, above all, shared goals for childhood professionals. A year later, the government legislated, in the Children Act 2004, to

- create integrated children's services departments by combining education and child and family social care functions
- bring these new services together with health and other childhood services by establishing Children's Trusts locally
- develop a set of shared working practices across these services
- increase the mutual understanding and common skills base of childhood professionals.

On the face of it, this was an entirely rational response to the failures in the Climbié case and the government's wider social inclusion agenda. The government's thinking appears to have been that children depended, to greater or lesser extents, on the services provided by the state and the voluntary sector. Currently, the quality and effectiveness of those services was severely compromised by the organizational barriers between them. If those barriers could be broken down, not only would catastrophic failures be avoided, but also all children would receive a better deal.

However, rational responses of this kind have a chequered history in this field. As an early review of the evidence base for the *Every Child Matters* proposals concluded:

> Structural reorganisation has traditionally been the dominant method of reform in children's services. It has mainly involved adjustments to the administration and management of the organisation, including greater or lesser decentralisation, increased or decreased specialization, the separation of the purchaser from the provider and divisions of responsibilities based on geography or function . . . In places, *Every Child Matters* is in danger of perpetuating the assumption that modifying the structure of services will result in a change of culture and better services for vulnerable children (pp.59, 70f). This cause-effect relationship is not supported by much evidence, however.
>
> (Warren House Group at Dartington 2004: 8)

In this chapter we will examine more closely whether these fears are justified. We will suggest that the pursuit of multi-agency collaboration is more complex than a rational perspective might seem to suggest. We will also examine what seem to us to be significant ambiguities and contradictions in the government's agenda. However, the picture is not entirely negative. The Dartington review quoted above concludes, not that multidisciplinary collaboration is impossible, nor that structural reorganization is irrelevant, but that reorganization is only ever part of the solution. We will, therefore, also explore some promising developments that seem to suggest what else needs to be done within the context of structural reorganization to make collaboration both possible and effective.

The problems of multi-agency collaboration

The principles on which multi-agency collaboration is based seem self-evident and are widely accepted to many of the professionals involved (Farrell et al. 2006; Payne 1998). In practice, however, many questions remain unanswered. For instance, the term 'multi-agency collaboration' covers a range of organizational forms and practices (Audit Commission 1998; Wilkin et al. 2003). We can see this in the *Every Child Matters* (DfES 2003b) reforms, where the same professional might well find her/himself employed by a local authority through its integrated children's services department, delivering services commissioned strategically by a Children's Trust, working for some or all of the time in a children's centre or school where professionals from different agencies are co-located, and contributing to ad-hoc teams supporting particular children and families. Each of these organizational forms is a site for collaboration, yet the legal status, governance, resourcing and working practices of each is different. If we add to this the legitimate local variations in these forms – Children's Trusts may have different partners in different places, children's services departments may have different degrees of integration, and so on – it becomes clear that the structures within which multi-agency collaboration take place are highly variable, even within what seems like a coherent set of reforms.

Not surprisingly, perhaps, roles and responsibilities within multi-agency collaboration are equally variable. A study by Atkinson et al. (2001) is unique in attempting to systematically examine the scope and success of multi-agency activity in which education authorities were then engaged. Frequently, respondents described roles and responsibilities as either 'simply evolving over time', or being 'the result of joint discussion among those involved'. On this basis it is understandable that 'confusion over roles and responsibilities' and 'competition between agency and individual priorities within the initiative' were among the most frequently reported challenges to multi-agency working.

This points to an ambiguity at the heart of attempts at collaboration. On the one hand, collaboration requires professionals to move beyond existing working practices and procedural arrangements in order to engage in the sorts of evolutionary and negotiated approach to role definition indicated above. This in itself may result in considerable role ambiguity, inter-professional tension, and the temptation to work beyond professional competence (Rushmer and Pallis 2002; Wasoff et al. 2004). Moreover, even where the structures of collaboration are clear, there may be considerable ambiguity over its purposes and working practices (Percy-Smith 2005; Stewart et al. 2003; Webb and Vulliamy 2001).

On the other hand, there is considerable research evidence that setting up collaborative arrangements does not in itself overcome the cultural differences between professionals from different backgrounds (Cameron and Lart 2003; Coxon 2005; Craig et al. 2004; Easen et al. 2000; Harbin 1996; Johnson et al. 2003; van Eyk and Baum 2002; Wasoff et al. 2004; Wilkin et al. 2003). There may therefore be limits to which professionals from different backgrounds are willing to renegotiate their roles, and fundamental differences in how they see the purposes of collaboration. Again, looking specifically at the *Every Child Matters* (DfES 2003b) reforms, simply creating integrated children's services departments does not in itself guarantee that teachers, social workers, educational psychologists, family support workers, youth workers and the rest will see the world in the same way.

These problems may be exacerbated by the practicalities of resourcing (Atkinson et al. 2001; Cameron and Lart 2003; Johnson et al. 2003; Tisdall et al. 2005; van Eyk and Baum 2002; Wilkin et al. 2003). Where partner agencies remain separate, there may be disputes over who contributes what resource to the joint venture. However, even within the single organizational and funding structures envisaged by *Every Child Matters*, there is no reason to suppose that there will not be internal disputes about the resourcing of different activities. Moreover, when, as in the current English context, many activities are funded on a short-term project basis, it is reasonable to assume that instability and tension will be increased as collaborative activities rise and fall, or as they struggle for resources against other activities.

Perhaps even more worrying is that the evidence for the impact of collaborative arrangements on outcomes for children and young people is far from convincing. It is not clear whether this is because of the absence of impacts, or the failure to undertake studies to search for them. As a review by Brown and White (2006) concludes:

> there appears to be limited positive evidence on outcomes from integrated working with much of the current work focusing on the process of integrated working and perceptions from professionals about the impact of such services.
>
> (Brown and White 2006: 16)

Likewise, Sloper (2004: 571) found 'little evidence on the effectiveness of multi-agency working itself or of different models of such working in producing outcomes for children and families'; other reviews have reached similar conclusions (see Cameron et al. 2000; Dowling et al. 2004).

All of this would seem to confirm the fears that structural reorganization may create opportunities for productive collaboration, but that it also generates significant anxieties, tensions and ambiguities without any guarantee of positive outcomes. As we turn now to the detail of government policy, we shall see that conceptualization of collaboration within New Labour reforms does nothing to resolve these problems and may, indeed, exacerbate them.

The ambiguities of government policy

Although we suggested above that the *Every Child Matters* agenda constitutes a rational response to the failures in the Climbié case and the wider concern with social in/exclusion, that is, perhaps, something of an oversimplification. The apparent rationality of breaking down organizational boundaries to promote multi-agency collaboration in fact conceals a good deal of ambiguity in current policy.

This ambiguity is evident in the origin of *Every Child Matters* (DfES 2003b). The Climbié case was a catastrophic failure in extreme and – fortunately – rare circumstances. The government at the time was very certain that there was a synergy between strategies for avoiding such failures in future and strategies for improving the well-being of all children:

> As Lord Laming's recommendations made clear, child protection cannot be separated from policies to improve children's lives as a whole. We need to focus both on the universal services which every child uses, and on more targeted services for those with additional needs. The policies set out in the Green Paper are designed both to protect children and maximize their potential.
>
> (DfES 2003b: 5)

However, such a statement begs the question as to whether the improvement in children's services 'as a whole' is a means to the end of improving children's lives 'as a whole', or whether it is simply a necessary basis for effective child protection procedures. For professionals on the ground, this raises questions about where the focus of their collective efforts should lie, which professionals should take the lead on which issues, and where, if at all, particular professional groups should recede into the background on issues of little direct relevance to their work.

The same ambiguity is evident in the formulation of desirable outcomes for children which provide a framework for professional collaboration. All children's services are expected to contribute to achieving five outcomes for children:

- **being healthy:** enjoying good physical and mental health and living a healthy lifestyle
- **staying safe:** being protected from harm and neglect
- **enjoying and achieving:** getting the most out of life and developing the skills for adulthood
- **making a positive contribution:** being involved with the community and society and not engaging in anti-social or offending behaviour
- **economic well-being:** not being prevented by economic disadvantage from achieving their full potential in life.

(DfES 2003b: 6–7, emphases in the original)

Whilst this formulation appears straightforward, it is, in fact, anything but. Whilst health, safety and achievement relate fairly clearly to aspects of children's lives in which particular services (health, social care and education) might be expected to take a lead, the situation is less clear in the cases of 'economic well-being' or 'making a positive contribution'. The former (which in any case rapidly became 'achieving economic well-being') begs the question about the role of economic, welfare and labour market policies, which lie outside the remit of even newly integrated children's services. 'Making a positive contribution', on the other hand, seems to be less of an outcome for children than a particular view of how adult society might like its children and young people to behave. Meanwhile, it is difficult to see where social development and personal relationships fit in, or why economic disadvantage is singled out as a barrier when ethnicity, gender and location might be equally disadvantaging.

Above all, *Every Child Matters* offers a list of desirable outcomes, but no indication of how these outcomes relate one to another. Which takes priority? Which ones form the necessary basis for which other ones? How do they support one another? Are there any points where they are in conflict? Such questions, no doubt, are perfectly capable of being answered, but they do mean that, for children's professionals on the ground, the outcomes framework offers much less clear guidance to practice than might be expected. In particular, they do little to ensure effective collaboration or to end territorial disputes when, say, education professionals argue that all other outcomes are subservient to 'enjoy and achieve', or health professionals that other outcomes are subservient to 'be healthy'.

The problem is compounded by the accountability of different professional groups for achieving different sets of targets. The system of public service governance set up by New Labour takes the form of centrally devised public service agreements for each government department. These are translated into a series of measurable targets which are then passed 'down the line' through intermediate bodies, such as local authorities, and so to front-line organizations and professionals (Dyson 2007). The perverse consequences of the culture of 'performativity' (Ball 2003; Broadfoot 2001) created by this system have been well discussed in the education literature (most recently in The Primary Review 2007). However, from the perspective of multi-agency collaboration, the problem is not simply that professional practice is shaped and constrained by often narrowly conceived targets. It is that different agencies and professionals either are accountable for *different* targets, or, where targets are shared, have different levels of responsibility for achieving those targets. In principle, for instance, social care workers carry some responsibility for children's educational achievements, just as teachers carry some responsibility for children's health. In neither case, however, are these professional groups likely to see themselves as having prime responsibility, or to put their more immediate concerns (child protection, or test and examination results) at risk to discharge these responsibilities.

We have argued elsewhere (Dyson and Raffo 2007) that these ambiguities and contradictions are anything but accidental. New Labour has tended to conceptualize disadvantage in a distinctive way. Using, particularly in its early years, the concept of 'social exclusion', it has argued that disadvantage is the result of a multiplicity of factors in people's lives. Poverty, which might historically have been regarded as the root cause of disadvantage, has been reduced in status to just one of these factors, alongside, for instance, poor housing, lack of employment, low aspirations, poor health-related behaviours, and low educational achievement. The appropriate policy response, therefore, has not been to make a concerted assault upon some supposed underlying cause, but to tackle each of the contributory factors separately. The *locus classicus* of this approach was the National Strategy for Neighbourhood Renewal, in which no fewer that eighteen separate Policy Action Teams (PATs) were detailed to formulate responses to the social exclusion experienced by people living in the most disadvantaged areas (Social Exclusion Unit 1998, 2001).

This approach has major implications for New Labour's conceptualization of professional collaboration. So long as these factors are seen as essentially separate, they call for separate interventions from different agencies and professional groups. Those interventions certainly need to be coordinated so that duplication of effort is avoided and professionals can offer each other mutual support. However, this does not necessarily imply any deeper sharing of purpose in the form, say, of a common approach to what is seen as a fundamental problem. Significantly, 'joining it up locally' was simply one among many PATs in the formulation of the Neighbourhood Renewal Strategy (National Strategy for Neighbourhood Renewal 2000), charged, significantly, not with developing the conceptual basis for responses to disadvantage, but with finding ways of rationalizing essentially separate policy responses at local level.

Taken together, these characteristics mean that multi-agency working is not as straightforwardly rational as repeated government exhortations might make it appear to be. In the context of separate targets and lines of responsibility assembled into loosely coupled lists of desirable outcomes or disadvantaging factors, collaboration may mean no more than a form of more-or-less enlightened self-interest. Different agencies may work together in so far – and only in so far – as this enables them to pursue their own goals more effectively – what one local authority officer described as like a set of 'cuckoos living in one nest' (Ainscow et al. 2008). Alternatively, collaboration may involve partners in meeting the formidable challenge of doing what national frameworks singularly fail to do – that is, developing their own 'vision and strategy' (Geddes 2006; National Strategy for Neighbourhood Renewal 2000) – that is, a sense of how outcomes fit together, how disadvantaging factors interact, and how some coherent shared response can be made.

What this analysis suggests is that New Labour's commitment to multi-agency working may in fact be badly underconceptualized. It offers accounts of desirable outcomes for children and young people, and explanations of why those outcomes fail to materialize for many. Yet these accounts and explanations are less convincing on inspection than they seem at first sight. It mandates collaboration, but fails to align other aspects of policy – notably, of accountability regimes – with this imperative. And it sets up collaborative structures, yet it is difficult to see what has been done to address the known problems with collaborative working that we identified in our review of the literature above. To those of us who have lived through the New Labour years, the pattern is, in fact, depressingly familiar – a high level of policy activity at the centre and an overwhelming desire to manage working practices on the ground, without the corresponding capacity to think issues through in depth or deliver workable solutions to practitioners. As in the Neighbourhood Renewal Strategy, the absence of a fully worked out 'vision and strategy' at the centre leads all too often to an injunction to practitioners and decision-makers at the local level to 'join up' the fragmentary mandates of national policy.

Despite this gloomy picture, the situation may not be entirely without hope. Precisely because national policy is underspecified and underconceptualized, it creates 'spaces' within which local practitioners and decision-makers can begin to work their way towards their own solutions. In many cases, no doubt, this space is one which the 'cuckoos' use to try to turn each other out of the nest. However, there are cases where this space is used productively, and which illustrate what multi-agency collaboration might look like in the right circumstances. It is to one of these that we now turn.

Some promising examples

New Labour's commitment to promoting multi-agency working is embodied as clearly as anywhere in its ongoing development of extended schools. Following from the Schools Plus report for the National Neighbourhood Renewal Strategy (Department for Education and Employment (DfEE) 1999c), successive governments have piloted various versions of what they call 'extended' schools, many of which we have been involved in evaluating (Cummings et al. 2004, 2005, 2006, 2007; Dyson et al. 2002). Latterly, the government has committed itself to a national 'roll out' in which every school will be involved in offering access to extended provision. Essentially, extended schools offer services to children, families and local communities over and above their core business of teaching the curriculum. Typically, they offer these services in partnership with other agencies and organizations, particularly those working with children and young people. They are seen, therefore, as key means of delivering the *Every Child Matters* and, in certain circumstances, on the neighbourhood renewal agendas (Department for Children, Families and Schools (DCFS) 2007).

All of this is particularly true of the Full Service Extended Schools (FSES) initiative, which ran for three years from 2003 with the aim in its original form of developing a full service school in each local authority area (DfES 2003e, 2003f). These schools were to deliver a range of extended services – childcare, out-of-hours activities, family support, adult learning, support for children and young people, community access to school facilities and so on – and were expected to do so in close collaboration with other agencies, which might well mean accommodating professionals from those agencies on the school site. Since the schools were overwhelmingly based in areas of significant disadvantage, they had the potential to act as hubs for multi-agency approaches to the problems facing many children and families in those areas, and to the regeneration of the areas themselves.

The attempts of FSESs to develop partnership working were as fraught with difficulty as our analyses above might lead us to expect (Cummings et al. 2005, 2006). However, some found ways round these problems (Cummings et al. 2007). Typically, such schools developed more-or-less clear analyses of the situations they were facing, linking the educational difficulties faced by many of their students to issues in families, in local community cultures, and in area demographics and economics. In many places, we were told that low educational achievement was linked to the disappearance of traditional heavy industries, the collapse of the local labour market, and consequent high levels of unemployment, poverty, ill health and family stress. Local people had lost confidence in themselves. In the absence of any obvious opportunities to find their way out of the current situation, and of any examples of education being used as a path to betterment, they lost faith in themselves as learners, and transmitted this disengagement and hopelessness to their children.

In response, many of the FSESs developed a four-strand strategy:

- activities aimed at providing swift access for students to a range of personal support
- activities aimed at promoting greater engagement with learning on the part of students
- extensive efforts to support and engage both families and local people
- activities aimed at engaging families and local people with learning.

The following account (from 'Hornham' School) is typical:

> A structure has been developed around a weekly multi-agency pupil referral panel meeting and a learning and support team to deliver intervention and support to the most vulnerable pupils and their families . . . [This comprises] learning mentors, two family support workers (one of whom is social work trained), a BEST [Behaviour and Education Support Team] manager (from a health background), members of the senior leadership team and an educational psychologist (EP). They work closely with a range of statutory, voluntary and community services and will signpost to other agencies whenever necessary. A wing in the school has been designated a learning support area, and it is from here (and the learning support unit and offsite provision) that learning mentors and other professionals operate for much of their time.
>
> The level of support for targeted pupils is very high. There are nurture groups for vulnerable year 7 pupils, key fund groups, youth engagement strategy activities, a buddy group, counselling support, sexual health clinics,

a nutrition group (run by a learning mentor and a health worker), and crime and drugs prevention work (in partnership with a community police officer). The school also has a Connexions-funded positive activities for young people (PAYP) worker who delivers one-to-one and group work support with targeted pupils, and supports pupils following the 'more appropriate' curriculum. As part of a trial in the local authority, aimed at reducing the number of pupils falling into the NEET [Not in Education, Employment or Training] category, Hornham has benefited from enhanced Connexions PA [personal adviser] input. So, PAYP pupils are offered 'entry to employment' placements at the end of the summer term and engage in work based learning to develop skills for employment . . . There is also BIP [Behaviour Improvement Programme] first day response provision for pupils at risk of exclusion . . .

Parent and community oriented provision includes: an outreach parent support group; lifelong and family learning provision; intergenerational work in partnership with Age Concern; environmental projects involving pupils and community members; and a police drop in for community members. Hornham has developed a close partnership with the local community centre and offers residents access to its web portal (which provides information on FSES and other provision in the area) from there.

(Cummings et al. 2007: 21–22)

As will be clear, this form of response involves a high level of multi-agency working. FSESs like Hornam would often employ, or recruit from local authority services, their own non-teaching education professionals – mentors, counsellors, education welfare officers, education psychologists, behaviour specialists, family support workers – and enable them to work alongside non-education professionals – social workers, health workers, police officers, youth workers – based in and around the school. Often, as at Hornham, these different professionals would share a physical base in the school, and their work might be coordinated through some formal team arrangements, complete with mechanisms for assessing cases and allocating tasks.

What seemed to be crucial, however, was that these professionals operated in what one headteacher called a 'zone in-between'. What he meant by this was that their work was located between the sorts of pastoral and support work schools could traditionally offer, and the more intensive and specialist interventions available by referral to external agencies. Referral, he argued, was a cumbersome process delivering limited results as agencies sought to guard their finite resources. By contrast, the 'zone in-between' approach involved creating the possibility for different professionals to work together at the point of need, responding flexibly and rapidly to problems as they arose. Although traditional referral routes might, in some cases, need to be activated, the multi-professional teams in schools were 'light on their feet', able to deliver low-level support in a way which averted the need for more formal procedures. They were able to pool their skills and resources, taking the lead on cases as appropriate, or developing joint strategies to be delivered flexibly. Moreover, because professionals from many backgrounds were involved, they were able to bring together packages of support in response to the complex, multidimensional character of the difficulties that individual students were facing.

We were given many examples of this approach in action. The following, provided by a Connexions personal adviser is typical and is worth quoting at length:

> [Name of pupil] was referred in year 9. Her behaviour in school was aggressive towards teachers and staff. She wasn't staying in lessons. She was a substance misuser and had outside issues with boyfriends and relationships with other young people. There was no family liaison. She was disaffected with school and at risk of exclusion. When I spoke to her I found she had very little self-esteem and she was involved in substance misuse. So the work I did involved home visits so parents were involved and I did self-esteem and anger management sessions [with the pupil] and linked in with the inclusion team so she could do 4 GCSEs in the unit [the inclusion unit in school where students get 1:1 support to complete GCSEs] and I supported her to and from her work placement. I also referred her to the substance misuse worker who comes into school . . . The inclusion team and I got her a taster course at a FE [further education] college in hairdressing and beauty so her timetable was a flexible package . . . When she left Year 11 she came here [the school] to apply to do an NVQ [National Vocational Qualification] in early years. Her attendance has been brilliant and now she is looking to work in social care and I've linked her with the social worker [in the FSES] to get a grounding in the job . . . [Without support] I don't think she would have finished school. She had no aspirations and wanted to work in the local caf[é]. It's really boosted her self-esteem and she is now thinking of helping other young people that she says 'were like me'. It's so great when it goes like this. It's the multi-agency staff that's given this input.
>
> (Cummings et al. 2007: 52–53)

What we see strikingly here is the way in which different professional resources – the Connexions PA, the substance misuse worker, the school's inclusion unit, the social worker – are brought to bear flexibly at the point of need. In particular, there is a good deal of overlap between their fields of operation: the Connexions PA is involved in school provision, counselling and family support; the school is involved in work experience and provision for disaffected young people; the social worker provides a work taster. Because of the multiplicity of resources and the flexibility with which they are used, they make it possible to respond to the multidimensional nature of the young person's difficulties, to construct new responses flexibly as issues emerge, and to multiply the effects of each intervention separately.

An emerging model

It is important not to romanticize the sorts of developments we have described above. By no means everything went as smoothly as in the case just cited, and we encountered tensions between agencies and disrupted relationships as well as resounding successes. In particular, one of the main reasons why multi-agency working seemed relatively successful in these contexts was the central role played by the school, yet this also meant that analyses, strategies and partnerships were driven perhaps too much by education professionals and educational perspectives.

Nonetheless, it seems to us that something important was happening in FSESs that might have implications for the field of multi-agency collaboration as a whole. To some extent, what was happening was entirely in line with – and undoubtedly supported by – the government's own model of multi-agency working. The structural reorganization of services under the *Every Child Matters* agenda was embodied in the multi-professional teams emerging in FSESs, and the framework of the five outcomes doubtless provided a starting point for their responses to particular cases and their development of more wide-ranging area strategies.

However, FSESs were doing much more, we suggest, than bringing centrally accountable professionals together within a loosely specified common framework. What seems to be crucial is that they were able to develop a local 'vision and strategy', both in relation to individual cases such as the one set out above, and in relation to their wider school population and area agendas. They were then able to create a set of inter-professional relationships and practices based on flexibility and mutual reinforcement. As a result, the potentially competing 'cuckoos in the nest' became, in some instances at least, genuinely collaborative partners.

We know from our own work that such examples of local collaboration based on a shared vision and strategy are not restricted to full service schools (Ainscow et al. 2008; Farrell et al. 2006). Moreover, the evaluations of two major multi-agency initiatives of recent years hint – and sometimes more than hint – that the inherent problems of collaboration in current policy contexts can be overcome. Sure Start, for instance, is an initiative in which agencies working with young children and their families in disadvantaged areas have been enabled to come together to deliver their services collaboratively and from shared sites. Initial outcomes from the initiative were highly disappointing. In typical New Labour fashion, the imperative to collaborate was clear, but the forms and practices of collaboration were underspecified, with the result that local programmes struggled to find coherent and effective strategies (National Evaluation of Sure Start 2005). However, the most recent findings suggest that programmes may be beginning to learn their way towards such strategies, and that the anticipated outcomes are finally beginning to emerge (National Evaluation of Sure Start 2008).

The Children's Fund was a similarly lightly specified initiative in which statutory and voluntary agencies were brought together in local partnerships to tackle the social exclusion of children and young people. The national evaluation here differentiated between 'stable' partnership boards and 'developing' boards (Edwards et al. 2006: 21ff). The former, in broad terms, did what we might expect from our analysis of the national policy framework, working through a process of limited collaboration, in which different partners were funded to pursue their own targets and few attempts were made to develop new understandings of local situations and strategies to address those situations. The developing boards, by contrast, acted as 'sites for cross-agency learning', developing not only new forms of collaborative networks, but also new analyses and strategies.

The implication would seem to be that, despite the stresses and ambiguities of the current policy context, it is possible for professionals and their agencies to work together in something more than a tokenistic and fragmented way. However, as the Dartington review pointed out, structural reform alone is not enough (Warren House Group at Dartington 2004). What is also needed is the space in which local professionals can begin to make sense of the situations they face and the strategies they need to address those situations. That space can only exist if professionals are free to work not only beyond organizational boundaries, but also beyond the separate priorities and targets that are imposed upon them centrally.

Although we suggested earlier that it was ironic that the National Strategy for Neighbourhood Renewal relegated the issue of 'joining up' to one report out of eighteen, that report in fact had much to say that was important. As we have done here, it argued that:

> Holistic government in particular places cannot be imposed top-down from a distance. If frameworks for co-operation are to be effective, they need to be more than lists of externally imposed priorities. They must also reflect the whole needs of communities and the priorities of local people. Joined up working must create room for personal initiative and creativity.
> (National Strategy for Neighbourhood Renewal 2000: par. 1.17)

This does not, it seem to us, demand a total withdrawal of central government from the field. New Labour has made important contributions by reaffirming the central importance of public services to the lives of vulnerable children and families, stating its commitment to multi-agency working as a means of enhancing the effectiveness of public services, and creating structures which weaken some of the more obvious barriers to collaboration. It could, we believe, now go further by making a serious commitment to localism, seeing itself as the creator and guardian of spaces for local decision-making, and letting go its attempt to micro-manage services through inflexible accountability mechanisms and multiple initiatives. In other words, the recommendations of PAT 17 in 2000 now have to be heeded:

> *Central government*, and in particular the failure of Departments to act corporately, has been responsible over the years for many of the factors

which make local joint working difficult. Examples include the fragmentation of delivery machinery, an uncoordinated flow of new initiatives, a proliferation of requirements for issue-led partnerships, too much central direction and regulation, and financial frameworks, performance indicators and measures that tend to reinforce 'silo' behaviour. A more co-ordinated framework for coherence and consistency of delivery is needed.

(National Strategy for Neighbourhood Renewal 2000: executive summary, par. 52, emphasis in original)

13 New Labour and breaking the education and poverty link

A conceptual account of its educational policies

Dave Hall and Carlo Raffo

Introduction

Evidence over many decades has shown that the family and socio-economic backgrounds of young people are major determinants of their subsequent educational attainments (Jencks 1972; Kelly 1995; Mortimore and Whitty 1997). The implications of this for young people are enormous. Put simply, the poorer the families they grow up in, the less well they are likely to do in the education system. Far from offering a route out of poverty, all too often education simply seems to confirm and replicate existing social positions. This chapter offers a conceptual account of the relationship between poverty and education which seeks to capture and frame the various explanations and theoretical understandings of this relationship. Although this conceptualization is one that speaks to connections between education and poverty in a range of international contexts, it is our intention here to examine the way in which New Labour policies embody aspects of this relationship. The chapter is based upon a conceptual framework that identified different clusters of explanations relating to the education poverty relationship; this formed a central aspect of a research literature review on poverty and education (Raffo et al. 2007). This review was undertaken as part of the *Joseph Rowntree Foundation Education and Poverty Programme* and, we believe, it offers the potential for new and distinctive insights into New Labour's educational policies.

Background

The relationship between education and poverty has been and remains at the time of writing absolutely central to any New Labour vision for the UK. In order to understand this, it is important to make brief reference to the political and policy origins of New Labour. New Labour by definition was shaped at its formation in the mid 1990s by its attempts to shake off previous policy commitments and aspirations to broad notions of socio-economic equality and to replace these with a 'new' vision linked to 'third way' policy solutions intended to harness both state intervention and market forces to create economic and social well-being (Newman 2001; Powell 1999). Accordingly the New Labour project can be seen as a reaction to postwar social, political and economic developments; an exercise in looking backwards and learning political and economic lessons from the past. In particular, as a rejection of the capacity of state economic interventions to generate levels of economic prosperity widely regarded as forming central aspirations for increasingly large proportions of the electorate. One important consequence of this was that the use of economic tools such as nationalization and the taxation system to radically redistribute income between different groups in society were largely eschewed. New Labour can also be viewed simultaneously as an attempt to look forward, an articulation of a new vision for society based upon equality of opportunity. In terms of education in general and links between education and poverty in particular this change of direction had two important consequences. First, as economic solutions to social problems largely went out of favour so social and educational interventions for the creation of a new society took on a new importance. Second, there was a movement away from policies intended to create social and economic equality in favour of a move towards a commitment to creating equality of opportunity so that all UK citizens could reasonably expect an equal chance to share in the rewards of prosperity. Both signified a new role for education. With an emerging understanding of the importance of educational qualifications in shaping the future life chances of young people it can be regarded as unsurprising that education featured as a key element even, it might be suggested, as a linchpin for New Labour.

This shift of emphasis placing education in a more central policy position meant that New Labour had placed a great deal of faith in education in terms of its capacity to act as a driver for change helping to create a new British society based upon equality of opportunity. As part of this the capacity of the education system and its institutions to offer children from socio-economically disadvantaged backgrounds the opportunity to gain educational qualifications equivalent to those of their more socio-economically advantaged peers became of paramount importance.

At one level it might be regarded as surprising that New Labour should place such a high degree of faith in the capacity of education to offer social trans-formation. Societies in economically advanced countries have for a number of years faced a paradox. Formal education in such societies is largely a public service available to all children and young people, regardless of family income. These education systems are generally well resourced, offer high-quality experi-ences, and are likely to have sophisticated mechanisms for targeting attention and resources to the most disadvantaged learners. It might be reasonable to suppose, therefore, that formal education will offer a route out of poverty for the most disadvantaged young people. Yet, as referred to in the introduction, studies continue to demonstrate the central importance of family background in determining educational outcomes

At another level New Labour's faith in the capacity of the education system to act as an engine of social change was based upon a determination to use an unprecedented range of targeted interventions in an increasingly centralized education system. Some of these such as the emphasis upon educational 'standards' in a narrow range of national tests linked to the National Curriculum can be viewed as a continuation of policies established under the previous Conservative administration. Others, in particular Excellence in Cities,[1] Connexions,[2] Sure Start,[3] Educational Maintenance Allowance,[4] and Full Service Extended Schools,[5] were a more identifiable break with the past. Viewed from this perspective New Labour's optimism in the capacity of education to deliver social transformation can be seen as more understandable. New Labour was adopting an approach to educational reform that could be viewed as innovative and with targeted initiatives aimed at those individuals and groups who had often benefited least from previous reforms.

Regardless of New Labour's intentions in education, there is a mounting weight of evidence that the policies pursued have not led to the outcomes imagined by their originators. Strong links between family background and educational attainments continue to be reported (Bell 2003; Bynner and Joshi 2002; Demie et al. 2002; UNICEF 2007). Each of the schemes described in the paragraph above has contributed to improvements in educational outcomes for the most disadvantaged but evaluations also suggest that these improvements have only been marginal at best (Cummings et al. 2005; Hoggart and Smith 2004; Kendall et al. 2005; Melhuish et al. 2005; Middleton et al. 2005). One reason is that, although there is widespread agreement that poverty and poor educational outcomes are related, there is much less agreement as to why that should be the case. Competing explanations – in terms of the differential distribution of educational opportunities, the cultures of poor communities, the dynamics of poor families, the quality of schooling in disadvantaged areas, and many more – have been advanced. Policy-makers and practitioners therefore have been and continue to be faced with a bewildering array of possible explanations, many of which seem to be supported by equally convincing evidence and argument. It can be viewed as hardly surprising in these circumstances that policy interventions are based variously on the latest explanation to be advanced, the one which is argued for most fiercely by its proponents, or alternatively that which is most politically convenient. Indeed, our analysis suggests that too many New Labour policy interventions have focused on the more accessible and amenable and with an overall approach that lacks coherence. We also argue that New Labour policies have largely eschewed or under played issues of power in a way that has undermined their transformative capacity.

Explaining the education poverty link: functionalist and socially critical perspectives

Raffo et al. (2007) undertook the review of the literature on the links between education and poverty in the form of a 'conceptual synthesis' (Nutley et al. 2002) of research evidence. It involved the identification of conceptual literature explicitly addressing the relationship between poverty and educational outcomes with the intention of identifying the conceptual bases (Burrell and Morgan 1979) out of which research related to this theme had emerged. The various literatures we considered included research texts, policy papers, evaluations and various other reports.

Arising out of the above process two broad conceptual understandings emerged. The first focused on the level at which the literatures cohered. Some studies focused either exclusively or primarily upon the individual, for example, by examining the characteristics of the individual or his/her relationship with teachers or peer groups. These studies were termed as being at the 'micro-level'. Other explanations examined the immediate social contexts of young people and consequently focused upon families, communities, schools and peer groups. These were termed as being at the 'meso-level'. Finally some of the research that was considered focused upon wider social structures and global socio-economic developments. Studies corresponding to this description were termed as being at the 'macro-level'. The second principal conceptual understanding emerging from the review relates the way in which the literature has addressed the nature, role and purposes of education. Two broad but different positions were suggested that were labelled as functionalist and socially critical. Both generally regard education as an overall 'good' for both individuals and society, but they differ in relation to what sort of a good it is and how it is to be produced.

Studies that could be labelled as 'functionalist' generally take for granted the importance of education in the effective functioning of society. When education is functioning appropriately it is seen as bringing benefits both to society as a whole and to individuals within that society. Such benefits include economic development, social cohesion, and enhanced life chances for individuals. For individuals and groups from poorer backgrounds however these supposed benefits often do not materialize. As highlighted above, explanations for these failures in education can be located at specific levels of analysis.

At the macro-level issues of class, race and gender are the focus of analysis and have recently been examined through discourses of globalization (Brown 1999; Lash and Urry 1994) and the network society (Castells 1996) and how these have generated particular forms of social exclusion for certain individuals, families and communities (Byrne 2005). These are manifested in aspects of spatial ghettoization (Meen et al. 2005), high levels of unemployment, poor housing, inadequate infrastructures and poor health for many individuals and families (Acheson 1998; Exworthy et al. 2003; Hastings et al. 2005) that, taken together, appear to compound poor educational attainment.

At the meso-level many studies focus on the social contexts within which young people are placed such as schools, families and neighbourhoods. These literatures can be conveniently categorized into those that focus generally on school factors and those that examine wider issues outside of school, such as peer groups, families and neighbourhoods. Much of the literature that focuses on school factors emanates from the school improvement and school effectiveness movement. These studies tend to examine how schools can develop particular strategies and approaches that can make a difference in areas of 'challenge' (Muijs et al. 2004). However claims made by studies utilizing this approach are criticized by others for not examining the influences of the social context of the school (Hallinger and Murphy 1986), the compositional make-up of schools (Thrupp 1999), the constraints that poverty exerts on schools and on teachers within such schools (Lupton 2005) and the nature of educational markets in such areas (Levacic and Woods 2002; Riddell 2005). These studies assert that without understanding some of the contextual issues associated with schooling in disadvantage, schools are only likely to have limited impacts on breaking the link between poverty and poor educational outcomes. Complementing these studies are a set of literatures that examine how schooling in disadvantaged areas is multifaceted and requires schools to work with other agencies to deal with some of the barriers to educational engagement that young people experience (Atkinson et al. 2005; Engestrom 2001; Milbourne et al. 2003; Webb and Vulliamy 2004).

Although school-focused research has provided numerous explanations and strategies for dealing with the failures in education, other studies have started from outside schools and have focused on how families and communities living in poverty experience life, and how these experiences then impact on the educational outcomes of young people living in those families and communities. Community-focused studies tend to examine the spatial ghettoization of particular poor neighbourhoods that include a lack of jobs and infrastructure in such neighbourhoods, poor opportunities for developing networks of trust within and between communities, a lack of appropriate role models within families which may have little or no history of work in such communities and pressure on very poor families to secure an income greater than that available from education and training. These issues are often viewed as reflecting a lack of appropriate bridging social capital and cultural capital[6] that have limited the capacity of people to realize their potential at school (Wikeley et al. 2007). In addition other studies examine how faith and ethnic minority communities and neighbourhoods living in poverty provide enhanced and differential levels of social and cultural capital. These capitals are seen as alleviating some of the material aspects of poverty by providing improved networked opportunities of support that lead to enhanced educational success for certain groups of young people (Carter 2003; Furbey et al. 2006; Kalmijn and Kraaykamp 1996; LaVeist and Bell McDonald 2002).

As well as literatures that focus more heavily on communities Raffo et al.'s (2007) review also examined meso-level research that examined families in general and parenting practices in particular. For example Desforges and Abouchar's (2003) study stresses the importance of 'good' parenting in edu-cational attainment. 'Good' parenting is defined as a combination of the educational aspiration of parents, educational support and stimulation for young people in the home, the provision of secure and stable home environments and participating with the school, all of which are seen as central to young people's educational success. However, Desforges and Abouchar (2003) also recognized that such notions are premised on issues of social class, maternal levels of education and material deprivation all of which are strongly correlated with poverty. These findings are also supported by Kellett and Dar's (2007) research for the Joseph Rowntree Foundation that demonstrates how young people from affluent backgrounds exude confidence in their literacy and that this confidence derives from a variety of family opportunities such as routine support for homework and parental oracy role models. By contrast Kellett and Dar's (2007) research found that young people from poorer backgrounds had few, if any, of these opportunities. These studies suggest the need for effective family support, and US child development literature in particular (Shonkoff and Phillips 2000) suggests interventions might profitably focus at the pre-school and early school ages.

Micro-level studies, in contrast to both macro and micro studies, tend to examine the link between education and poverty in terms of dysfunctions associated with individual learners. Because the level of analysis is on individuals the focus is either on how individual young people living in poverty choose not to engage in education or on how poverty is the result of predetermined capabilities inherited by young people through their genes that predisposes them not to achieve in education and therefore reduces their life chances (Herrnstein and Murray 1994). These latter studies have been strongly and widely critiqued both methodologically and morally. However, those former studies that have focused on young people's agency have recognized how this has been informed by new forms of risk and individualization (Beck 1992; Giddens 1991) which have provided new opportunities for young people to shape their biography, including the development of particular learner identities vis-à-vis education (Archer and Yamashita 2003). However, much of this literature also recognizes that the possibilities for exercising agency by young people living in poverty is constrained: first, by restricted networks of influence linked to an inability to benefit from mainstream formal educational provision (Raffo 2006), and second, by other constraining proximal family, peer and neighbourhood factors. A particular approach to examining young people's life course linked to developmental psychology also recognizes that individual young people living in poverty can beat the odds and can demonstrate an agency that appears unfettered by constraining factors and what they define as 'risk' factors. These studies suggest that there are moderating factors that help to create resilience against these risk factors. Writers in this field examine the impact of particular risk factors of poverty, such as parental mental health (Ellenbogen and Hodgins 2004) and community violence on young people and their educational outcomes. At the same time they examine how certain protective factors such as caring and warm adult relationship (Luthar and Zelazo 2003), effective teacher–student relationships, or the aspirations of parents (Schoon and Bynner 2003) can at times moderate some of these risk factors through creating forms of individual resilience that result in improved educational outcomes.

The second position, which we label here 'socially critical', doubts whether the benefits of education can be realized simply by overcoming specific problems in its contribution to current social arrangements. From this perspective those social arrangements are themselves inherently inequitable, and education in its current form both reflects and replicates unequal distributions of power and resource. The failure of education to produce benefits for people living in poverty is not simply a problem in an otherwise ordered and well-functioning system, but is a result of the inequalities built into society and the education system alike. It follows that, if educational benefits are indeed to be realized, a form of education is needed which is critical of existing arrangements and which can both challenge existing power structures and enable democratic development. Macro-level studies that are socially critical raise wider questions of power, hierarchy, social control and cultural reproduction (Bourdieu and Passeron 1977; Bowles and Gintis 1976). More latterly socially critical studies at this level of analysis have focused on either demonstrating how global and national social and economic structures determine educational provision and achievement for the middle classes (Lipman 2004; Morrow and Torres 2000; Ozga 2000; Rivzi and Lingard 2000) or have provided a critical analysis of neoliberal educational policy interventions such as choice and the market in the way that they favour the middle class because of their enhanced cultural capital at the expense of the poor (Gewirtz 2001; Harris and Ranson 2005; Smith and Nobel 1995). Many of these writers assert that education has largely not been developed to enable and educate all young people in a manner that might challenge existing social structures (Gilborn, 2005; Ladson-Billings 1995, 1998; Maguire, 2006).

The socially critical perspective at the meso-level contains studies that focus on neighbourhoods, community radicalism, different school curricula and culture and the potential that these have for changing wider power relations. At one level these can be summarized as research studies that have focused on issues of place. Certain studies have highlighted forms of cultural exclusion (Bauder 2002; Sibley 1995) experienced by particular groups of people in particular neighbourhoods. Others have critiqued a deficit and passive representation of place and people in those places (Franklin 2000; Gulson 2005; Lister 2004; Miron 2006). Complementary studies have provided enriched ethnographic accounts of life in disadvantaged neighbourhoods and communities (Seaman et al. 2006) that demonstrate high levels of resilience and support for young people in such communities. At a different level other studies have emphasized more radical and democratic approaches to education that have challenged and changed existing power relations. These include studies that focus on more democratic ways in which teachers and pupils interact; aspects of school curriculum that advocate critical pedagogies, student voice and the way school governance relates more directly to community needs (Connell et al. 1992; Fielding 2006; Friere 1970; Thomson 2002). Other work in this area focuses more specifically on community radicalism in 'answering back' and creating equitable educational opportunities (Anyon 1997, 2005). Since many of the writings from a socially critical perspective focus on the social, there is little in the literature where the main level of analysis is on the individual and at the micro-level. Certain radical developmental psychologists have worked on the interface between a focus on the individual and the impact of community but often in response to what they see as a conservative bias in much mainstream developmental psychology (Holzman 1997). In addition there is the work by Davies (2006) and Youdell (2006) who draw on the philosophical work of Judith Butler and focus on the way in which the individual pysche develops. They argue that identities are heavily shaped by external power relations which constrain or enhance the possibilities that individuals can achieve. In many respects these ideas are foregrounded in Frankham and Edwards-Kerr's (2007) study. They document through detailed ethnographies the importance of authentic and power neutral relationship building processes between young people and adults as a precursor for active engagement with education. These ideas suggest that educators and policy-makers need to take responsibility for the way in which taken-for-granted practices and discourses can limit individuals' life chances.

Synthesizing socially critical and functionalist perspectives

Table 13.1 provides a synthesis of the two perspectives. Explanations from a functionalist perspective focus on the dynamics that generate social exclusion and highlight how certain individuals, families and communities are marginalized and potentially made poorer by a lack of access to education. From a macro perspective, there are studies that suggest that structural barriers create a lack of resources for neighbourhoods and for individuals and families that live in those neighbourhoods. This lack of resources is linked to unemployment or poorly paid employment and is exacerbated by the poor infrastructures of health, housing and transport in such neighbourhoods. At the same level of analysis but from a socially critical perspective, the main issues tend to cohere around the nature of power and in particular how global economic structures and power inequalities result in poorer educational outcomes for certain class, gender and ethnic groups. Taken together these perspectives suggest the need for educational intervention strategies not only to deal with barriers to educational access, aspiration, progression and opportunities but also to question how global capitalism and neoliberal educational policies are potentially creating barriers for particular individuals and groups through an exercise of power that benefits some individuals and groups and marginalizes others.

From a meso-level functionalist perspective we have described explanations that have highlighted inhibiting factors for poor families, communities, peer and ethnic groups around issues of parenting and a lack of social and cultural capital. From a socially critical perspective, we have been reminded how discourses about family and community engagement with education can often be deficit oriented and victim blaming. Again at the meso-level other functionalist studies have concentrated on how to improve schools per se and/or improve access to schools by developing effective multi-agency working. As

Table 13.1 Education and poverty: a summary of the synthesis of explanations

Level of analysis	Sites	Functionalist explanations	Socially critical explanations
Macro	National and local economy, social structures, 'the system'	Globalisation and changes in local and national economies Resultant social exclusion Tax and spending on public services Reductions in child poverty	Education reproducing inequality, social disadvantage and poverty Challenging politics of choice, standards, middle-class values and the market Ethnic disadvantage
Meso	Neighbourhoods, peer groups, school systems	Work or unemployment Income and wealth Health Neighbourhoods and ethnicity Parenting Schools operating in challenging circumstances School improvement Multi-agency working	Curriculum Teaching practices Leadership and engagement Reinterpreting 'disadvantaged neighbourhoods' Parenting and resilience Identities are heavily shaped by external power relations which constrain or enhance the possibilities that individuals can achieve
Micro	Individuals	Providing choices and social capital to encourage and support education (e.g. mentoring) Risk and resilience	

well as these organizational and procedural improvements, studies from socially critical perspectives remind us that deep learning may not be fully realized unless schools develop a much stronger engagement with student voice, the development of critical pedagogies and enhanced authentic community engagement.

At the individual micro-level functionalist explanations have explored identity and the role of individual choice and at the same time examined how the risk that individuals experience living in poverty can be ameliorated through moderating variables that create resilience. Social critical perspectives have also reminded us how proximal power relationships in schools and beyond, between young people and teachers and other significant adults, can both enhance and constrain a sense of self that may lead to disengagement from, and disaffection with, education.

An examination of New Labour educational policy through the mapping framework lens

When New Labour initiatives are examined, important insights can be gained into why New Labour has struggled to overcome the intransigence of links between educational attainment and the socio-economic circumstances of young people and their families. In particular, it becomes clear how New Labour policies embody specific explanations and/or groups of explanations highlighted above. For example the Sure Start initiative, which was set up to enhance the functioning of children and families living in disadvantaged areas by improving services provided in local programme areas, can be couched in terms, among other things, of functionalist explanations that focus on family processes and early child development issues. The Excellence in Cities initiative has a number of strands of activity that in many respects focuses on individual pupil development within the school through the use of learning mentors, ICT and talented and gifted curricular. This implies an explanation predominantly located in terms of functionalist school improvement that focuses on resilience building activities and enriched environments.

These examples of New Labour policies in many ways demonstrate a diversity of explanation about connections between education and poverty and offer very different ways of intervening in this relationship. What they have in common though, we would argue, is an acceptance of a particular perspective about the nature and purposes of education and a focus on specific levels at which explanations, and their corresponding interventions, are intended to improve education in areas of poverty. First, the perspective underpinning the initiatives documented can be viewed as essentially functionalist in that education is seen as a 'good' and as a prerequisite for the development of economic and social well-being as these are currently configured. Sure Start, Excellence in Cities, and many other interventions developed by New Labour to deal with educational equality of opportunity are about enabling young people to improve how they engage with education to improve their educational outcomes and hence their life chances. The nature of that education and, for example, the way in which it might be made sense of within the lives of affected young people, that is reflective of a socially critical approach, is not fundamentally questioned. Second, we would argue that there is an implicit and largely incoherent theory of change in the way such varied initiatives are seen as having the potential to address the connection between poverty and poor educational outcomes. This is reflected in the disparate functionalist meso-level explanations and interventions that these initiatives embody and that focus separately on improving the educational processes in schools and on providing particular and yet separate types of support for either young people, their families and/or their communities in order that they might be enabled to maximize their opportunities within school. What this general approach also overestimates, we would argue, is the extent to which disparate meso-level interventions can resolve interlocking set of problems that act to prevent some groups of young people from securing the educational attainments of their more socio-economically advantaged peers.

An important implication of the mapping framework described above is that it becomes legitimate to ask how any given educational intervention designed to positively address the connection between education and poverty maps onto the full range of factors which various explanatory theories show to be implicated in the poverty–education link and to question how it plays out in particular contexts. From this perspective New Labour's focus on schools as the prime agents of change is flawed in terms of dealing with the problem of educational inequality. This is because the focus here is almost exclusively at one level, the meso-level, and located within one site, and the specific educational processes linked to that site. Of course improvements in schooling have been and no doubt continue to be made but in the most optimistic of analyses these improvements offer the hope of at best marginal change (Mortimore and Whitty 1997). Our analysis suggests two main reasons for this. First, this focus on the school as a lever for change has not typically taken into account in a considered or integrated way other meso-level factors either from functionalist and socially critical perspectives. These include variables such as various risk factors linked to communities experiencing poverty, the importance of parents in preparing and supporting young people through education, or the need for education to work with other public sector services. It also includes accounting for student voice, developing authentic and democratic engagement with schools' communities and developing critical pedagogies of engagement with young people.

Second, New Labour policy on schools possessed no means of recognizing factors at work at other levels of analysis. It did not appreciate how the forces of globalization were impacting on certain communities, nor did it see how schools or education might take part in the redevelopments of those communities through various regeneration initiatives. Consequently, schools have not been encouraged to see themselves as an embedded part of social and economic policy but merely there to uncritically contribute to it. In addition, the prime focus on schools as agents of change did not recognize how changing transition experiences associated with increased levels of decision-making and choice were becoming ever more important in the lives of young people and how these were then influenced by particular networks of people that were often separate and external to the school. In other words New Labour's policies approach potentially had a limited theory of change based on a limited set of factors that focused on institutional issues. The same type of arguments could be made of any one of the other interventions highlighted above, be they Sure Start or Excellence in Cities or any other initiative as they are currently constituted. Each one in their own way focuses on particular sets of issues aimed at particular levels of intervention, from a particular perspective without scoping into a wider analysis. Of course, it is often in the nature of individual initiatives that they are not able to take account of the type of complexity referred to in our framework, but New Labour educational policy has lacked any sense of a wider coherence that might enable a range of initiatives to work collectively towards addressing the socially replicating effects referred to throughout this chapter.

Conclusion

Based upon the analysis presented in this chapter, it seems to us that New Labour educational policies, if they are to make more progress in positively addressing the existing social and economic basis of educational inequalities, must attend to some fundamental issues. New Labour policy-makers have struggled to generate coherence between their educational interventions. The issue here is how to make multiple interventions coherent, how to sequence them chronologically, and how to prioritize the most effective or most important interventions among all those which might or should be undertaken. This is as opposed to a 'magic bullet' approach that places an exuberance of trust in single and particular types of policy interventions and a scattergun approach that hopes, often beyond reason, that separately or together a range of educational interventions might make a difference.

The research evidence offers some guidance on these matters. There is work which evaluates the effectiveness of particular interventions or estimates the impact of particular factors on the poverty–education relationship. Such evidence is always likely to be partial, given the complexity of factors involved, the difficulty in measuring the impacts of some of these factors, and the inevitability that past interventions are located in sets of circumstances which might be significantly different from the point in time at which New Labour policy-makers have to take their decisions. We believe, therefore, that New Labour policy-makers need to develop in as careful and robust a manner as possible their own explicit theories of change through careful monitoring of how a coherent and integrated set of interventions actually impact on the various factors towards which they are directed. This, of course, contradicts much of what we know about the policy process under New Labour, where more immediate pressures and opportunities tend to militate against a considered, reflective and long-term approach.

The research evidence points firmly to the need for extensive and complex policy interventions if the established and longstanding relationship between poverty and poor educational outcomes is to be disrupted. No single explanation for why learners from poor backgrounds do badly in educational terms emerges from our work. Rather, a set of multiple factors are implicated at each of what we have called the micro-, meso- and macro-levels. This suggests the need for a set of interventions which address the full range of factors from both functionalist and socially critical perspectives *and* which operate at all three levels. Instead of this New Labour educational policy has focused mainly upon the functionalist meso-level with precious few indications of any serious intent to contemplate the more fundamental changes that are necessary to intervene at the macro level and some of the more critical issues highlighted at the meso-level. Policies to address or ameliorate the widening inequalities of income and wealth that have become a marked feature of New Labour's tenure, for example, have been rejected. As well as making macro-level changes it has largely been equally difficult for New Labour policy-makers to find ways of intervening at the micro level, or, indeed, in those meso-level factors that are not directly within their control. For example, it is one thing to target some limited additional resources into schools; quite another to change the ways in which particular families or adolescent peer groups function.

From a socially critical perspective the relationship between poverty and education is only likely to be disrupted if fundamental issues of power and interest, advantage and disadvantage are addressed. Simply tackling the presenting 'problems' of poverty and education will, this perspective suggests, ultimately prove to be ineffective if underlying inequalities are permitted to reproduce these problems in other forms. Policy-makers, like so many other actors in this process, are implicated in these inequalities, but viewed from a critical perspective all citizens are policy-makers and all are involved to a greater or lesser extent in formulating policy interventions. This suggests that in those situations where particular explanations of poverty and education dominate the thinking of elected and appointed policy-makers, it may be that the grassroots movement in schools, classrooms and communities offer significant potential in formulating and enacting policies to address the relationship between education and poverty. In this respect, it is impossible to overlook the irony of the current situation in England where as a direct consequence of the centralized nature of New Labour education policies opportunities for such grassroots resistance have become significantly more restricted.

The issues of coherence, scope and power outlined above and underpinned by the mapping framework detailed in this chapter offer clear insights into reasons why New Labour policies have to date struggled to cope with intergenerational replications of educational disadvantage despite avowed policy intentions and a range of carefully targeted policy measures. This helps to shed light on why one of New Labour's principal policy aims, equality of opportunity, is proving so elusive and highlights why breaking or ameliorating links between education and poverty are likely to prove so difficult. Nevertheless, these same issues of coherence, scope and power do, we would argue, offer policy-makers, in whatever guises, some guidance as to how future interventions may achieve more success in helping to break down this longstanding relationship.

14 Using research to foster inclusion and equity within the context of New Labour education reforms

Mel Ainscow, Alan Dyson, Sue Goldrick and Kirstin Kerr

Introduction

In recent years, inclusion has become a policy emphasis in many countries as education systems struggle to respond to the United Nations 'Education for All' agenda (Ainscow et al. 2006b). In England, Labour governments have published a range of guidance documents to schools which imply not only that schools should educate increasing numbers of students with disabilities, but also that they should concern themselves with increasing the participation and achievements of all groups of learners who have historically been marginalized.

At the same time, Labour governments have pursued a second, more powerful agenda. This has focused on what has come to be called 'the standards agenda', an approach to educational reform which seeks to 'drive up' levels of attainment. It is hardly surprising, therefore, that observers of the English education scene have detected significant tensions as schools attempt both to become more inclusive and to respond to these features of the standards agenda.

In this chapter we reflect on our attempts to use processes of research to support attempts to address this policy tension. In so doing we explain our efforts to create an effective methodology and explore different ways of conceptualizing the agenda for our work. This leads us to conclude that inclusion is limited as an organizing notion by its history in the field of disability and special educational needs. Rather, we see equity as a more useful lens through which to analyse and understand the state of education systems. We also argue that the approach we are proposing sits uneasily within the current government's approach to educational reform.

Researching the English context

Like many other countries, England has been making extensive efforts to improve the quality of its public education system. Over the past few years this has involved a series of national reforms. As we have monitored the impact of these initiatives, we have remained concerned about their perverse effect on certain groups of learners, particularly those from economically disadvantaged backgrounds (Ainscow et al. 2006c, 2006d). In particular, we have documented how the development of an educational marketplace, coupled with an emphasis on policies fostering greater diversity between schools, has created a quasi-selective system in which the poorest children, by and large, attend the lowest performing schools.

Educational research has, of course, had much to say about the disjuncture between reform efforts and equitable outcomes. However, there is a strong sense among researchers that their contributions are ignored by policy-makers whenever they become too probing (Gunter and Thomson 2006a). In this situation, there have been numerous efforts to bring research, policy and practice closer together, tapping into a *research and development* tradition which sets out to solve problems generated by practice. Closely related to this approach is the tradition of educational *action research*.

There are many similarities between these two approaches. However, they differ in the way they relate research to action. Put simply, research and development approaches tend to find the solutions to the problems of practice outside the practice situation itself (for instance, in prior research or theorizing) and then refine those solutions in the practice situation. Action research approaches, broadly speaking, begin by researching the practice situation to see what solutions might be found therein, and only later (if at all) systematize and theorize what they have found with a view to its transfer to other situations.

In a situation where policy and practice are struggling with issues in equity, and where researchers feel they have something to contribute to these issues, attempts to bring research and practice together begin to seem particularly attractive. From the perspective of researchers, in particular, they open up the possibility that the distinctive forms of knowledge made available by robust research processes might at last be used to make the education system, not only more efficient and effective in a technical sense, but also more socially just. However, in reviewing established traditions of action research, and research and development, we have also started to question just how far these methods can be used effectively to address challenges in education around issues of inclusion and equity.

Our work at the Centre for Equity in Education (CEE) is located at the heart of these concerns. We are committed to doing research that makes a difference. We seek, therefore, to impact directly on policy and practice and to adopt a social justice stance in making these impacts. In order to do so, it seems necessary for the CEE to move from opportunistic engagements with practitioners and policy-makers towards the development of a robust set of processes – a methodology – which can be used consistently across a range of contexts and which, ideally, does not require the presence of CEE personnel, nor, indeed, the immediate presence of any researchers.

In what follows, we discuss three projects which have helped to move our thinking and processes of engagement towards a methodology we call *Development and Research* (D&R). As we move through these accounts, we will discuss the issues to which they give rise, and conclude by setting out a series of propositions which constitute the current basis for our work.

Focusing on inclusion

Much of our early work focused on the development of inclusive practices. By this, we mean practices which seek to maximize the presence, participation and achievement in local mainstream schools not only of learners with disabilities, but of all children at risk of marginalization.

Our collaborative action research network, 'Understanding and Developing Inclusive Practices in Schools', involved 25 urban schools, their associated three local education authorities and three universities. Between 2000 and 2004, we explored ways of developing more inclusive practices in the schools through investigating the barriers experienced to such changes in the various contexts, and the methods used to overcome these barriers.

It is probably fair to say that we embarked on this process with a good deal of practical experience about how to work with schools, but with relatively weak theoretical foundations for that work. Much of what we did, therefore, was on a 'trail and error' basis, as we explored ways of engaging schools in issues around inclusion.

The form of the project arose partly out of a set of explicit assumptions, grounded in both our own professional experience and in the wider research literature. We had worked on development projects with schools many times in the past, and knew something about what keeps schools engaged, and what produces change. The decision to invite schools to identify teams rather than lone project leaders, for instance, came from experience elsewhere (Ainscow 1999). Likewise, as we indicated earlier, there is a long and productive history of action research reported in the scholarly literature. However, it is clear in retrospect that we added our own emphases and assumptions to this prior knowledge. For instance, although there is a literature on critical approaches to action research (Carr and Kemmis 1986), we were faced with a particular challenge. As indicated above, we saw inclusion as a value and set of practices about which something was already known. Moreover, as established authors and researchers in the field, we had played our part in generating this prior knowledge. We also knew, from our own work and from other work in this field (Clark et al. 1999; Dyson and Millward 2000), that acceptance of the value and practices of inclusion was frequently resisted by practitioners who saw themselves as having other priorities and as working within constraints that made inclusive practice impossible. This was particularly the case in the then current English policy context where a focus on standards was being imposed on schools by central government (Blair 2005).

We therefore needed a means of releasing practitioners from the constraints of national policy and enabling them to change their value positions and assumptions. We saw the use of research evidence as offering this means. We made the assumption that, when practitioners were confronted by evidence about their own practices, they would – with appropriate encouragement from their 'critical friends' – begin to recognize the non-inclusive elements of those practices and would find ways of making them more inclusive. In practice, this is often what did, indeed, happen. However, in retrospect, we believe that this way of working owed more to our own implicit assumptions than to any robust evidence.

The outcomes of the inclusion project have been widely reported in the scholarly literature (Ainscow et al. 2004a, 2004b, 2006a, 2006b; Dyson and Raffo 2007; Dyson et al. 2003; Howes et al. 2004, 2005). In terms of the development of a methodology for enabling research to contribute to more equitable policy and practice, the main lessons were as follows:

- It is possible to infuse a critical dimension into a collaborative action research project, so that issues of social justice (in this case, a focus on inclusion) are considered as practitioners shape their action.
- The critical friendship of 'outsiders' (in this case, ourselves as researchers) is a way of keeping these issues on the agenda. However, equally if not more powerful is the role of outsider-researchers in enabling practitioners to collect and engage with evidence about their practice. Such engagement is capable of bringing about significant changes in practitioner thinking which is reflected in changes in practice.
- Where such changes take place, it is useful to think of them as the result of an 'interruption' to continuing practice which brings about a transformation from 'single-loop' to 'double-loop' learning (Argyris and Schön 1978, 1996); that is, from learning which enables practice to be improved incrementally to learning which shifts the assumptions on which practice is based.

We also learned some of the problems inherent in this way of working. For instance:

- Although transformations in thinking and practice occurred, they were far from universal. Some practitioners and their schools continued in their established course with little deviation.
- Although we understood 'inclusion' as a broad social justice issue, some practitioners interpreted it in rather narrow terms – for instance, as being about improving the attainments of low-attaining students. Because we did not offer practitioners a robust model of inclusion as a set of principles on which practice could be based, we were very much in the hands of teacher interpretations.
- In time, the research process generated a model of inclusive practice. However, this was at a generalized level. It did not form the basis for any impact on policy, and was not readily transferable as it stood to other contexts.

Rethinking our agenda

Our current work takes the form of a series of collaborative projects with policy-makers and practitioners that are similar to the inclusion network, but try to build on what we learned from that project. In particular, where the inclusion project worked out its methods to some extent by trial and error, we are seeking to found our current work on a robust and explicit methodology, which we characterize as D&R.

In the inclusion project, we were clear that we wished to understand something about the development of inclusive practices in schools. However, it was only as the project progressed that we came to understand that there were different types of knowledge about such practices. One was the knowledge that we as researchers had about the meaning of inclusion, the practices that might realize inclusion, and the actions of practitioners in attempting to realize inclusive principles. Another, however, was the knowledge and understanding that practitioners themselves had about these things – ranging from knowledge of 'what works here', to understandings of inclusion that might be very different from those that we as researchers held. Yet another was the knowledge that might be generated jointly by researchers and practitioners and made available to peers in other situations and at other times – in other words, generalizable and transferable knowledge.

We have, therefore, subsequently reconceptualized our work. We now see it explicitly as a process of knowledge-generation, occurring when researcher and practitioner knowledge meet in particular sites, and aimed at producing new knowledge about ways in which broad values might better be realized in future practice. Whilst this conceptualization still draws on notions of action research – particularly, 'critical collaborative action research' – and of research and development, it does not equate precisely with either. Unlike action research, it is not focused simply on particular sites, but seeks to generate generalizable and transferable knowledge. Unlike research and development, it does not assume that the contribution of researchers to this process is prior to that of practitioners. In other words, researchers do not design practices that are then implemented by practitioners.

We envisage researchers not as pre-hoc designers but as ad-hoc supporters and post-hoc model builders. Their role is to support practitioners in developing the best possible propositions about what will promote equity in a given situation. This involves bringing to bear knowledge gained from prior research, but, given the uniqueness of particular situations and the general nature of values, this cannot amount to a 'design'. Moreover, what emerges from practitioners' attempts to act on these propositions is not a finely tuned and context-independent set of practices which can be transferred wholesale to other sites. Rather, the practices developed in one site, together with their underpinning rationale, become an elaborated set of propositions to be put forward in other sites. We call these elaborated propositions 'models', and the whole process we refer to as one of D&R to indicate the different relationship between the two terms from that implied by 'research and development'.

Underpinning this conceptualization is what we believe to be a clearer understanding of the role of values and principles in our work. The inclusion project was values-based in that we saw inclusion as an overarching educational value. However, the place of that values base was somewhat undertheorized. We tended to assume either that practitioners would share our values, simply because they opted into the project, or that we would find some means of 'converting' them to our views. What we learned from the project was that neither of these assumptions was correct and, more particularly, that it makes little sense to separate out technical knowledge from the sets of values and assumptions in which such knowledge is embedded. Inclusion, therefore, is neither a disembodied value nor a value-free set of practices, but rather an understanding about how to realize particular values in particular sites of practice (Artiles and Dyson 2005).

It follows that we now see values as central to our engagement with policy-makers and practitioners. The initial situation analysis in which we ask them to engage, therefore, is not an analysis of 'what is working' in their contexts, but an analysis of the extent to which particular values are actually being realized. This means that the learning which we seek to promote, the new knowledge which we seek to generate, and the 'models' in which we seek to embody that knowledge are not merely technical in nature, but are about how values can be embodied in situated practices. The change process in which we engage with practitioners, moreover, is not simply a change in practice, but a change in the values which underpin practice and/or in understandings of how those values can be realized in particular situations. This is very different from – and, we suggest, much more challenging than – the technical developments which seem to characterize research and development approaches, or those action research approaches which focus only on practitioners exploring their practice within their own frames of reference.

At the same time, we now take equity rather than inclusion as the under-pinning value for our work. This follows from our clarification of the role of values. We see our task not as being to promote a single, narrowly defined values position, much less to promote a particular set of practices that we see as embodying our preferred value. Rather, it is to reinforce broadly defined social justice concerns in an education system which acknowledges such concerns, but, in our view, fails to act upon them adequately. From this perspective, it is helpful to be able to engage with practitioners and policy-makers in terms of some broad but explicit principle.

Although in England serious attempts have been made to broaden the meaning of inclusion, our view is that it struggles as a concept against its conceptual origins in the field of disability and special education, and that it does not fully address, therefore, the fate of learners who do badly in and out of the education system because of their disadvantaged social backgrounds (Booth 2003). It seems to us that the principle of equity signals a broader set of concerns while yet being capable of an explicit articulation.

It follows that we have done a good deal of work in trying to map out our understandings of equity as an overarching concept which includes but goes beyond inclusion (Ainscow et al. 2006c, 2006d). The result is that we tend to agree with Braveman (2003) that equity is not a unitary concept that can be applied to all situations. Rather, we view it as an overarching – if somewhat generalized – value of 'fairness' or 'justice', which provides a series of lenses through which different situations can be examined.

Development and research

With these thoughts in mind, we now provide brief accounts of two ongoing D&R projects in order to illustrate what our direction of travel means in practice. These examples also throw light on some of the difficulties we face in using D&R in the current English policy context.

Equitable school development

Recent years have seen extensive efforts to encourage greater cooperation between schools. One such collaborative arrangement involves a network of four urban secondary schools. Faced with a local authority context in which a history of selection, including the presence of faith schools, had left them feeling at the 'bottom of the pile', these schools have been working together to explore ways of making their provision more equitable. One of the schools is relatively successful in terms of examination results, while the other three serve disadvantaged communities and have differing degrees of success. Two of the schools are seen as being unsuccessful and struggle to enrol students. These schools are, therefore, more likely to admit young people from less supportive families, students who have been excluded from other schools because of difficult behaviour, and others who arrive from outside the country, including refugees and asylum seekers.

The network has existed for some eight years. However, while the headteachers had developed very good working relationships, they felt that the impact of the joint endeavour was quite limited. They concluded that there was a need to develop ways of working that would challenge practices, assumptions and beliefs of staff and governors, and which would help to create a stimulus for further sustainable improvement. As a consequence, in 2006 they approached CEE to support and facilitate the use of research to strengthen their network.

The work of the network is focused around the following questions:

- Which of our learners are most vulnerable to underachievement, marginalization or exclusion?
- What changes in policy and practice need to be made in order to reach out to these students?
- How can these changes be introduced effectively and evaluated in respect to student outcomes?

Staff research teams were set up in each school. Using a D&R process, university researchers worked with these teams, challenged their interpretations and encouraged them to think through the wider implications of their work. Occasionally, the teams from the participating schools came together to report progress and interrogate each other's work.

The developments in each school focused on particular groups of 'marginalized' students, for example: students who did not attend lessons; students transferring to the school in the middle of the year; 'quiet' students who escaped their teachers' attention; students who were underattaining; and students from minority ethnic communities who presented challenging behaviour. Many of these groups were not the subject of existing school or national policy concern, and their identification suggests that many equity issues remain largely invisible in schools.

The project has shown how evidence can challenge staff understanding of the barriers experienced by some of their students. In all four schools, marked shifts became evident at both the individual and team levels, as evidence contradicted and elaborated prior understandings. The teams sometimes encountered opposition from colleagues who refused to accept the meaning of the evidence they had generated. In such contexts, evidence generated from student 'voice' proved to be particularly powerful in challenging established meanings.

It was significant that, in each case, the relatively narrow initial focus widened as a result of the process and the schools began to address more fundamental issues of school improvement and equity. The extent to which this happened was shaped significantly by the willingness of school leaders to allow these issues to be explored and by the wider culture of the school. Each team found ways of developing its practice in response to the process. However, external policy constraints opened some channels of development while closing many others.

This account is, in many senses, very encouraging. It demonstrates the potential of groups of schools to work together, using various kinds of evidence to challenge inequities within their organizational contexts. At the same time, local historical factors continue to limit the impact of their efforts. In particular, trends within the 'marketplace' of the local education system make two of the partner schools extremely vulnerable, so much so that it has now been decided that one of the schools will close down in the next two years. Meanwhile, while headteachers in some of the other local schools have expressed an interest in joining the network, there are intense pressures on all of the schools to look after their own individual interests.

In this context, officers from the local authority have, until recently, had little influence. It is encouraging, therefore, that senior officers have begun discussing the implications of what has happened in the network for the changing role of the authority. However, these discussions seem likely to bring to the surface tensions regarding the control of development agendas, something that is even more apparent in our next example.

An authority-wide strategy

This initiative was instigated in 2006 in a relatively small authority. The aim is to develop a borough-wide strategy that responds effectively to the following challenges: school attendance, which was below national levels at all phases of education; the number of students permanently excluded from mainstream education was higher than the national average; attainment below national levels at all phases of formal education; and low aspirations, as manifested in the low number of young people who enrol or graduate from further and higher education.

In agreeing to work with CEE on this agenda, senior staff in the authority believed that there was a need for deep changes in thinking, relationships and practices within the education service, and across all departments and services that work with children. It was also felt that new relationships were needed with other interested organizations and support across the wider community. Consequently, there was a need for effective leadership and well-informed strategic action.

A steering group was set up, comprising headteachers from all phases of education, a local councillor, local authority representatives, parent governors and researchers from the University of Manchester. Together they designed a unifying strategy for learning across the borough, from early years to post-16 education. The overall focus is on improving learning for everybody living and working in the community. From the start, the steering group decided that a focus on schools and leadership, within and across the schools, was needed to initiate the implementation of the strategy. However, repeatedly the group returned to the importance of the other stakeholders in ensuring its goals. To this end, the steering group devised an explicit working strategy to implement the desired changes. It involves a rationale that articulates the educational challenges facing the borough, its aspirations and intended outcomes in relation to moving in more equitable directions for education, and how the strategy works in practice.

Central to the strategy is a *framework for learning* that was created to provide a means of prioritizing actions, gathering and engaging with evidence, and evaluating the ongoing impact of interventions. This framework is intended to steer interventions towards a central focus on learner experience and to strengthen collaboration processes across the borough.

In order to have one overall strategy that allows for local contexts, a tight–loose approach was adopted. With this in mind, five area networks were created and each was provided with a detailed needs analysis that outlined main areas of disadvantage. Using this as a foundation, each school was expected to formulate a set of research questions in relation to the overall agenda for improvement. The coordinated implementation of this overall approach aimed to create a common language of practice across the authority that would help to foster the sharing of experiences and ideas.

There is much to commend about the way in which this local authority is attempting to rethink the way relationships between different stakeholders in order to develop more equitable educational arrangements. However, progress so far has been rather limited, not least because of the way a combination of local historical factors and contradictory national policies have created barriers to progress. Most significantly, the formulation of the five area networks was not favoured by some of the headteachers. Some argued that the areas should be based on previous collaborative structures. Others felt that collaborative arrangements for school improvement efforts should not be confused with districts that are intended to foster multi-agency working. As a result, the steering group felt it necessary to abandon the idea of the five areas and to concentrate on strengthening school-to-school networking, leaving the goal of wider participation for the future.

Drawing out the lessons

These two projects clearly have much in common with the inclusion project described earlier. However, they differ from the inclusion project in at least one important way. Put simply, there is a clearer framework within which the project is set. In the inclusion project, schools were issued with a rather open invitation to develop some aspect of inclusive practice, and researchers tracked and supported their action in this respect. In the later projects, there is a clearer initial specification – through organizing questions in the first example, and the framework for learning in the second – of what would count as a more equitable state of affairs, and participants are asked to review and develop their practices in the light of this specification. Organizationally, these initial specifications are arrived at by working with a practitioner steering group. Once formulated, however, they create a shared agenda within which all participants – practitioners and researchers – can talk to each other about their work, even when they are working on apparently separate issues in their own contexts. That same agenda then offers a means of identifying the sort of evidence that is needed – that is, evidence that will illuminate the current state of affairs in relation to the specification of a more equitable state. It also offers a means of identifying the sorts of outcomes that will make the project successful in participating sites – that is, new understandings and practices that move closer to the more equitable state of affairs – and that may lead to the development of what we have called 'models' that can be implemented elsewhere.

Our engagement in D&R projects of the kind described here is, in itself, a D&R project. We have not embarked on this work with a predefined set of methods, nor even with fully elaborated theoretical propositions, so much as with hunches, lessons from past experience, and disparate theoretical resources. As we proceed, we are seeking to develop a theoretically and practically robust set of practices. Currently, for instance, notions of what Kemmis, following Habermas, calls 'communicative action' (Kemmis 2001), and of 'double loop learning' (Argyris and Schön 1978, 1996) seem particularly helpful in understanding the processes in which we are engaged. We are setting out to enable people with different assumptions, experiences and backgrounds, who happen to be engaged in the same sites of practice, to talk and debate together in order to develop understandings that are sufficiently shared for them to be able to act in a coordinated manner. However, we are also seeking to create a situation in which any consensus at which they arrive can be problematized by the diversity within the group of actors, by the evidence about their practices which they collect, and by the provocations of researchers acting as critical friends. In this way, we anticipate that their shared 'single loop learning' about 'how to do the same things better' will be complemented by 'double loop learning' which questions the aims of and assumptions underpinning current practice.

Interesting as these theoretical propositions are, they represent only a step along a continuing journey. At this stage, therefore, it seems appropriate to conclude this chapter, not with a definitive statement of our findings to date, but with a series of *working hypotheses* about where we are and where we are going. These hypotheses, which will be tested, elaborated and refined as our work progresses, are as follows:

- CEE exists to help find ways in which to make education practice (including policy as a form of practice) more equitable. Since 'equity' is a value, its work is therefore always premised on values which it tries to make explicit.
- Its approach to D&R starts from a position of both certainty and indeterminacy. The certainty comes from the explicit values on which it is based, and from existing knowledge, from the CEE's previous work and from the research literature, about how those values might be realized in practice. The indeterminacy stems from the broad nature of the values on which the CEE's work is based, which means that their precise form in any given situation is unclear, and from the uniqueness of complex situations of practice, which means that solutions cannot be transferred from one situation to another without some degree of adaptation
- It follows that the CEE's D&R process is inherently cyclical. A first 'rough draft' of what particular values might mean in practice and in a given situation is a starting point for a process of inquiry into the extent to which those values are realized in current practice and into how practice might change to realize those values more fully. This then leads to an attempt to change practice in these ways, and to monitor what happens as a result. In turn, this leads to a clearer specification of what the values might look like in practice and in this particular situation. So the process continues.
- Because of the indeterminacy on which this process is based, it necessarily involves research-like activities. Because of the certainties on which it draws in terms of what is already known, it necessarily involves scholarly activities to identify, analyse and synthesize prior knowledge. This combination differentiates D&R from R&D (where the desired outcomes are known

and certain means of realization can be engineered) and from action research (which need not draw on scholarly resources).

- The CEE's D&R methodology involves a distinctive relationship between the practitioner role and the academic role. The practitioner is a primary actor in the situation where values of equity are to be realized. The CEE assumes that such actors exercise agency and that they bring to bear on the situation their assumptions about values and practice – i.e. 'what matters' and 'what works'. They do this both as individuals and as participants in socio-cultural groups which are themselves located in policy, political and social contexts. It follows that the D&R process has to engage with these actors and with the contexts in which they operate. There is no prospect of solutions being 'engineered' at a distance from these actors and then delivered to them for 'implementation'. The CEE's D&R process, therefore, is different from more common 'engineer-and-adapt' processes. These take into account the need to adapt engineered solutions to local circumstances, but fail to take into account the socio-cultural contexts within which those solutions have to be implemented.

- In the CEE's process, academics count as secondary actors in the situation, i.e. they can act on that situation, but only through the mediation of practitioners who are the primary actors. However, academics make two distinctive contributions: first, they have access to resources (research skills, research literature, experience in other contexts) which practitioners might in principle have access to, but which in practice are often denied them, and second, they are defined by their distance from practice and therefore from the assumptions on which practice is based. In other words, they belong to a socio-cultural group which is precisely not that of practitioners, and which is, therefore, able to draw on different sets of assumptions and open up different possibilities.

- The different roles and different socio-cultural contexts of practitioners and academics create a complex set of power relations which have to be factored into D&R explicitly. Practitioners derive their power from being primary actors; they can cause things to happen or to cease to happen in a way that is denied to academics. Academics derive their power from standing at a distance; they can problematize the actions of practitioners. At their most productive, these power relations lead to dialogue in which the academics' views are informed by the realities of practice, and practitioners' views change in response to 'outsider' critique. At the least productive, academics mistake their distant position for superiority and claim moral and intellectual authority over practitioners, while practitioners dismiss academics as ignorant and resist their critiques. Managing these relations is crucial to any D&R process.

- D&R also has to take into account its own contextual situation in relation to other actors and stakeholders in education. Even where practitioners and academics interact productively, they constitute just two of the groups with interest in the situation. Their assumptions are not necessarily shared by other interest groups. Their actions are constrained by those who have power over them and constitute an exercise of power over others. The former are most obviously those decision-makers who are outside the practitioner–academic partnership but are nonetheless able to shape the situation in which that partnership operates. They will often be national policy-makers. The latter are those who participate in the situation but cannot exercise control over the practitioner–academic partnership. They will often be students, families and communities. The CEE's aim of promoting equity requires it to pay particular attention to this latter set of relations.

A final thought

The implication of the arguments that we have presented in this chapter is that D&R provides a potentially powerful means for supporting movement towards greater equity within education systems. At the same time, there is much more work to do in order to articulate a firmer rationale for using such an approach in complex and, at times, perverse policy environments of the sort that exist in England.

As our examples show, the use of D&R is very difficult within the context of the New Labour reform agenda, with its emphasis on narrowly conceived national targets and centrally driven improvement strategies. This is why we have argued elsewhere that governments must recognize that matters of detail regarding policy implementation are not amenable to central regulation (Ainscow et al. 2006c). Rather, these have to be dealt with by those who are close to and, therefore, in a better position to understand local contexts. They should be trusted to act in the best interests of the children and young people they serve. National policy frameworks can support this through long-term financial arrangements, and the use of equity informed targets and principles, which encourage the collaboration between education providers and their communities that is essential to the development of effective strategies for fostering inclusion and equity.

15 Debating New Labour education policy

John Smyth and Helen M. Gunter

Introduction

In this chapter we are not going to attempt to review all aspects of New Labour education policy reform or how the various chapters in this book have sought to address that. To do so would be to lose an important opportunity, and besides it would be far too constraining, and ultimately unsatisfying for the reader who would be left with too many loose and unconnected threads. Our intent is both more modest and more ambitious – we want to articulate the defining aspect of New Labour education reform, comment on the consequences that flow from it, while offering a different vision. In doing this we have drawn not only on our own work but also from colleagues outside of Manchester to show that we are not alone but speaking from among a knowledgeable wider research community.

Testing, testing, testing

In getting to the heart of New Labour policy there is no better place to start than with the words of the *then* leader himself, Tony Blair. In a speech at Ruskin College, Oxford on 16 December 1996, Blair waxed eloquently that:

> Education is about more than exams . . . education is about opening minds not just to knowledge but to insight, beauty, inspiration.
>
> (Blair 1996)

In light of the New Labour's record on turning the education system into a testing system, Blair's statement must rank as one of the most duplicitous statements ever uttered by a politician anywhere in the world, rivalled only by Blair's other famous dictum that New Labour was committed to three priorities 'education, education, education'.

As Warwick Mansell, chief education correspondent for the *Times Educational Supplement* put it in the opening pages of his book *Education by Numbers: The Tyranny of Testing* (Mansell 2007a):

[These words] will strike those with knowledge of the reality of classroom life today as hugely controversial . . . [f]or England's children are now the most tested in the world.

(Mansell 2007a: xiv)

Mansell (2007a) points to what lies at the heart of New Labour's entire education project:

In truth, testing children has been the government's defining educational policy.

(Mansell 2007a: xiv)

To assess New Labour's contribution to education we need to start with this most defining aspect of its contribution, because in a real sense, everything else flows from it. Mansell's argument is worthwhile persisting with because of the way it focuses attention on the broader public policy issues. But before we do that we should briefly position Mansell. He is a moderate, temperate, careful but interested and well-informed critic and commentator. When he started out covering for *The Times Educational Supplement* what was happening in England with respect to testing, Mansell (2007b) admits that 'the idea that [testing and publishing results] would be effective in transforming classrooms seemed persuasive'. His conversion from an ardent acceptor of the need for accountability to paid-up sceptic of the New Labour version, is now complete, and as he put it:

after four years of charting its side-effects, I am convinced that it is doing huge harm to our schools . . . The question then, is not whether schools need to be held accountable, but whether the current system is serving pupils and the nation well . . . [T]he answer is a resounding 'no' [and] a radical rethink is needed.

(Mansell 2007b: 1–2)

In the measured (sic) way he presents his argument, Mansell (2007a) admits that not all aspects of education under New Labour has been a disaster, and he praises:

The government's investment in technology . . . [its] impressive commitment to improving staffing levels . . . [and] the long-overdue refurbishment of many run-down buildings.

(Mansell 2007a: xvii)

Mansell (2007a) is also clear on the aspects of New Labour he is not prepared to be critical of, for example:

that the government's pre-occupation with results is necessarily harmful because it has negative implications for teachers . . . [or] that testing, in itself, is a bad thing.

(Mansell 2007a: xvi)

Invoking the term 'hyper-accountability', a notion that appears to have originated with Christopher Hood during the examination of his witness statement to the Select Committee on Education and Employment on 24 February 1999, Mansell (2007a) argues that when stripped to its essentials hyper-accountability amounts to portraying everything in terms of numbers. Put simply, in respect of education test results are used to drive everything, and are supposedly a

> rich source of information for families . . . [as well being used to] hold teachers, heads, officials and ultimately ministers to account for school performance . . . [and by] implication schools will be forced to try and raise their test results, and standards, as measured by the tests, will rise.
>
> (Mansell 2007a: 15)

Putting this in historical perspective Mansell (2007b) says:

> The need to maximize exam results now defines how teachers and schools behave to an extent not seen since Victorian times, when schools were funded according to how well their pupils fared in simple 3Rs tests . . . Yet [it] is far from clear that this [current preoccupation with testing] is improving in any sense other than helping teachers and politicians raise the narrow statistical indicators by which they are judged.
>
> (Mansell 2007b: 1)

This fanatical, almost 'Stalinist' (Mansell 2007a: 7) obsession with centralized measurement constitutes an effort to monitor the activities of everyone involved in teaching and the subliminal message being conveyed through this policy trajectory is that test results as constituted through league tables 'serve to impress on schools that they can never forget about their bottom line . . . or risk losing the custom of parents' (Mansell 2007a: 7). This seems to not only be an attempt to hold schools and teachers to account but in the process 'to [completely] define the success of . . . schools in terms of test scores' (p. xvi). To not put too fine a point on it: 'Teachers are forced not merely to pay attention to results. They live or die by them' (p. 14). The striking irony of hyper-accountability, according to Mansell (2007a) is that:

> While it is clear that all the other actors in the complex system described above benefit, directly and without qualification, from improving test results, this is not necessarily true in the case of those it is meant to be serving; the pupils.
>
> (Mansell 2007a: 15)

With pupils in year 6 in primary schools in England estimated by the Qualifications and Curriculum Authority to be spending 10 hours a week of class time between January and May each year doing nothing other than preparing for tests (Mansell 2007a: 33), there are real questions about whose interests are being served here.

Fear and uncertainty as a policy driver

What is driving this hyper-accountability policy agenda according to Yarker (2008: 19) are the 'huge financial resources . . . made available to the education system [and] so demonstrable results had to follow'. Figures cited by Mansell (2007a: 23) show that in England the rise in educational spending was 'from £45.1 billion (at 2005/6 prices) in 1997/8 to £68.5 billion in 2005/6'. These dramatically increased stakes meant that New Labour had to 'be seen to have influence over how these resources were allocated, and to be able to point to results in return for its largesse'. In other words, what was driving it was a 'political imperative', for government had to have 'instruments' with which 'to demonstrate improved outcomes in return for rising spending' (Mansell 2007a: 22–23). The incredibly high price being paid for properly resourcing a public education system – something that should be happening as a matter of course – is only beginning to be fully understood. The relay for the transmission of this political fear works like this:

> the test-driven accountability structure is the price education is paying for increased funding . . . [and this is being] very effectively transmitted into classrooms, as pupils and teachers are made anxious over results.
>
> (Mansell, 2007a: 23)

It is highly questionable as to whether public policy initiatives ought to be judged according to whether (and to what extent) they achieve arbitrarily determined standards and instrumental devised ends, or whether they produce positive social change – and ascertaining the latter is not a simple or a neutral process in a democracy. Newman (2001: 39) captured the essence of this idea when she said: 'governance in liberal democracies is always likely to be characterized by multiple and potentially conflicting models'. Giving an especially positive reading, she says in the case of New Labour that the distinctive emphasis has been towards an 'open system and self-governance' characterized by 'devolution, partnership, policy evaluation, long term capacity-building and democratic renewal'. However, she says, 'this emphasis is cross-cut by residues of, and even intensification of, other styles of governance' (Newman 2001: 39) – most notably, ones that are marked out by rational goals of 'maximization of output' and 'economic rationalism', and modes of hierarchy such as 'standardization' and 'accountability' (Newman 2001: 38). The tensions between and among these competing models of governance become particularly exacerbated when 'government [is] determined to deliver fast and visible change to satisfy the electorate and secure re-election' (p. 39). In a word, the problem with New Labour, as put by Newman (2001), has been in the way it has dramatically tipped the balance between these policy models.

We want to demonstrate now the devastating effect this tipping the policy model balance can have, and we want the reader to keep in mind the situation described above around the fanatical preoccupation with testing. To make our point in the most dramatic way possible, we want to step outside the area of education and draw our example from the field of health care. The instance, as retold by Parker Palmer (2007), comes from a US context, but it could equally apply to England or any other country that has followed the same broad policy pathway:

> On January 10, [2002] a healthy 57-year-old man underwent a liver donation procedure that successfully resected approximately 60 per cent of the right lobe of his liver in preparation for transplanting that liver into his brother, a 54-year-old man who suffered from a degenerative liver disease. After what was described as a technically uneventful transplant, the donor patient seemed to do well on the first post-operative day. He began to manifest some tachycardia [abnormally rapid beating of the heart] late on the second post-operative day. Early on the third post-operative day, he began to hiccup and complained of being nauseated. He was given symptomatic treatment. Later that day he began to vomit brownish material. He became oxygen desaturated [lacking adequate oxygen in the bloodstream] and was placed on 100 per cent oxygen by mask. He continued to vomit, aspirated and suffered a cardiac arrest from which he was not resuscitated and he was pronounced dead on the third post-operative day.

Three months later, the state health commissioner issued an incident report that said:

> The hospital allowed this patient to undergo a major, high-risk procedure and then left his post-operative care in the hands of an overburdened, mostly junior staff, without appropriate supervision. Supervision of medical residents was far too lax, resulting in woefully inadequate post-surgical care.
>
> [Palmer goes on] I do not doubt that the hospital, inadequate staffing, and lax supervision are to blame for the tragedy. Nor do I doubt the importance of fixing systemic problems. But I am struck by the impersonal quality of this analysis, as if no one involved had a name: The report assigns culpability to common nouns, not people. When systems analysis is our only approach to situations such as this, it becomes a sophisticated way to know what has occurred but not recognize its meaning.
>
> Two details captured my attention as I learned more about the organ donor's death. First, a surgical resident with 12 days of experience in the transplant institute had been left alone to attend to this man and 34 others in intensive care during a critical three-hour period when the patient developed serious symptoms.
>
> Clearly, the resident could not give her charges the attention they needed; she later described herself as 'feeling "overwhelmed" by the responsibility of caring for so many patients.'

Second, the donor's wife was with her husband during the entire post-operative period. Her description of his death is heart-wrenching: 'I was present . . . while my husband coughed up blood for two hours before he finally choked on it and died. [I] begged for attention to his condition and got none.'

(Palmer 2007: 2)

Now, the point to this tragic story, as Palmer (2007) put it, is that it is a graphic illustration of an inability to confront 'institutional inhumanity'. It is no doubt true that the medical resident was inexperienced, overworked, and was rushing from patient to patient, but the more pressing question is:

> What kept her playing her role as an obedient underling in this tragedy instead of speaking truth to power? What kind of action might she have taken to bring reinforcements running? . . . I am not talking about becoming a whistle-blower after the event. I am talking about acting ethically and courageously in the moment, while there is still something to be salvaged, instead of waiting for a review board to ask what went wrong.

(Palmer 2007: 3)

It is too simple to say that this person was a pawn and that her superiors had power over her career. What lies behind it, says Palmer (2007), is 'institutional pathology' – that is to say, the way all of us in institutions become complicit in believing that the institutions we work in are 'external to and constrain us'. In other words, we act as if there is a 'hidden curriculum . . . [that] portrays institutions as powers *other* than us' (Palmer 2007: 4). We become 'co-creators' of these 'institutional pathologies' when we give institutions more power over us than they really have. We are taught to hide our feelings, to not reveal anything of our emotions, and hide behind the screen of appearing to be in charge at all times, 'and we fear that feeling too deeply will cause us to lose control' (Palmer 2007: 5).

If we draw the discussion back to education and specifically the policy ensemble around testing from Mansell that we raised at the start, then we can see that there are some uncanny resemblances between what Parker is alluding to and what is happening in education around policy issues. Yarker (2005) put this as poignantly as anyone, when he asks:

> 'How far is it proper for a teacher to stay silent or be silenced and disregard their personal views in the implementation of education policy?' he raises questions we are often too busy or too apprehensive to consider. And yet, 'What we teach is ourselves'. It is our relational engagement with young people that is at the heart of education.

(Yarker 2005: 169)

At one level, this sounds like a call to teacher activism, and in a sense there is an element of truth in that. But equally, it is a question that goes to the very core and being of what it means to be a teacher and what it is that students learn from teachers. What Yarker (2005) is saying is that students learn from us as professionals, what we stand for, and how we act morally and politically as much, if not more, than they learn the disembodied content we dish up to them. How teachers respond, react to, resist or embrace educational policy provides a profound lesson to our students. Others may have an agenda in trying to construct teachers as compliant technicians, but the reality is that teachers are moral and political actors, and that pertains as much to how they react to what is happening to schools, teachers and students, as it does to how they engage students with wider social issues. For a teacher to impose adult performance management on children in childhood is an abdication of their responsibilities for children as children. Yarker (2005) put this eloquently:

> Who the teacher is remains central to the activity of teaching because we are more than our practice. What we teach is ourselves. Consciously and unconsciously we teach our stance towards our students, our subject (and indeed the whole domain of knowledge and the activity of the world) and towards what it is to inhabit the role of being a teacher. Our practice as teachers always has this as its surplus. Students will determine whether or not they will learn from us not solely by what we do in the classroom, but also by the way we inhabit and reconstruct the role of teacher.
>
> (Yarker 2005: 171)

When fear becomes the underlying motivator in public policy as appears to be the case of testing under New Labour, then the inevitable result is the 'corrosion of character' (Sennett 1998), or as Yarker (2008) put it, 'personalized corruption' as teachers are forced into responses that can impugn their professional integrity. Once the overall policy direction has been set, as the US experience amply demonstrates (see Nichols and Berliner 2005, 2007), various forms of 'test pollution' (Haladyna 1992), 'high-stakes cheating' (Yarker 2008: 120), and forms of test-related 'civil disobedience' (Nichols and Berliner 2005: 23) come into existence as teachers and school leaders try to 'resist a system they see as corrupt and unfair' (Nichols and Berliner 2005: 24). To a degree teachers become caught up in what Yarker (2008) calls various forms of 'self-betrayal' and 'complicity' in their response to a policy-driven system not of their own making. These are not in the end the 'vital signs [of a] vibrant society', to borrow a turn of phrase from Emerson (2006).

Chickens coming home to roost

New Labour has accepted neoliberal thinking and in turn has itself been shaped and produced. Blair and Brown, for all their disagreements, have been structured in a context where the temporary settlement of a welfare state was broken from the 1970s onwards. As Marquand (2008) has explained:

All the great hallmarks of the Thatcher counter-revolution – privatization, marketization, centralization, consumerism, a shrunken public domain and a growing gap between the super-rich and the rest – are still in place. There is nothing surprising, or even particularly shocking, about their survival. They are the hallmarks of renascent capitalism everywhere, from Moscow to Manhattan. The notion that Blair and Brown could have embraced a vastly different socio-economic model if only they had been braver or more far-sighted belongs to Neverland. (So, of course, does the notion that David Cameron will be able to do so.)

(Marquand 2008: 55)

Thatcherism took sustenance from the recognition that, in King's (1976) terms, Britain had become harder to govern, where politicians had stopped deciding and 'in the 1970s they merely grope' (King 1976: 25). The strategy was to attack the nature of public service where no one could or should 'care' about others or act in the public interest. Consequently, the public was constituted through an aggregation of private interests rather than as a moral conceptualization of the social and the collective. Neoliberalism as the 'financialization of everything' (Harvey 2007: 33) is a political project where commonsense ideas and seductive claims of the good life can travel into homes and workplaces to generate positive approaches to labour and life. Popular culture can single out and airbrush the successful as 'celebrity' onto the front cover of magazines, and offer the positioned ordinary person the opportunity to join in through makeovers where they can feel but rarely are authentically included (Gunter and Thomson 2006b). Indeed, as Harvey (2007: 19) states, while the ideas of neoliberalism are pervasive and attractive, 'when neoliberal principles clash with the need to restore or sustain elite power, then the principles are either abandoned or become so twisted as to be unrecognizable'. Consequently, social injustice remains as the class system, along with barriers related to gender, ethnicity and religion, continues to privilege through the sorting of who or what matters.

Neoliberalism creates fear where all is at risk. The social security of collectively supporting those who have needs at a particular time (and which I as taxpayer and we as taxpayers may have at another time) has been broken, and this has permeated into civil society where we are on camera at all times, and where cultural messages are about the science of detection and the proofs of pseudo-scientific measuring of social life as effective and efficient. There is a denial of politics and dialogue. There is nothing to talk about because the goal of capital accumulation is obvious and the means by which to do it is based on admired practice. This is the in-built defensive mechanism where contrary ideas and arguments are automatically positioned as a product of the very system that neoliberalism has declared unmodern:

The process of neoliberalization has, however, entailed much 'creative destruction', not only of prior institutional frameworks and powers (even challenging traditional forms of state sovereignty) but also of divisions of labour, social relations, welfare provisions, technological mixes, ways of life and thought, reproductive activities, attachments to the land and habits of the heart. In so far as neoliberalism values market exchange as 'an ethic in itself, capable of acting as a guide to all human action, and substituting for all previously held ethical beliefs', it emphasizes the significance of contractual relations in the market place. It holds that the social good will be maximized by maximizing the reach and frequency of market trans-actions, and it seeks to bring all human action into the domain of the market.

(Harvey 2007: 3)

This works in what seems to be perverse ways, and so Furedi (2006) talks about how he is prevented from taking a picture of his son playing football 'in case they fall into the wrong hands', and recounts the story of how someone drove past a toddler walking through a village, he did not stop through fear of being accused of abduction and moments later the child drowned. The market operates in ways that deny relationships in any other way than securing advantage over another person through profit in some way. Trust is reduced to the turn of a card or the exercise of power to subjugate someone who is always the opponent. This works as an example of 'an ordinary tyranny' (Gunter 2007) where normalized practices (minding my own business, doing the best for my family, making a difficult situation work, accepting that you or your child is in danger) operate in open and transparent ways to create the conditions in which people do not care about others but about the processes that might damage their private interests. The regulation of risk is based on the protection of property rights, trade, and the security of money (Harvey 2007), and the state is required to protect the population from invasion, and other dangers such as the cattle disease BSE, Foot and Mouth, Bird Flu, Terrorism. The transfer of what Hood et al. (2004) call 'risk regulation regimes' into everyday social encounters through biometric data identity cards, surveillance cameras and presumption of guilt by association with particular types of religion, dress and home, means that we are ever ready to be pulled apart, captured as data, measured and described through computer software as a credit worthy risk or not.

Neoliberalism does not come naturally. People are positioned as risk averse and so they need to be told and trained, and the ideas are packaged as seductive but realizable products in self-help guides – all can purchase and win:

> For any way of thought to become dominant, a conceptual apparatus has to be advanced that appeals to our institutions and instincts, to our values and our desires, as well as to the possibilities inherent in the social world we inhabit. If successful, this conceptual apparatus becomes so embedded in common sense as to be taken for granted and not open to question. The founding figures of neoliberal thought took political ideals of human dignity and individual freedom as fundamental, as 'the central values of civilization'.

In so doing they chose wisely, for these are indeed compelling and seductive ideas. These values, they held, were threatened not only by fascism, dictatorships, and communism, but by all forms of state intervention that substituted collective judgements for those of individuals free to choose.

(Harvey 2007: 5)

New Labour has accelerated this 'choice' in a constructed marketplace and paradoxically had to regulate those who had to learn to do it so that the market would work. New Labour had to take risks to encourage risk taking to make learning risk free. This accelerated what the Thatcherite governments had done (e.g. Coopers and Lybrand 1988) through how the school as a small business needed to provide data for their customers. There are two aspects to this that are worthy of emphasis here. The first is the emphasis on data, and the second is personalization.

The document *Smoking Out Underachievement: Guidance and Advice to Help Secondary Schools Use Value Added Approaches with Data* (DfES 2004b) (we could write a chapter just on the title!) provides guidance for secondary school practitioners on how to collect, analyse and use data to support pupil performance. As teachers we do this all the time and we think data is one among many ways in which progress can be examined. There is much in this document that is seductive, in one easy lesson the teacher or school leader can read through what to do, how to do it, and why it is necessary. We can just imagine how in a highly charged performance culture being directed in this way can help you get through the mountain of work in ways that modify the risk of getting it wrong and being named and shamed:

> At the end of the guidance teachers should have developed their thinking from being a teacher of 10 classes of 30 pupils to being teachers of 300 individuals with individual learning needs and strengths.
>
> The guidance should support them in analysing how pupils learn and encourage a move away from the haphazard approach of getting differentiated teaching and learning styles into each lesson. It should promote more meaningful and effective reviews with pupils and inform target-setting and target getting.
>
> It will broaden schools' knowledge on past and current performance and give good indication of future performance.
>
> (DfES 2004b: 4)

We have deliberately replicated the layout as single sentence paragraphs are key to the communication of the message that this must be done and can be done.

Drawing on Raffo and Gunter (2008) we confirm that making the market work requires a functionalist approach to the rationales for change and the narratives that surround what must be done. Hence children and their learning must be calculated, and all must be involved in such mathematical processes because 'value-added data is for everyone in school concerned with the progress made by pupils. Classroom practitioners will use data in different ways, as they will be asking different questions of it' (DfES 2004b: 7). The questions to be asked are about: 'how' is something (e.g. standards) the case? 'Who' is responsible (e.g. strong/weak teachers/departments)? 'Can' something (e.g. measuring impact) be done? 'Are' things (e.g. teachers) good enough? (p. 9). Such questions can lead to data that parents are expected to use to exercise consumer choice, but there are also questions that are not being asked.

The different kinds of questions that need to be asked are of a kind that say: what is missing in the 'smoking out process', and *why*? Why is it that the school is at the bottom of the league tables, is it because the school is no good or because of other factors, not least how league tables are constructed? While the document is about data it is not about research. A researching school might ask questions about the social and economic mix of the locality. Particularly an inquiry might be framed around how advantage and disadvantage work and how the school is located within this and what it means for how it builds a socially critical approach to education and change. Here the rationales are about the way the system works to include and exclude, and the narratives are about creating opportunities for participation. This would require teachers and school leaders to establish research-based relationships with their students (rather like we do), and to be researching professionals by having access to higher education programmes, researchers and reading that would enable schools to set a different agenda to the one they are being required to comply with.

Personalization is interconnected with this, and again as educators it is central to our repertoire of approaches to teaching and learning. We have been energized by much of the talk about this as it intuitively speaks to our professional values. It has become part of the normalized discourse. However, like the directive to gather a particular type of data in order to make the school, workforce and students operable in the marketplace, we are deeply troubled by personalization as another requirement that begins with consumerist practices as its goals. It has become what one of us has called an 'aerosol' (Smyth 2008a) word that is seen everywhere, its meaning is assumed, but it has through the process been rendered meaningless. We agree with Fielding (2007) that:

> There are at least ten reasons why one should look at personalization with some skepticism. These are that it in its current forms it tends to be ahistorical, superficial, insular, technicist, conservative, individualistic, hyperbolic, episodic, calibrated and dishonestly vacant.
>
> (Fielding 2007: 2)

Fielding goes on to explain that much of what goes on in the name of the personal is actually functional, and in particular, relationships not only are damaged but also rendered different from those we would wish to practise:

> relationships are important; the voices of students are elicited and acknowledged; community is valued, but all primarily for instrumental purposes

within the context of the market-place. Social and, indeed, personal relationships are reduced to social capital; 'having relationships' moves subtly towards 'doing relationships', towards relationship management.

(Fielding 2007: 5)

It seems to us from our articulation of New Labour education reform that there are some emerging issues that need to be opened up to dialogue and research regarding the interplay between data, personalization, standards and performance regimes. First, students are positioned as the objects of reform who are the producers of data that proves that elite adults (teachers, headteachers, ministers) are performing and meeting targets. Research is needed to expose how new trajectories that are personal and social operate to achieve educational outcomes (see Fielding 2006; Smyth 2006, 2007, 2008b; Thomson and Gunter 2008). Second, as Hartley (2007b) has shown, there is a tension between centralized regulation of standards and consumer choice in a marketplace. Drawing on Gee (2004), Hartley (2007b) shows that this could be handled by separating the basics that all children, particularly poor children, need to have to operate in the marketplace as workers and consumers (literacy, numeracy). This could be extended to the 'residualization' of provision for those who cannot buy their own personal services for welfare, health and security:

The inference to be drawn from this is that there *will* be a personalization, but only of the 'basics', defined and monitored by government. Any further personalized 'add-ons' would have to be co-customized *and* co-funded. At this stage, for the government to have emphasized *co-customization* or *co-funding* might have attracted yet more criticism that education is falling further into the reaches of the market. But to refer merely to *personalization* does not go against the grain of consumer culture, and it leaves the way forward towards co-customization and co-funding.

(Hartley 2007b: 8, emphases in the original)

So what needs to happen is for this to be named and the trajectories understood. There are two aspects: first, following Fielding (2007) is that the nature of 'personhood' needs to be at the centre of educational purposes, and so there is a need to ascertain how children feel about growing up in England; second, following Gunter and Forrester's (2008) findings on knowledge production and policy-making, those who have hitherto been positioned as enemies and/or recipients need to be included in the dialogue as knowledgeable people rather than as troublemakers, for several reasons. They answer back. They show other ways forward. They have evidence about how other ways of doing things work.

Conclusion

The defining aspect of New Labour's education policy has been a denial of politics and a promotion of the market. The interplay between structure, culture and agency is not new to New Labour or to any successive governments. How this is to be handled and how political practice is rebuilt and re-energized is a reasonable starting point. This will not be easy because politics is 'inevitably destined to disappoint because it is about the tough process of squeezing collective decisions out of multiple and competing interests and opinions' (Stoker 2006: 1). Whereas the market gives the illusion of always winning for the self, with the added incentive of not having to engage directly with the losers, politics makes the losers the winner's responsibility. We have to rework winning as being both social and individual, because as Stoker (2006) argues, politics matters:

> politics can provide a means of getting on with your fellow human beings that aims to find a way forward through reconciliation and compromise without recourse to straightforward coercion or outright violence. It provides a way to live in an ordered manner with your neighbours, but one that unavoidably often calls on you to sign up to deals and compromises that might not be your first or even tenth choice, but which nevertheless have something in them that enables you to put up with them. It might not be very inspiring, but when it works politics delivers one great benefit: it enables you to choose, within constraints, the life you want without fear of physical coercion and violence being used against you. Politics creates space for human choices and diverse lifestyles. Politics, if done well, creates the positive context and stable environment for you to live your life. That's why politics matters.
>
> (Stoker 2006: 7)

What we wanted in 1997 was for New Labour to do politics well and to help us all do it well.

In rounding off this chapter we have one final necessary and important point to make. We realize that the marketization of everything means that the chapter we have written will not necessarily be understood for its intentions and possibilities. This is because there are no data, no score-card, and no bullet-pointed solution. No rhetorical language (a world-class education system) and no normative demands (to make the system work better). There are ideas, analysis and argument, but in a world used to electronically presented data this type of chapter is open to dismissal. There is an automatic censorship device in neoliberalism regarding irrelevant, wacky and dangerous ideas. We can rehearse the argument ourselves: this chapter is a form of 'oppositional escapism' (Fielding 2007) where we entertain ourselves and do little to help policy-makers and practitioners know what to do on a Monday morning. Unlike neoliberal gurus we would never presume to do this as we approach this very important work of decision-making and action in the interests of children and the nation as a form of conceptually informed practice. It is not for us to tell people what to do, but to develop the ideas, to speak to the agenda, and to think through the tough issues with people. This is how we approach our Monday morning when we practise education. Our aim in our research is, in Bourdieu's (2003) terms, to 'restore politics' because it is our job in higher education to speak out and for the polity that we are a part of. We might not always get it right, we might not always speak in ways that are intelligible, but we will not be quiet and we will not succumb quietly to emerging forms of intellectual rendition.

16 Reflections on reform

Perspectives and challenges

Christopher Chapman and Helen M. Gunter

Introduction

As noted in the Introduction, this book has set out to present and examine aspects of New Labour's reforms to the provision of public education in England. In this sense the contributions explore the English system as a type of laboratory where the pace of experimentation has been frenetic (Finkelstein and Grubb 2000). Drawing primarily on our research and development activity at the University of Manchester, we have explored New Labour's reforms across four key strands for change:

- standards and accountability
- workforce reform
- choice and diversity
- *Every Child Matters* agenda.

The chapters clustered around each of the strands should be viewed as a set of interrelated essays that have emerged from a sustained programme of research rather than a set of chapters reporting the findings from a single research project. With this in mind, it is unsurprising that the chapters present a range of perspectives, both in the field and among the contributors. We consider this diversity as a distinctive feature of this book and illustrative of the range of approaches to educational research at Manchester.

In this concluding chapter we, the editors, start by summarizing the nature of these differences in relation to the four strands. This leads us to define two overall positions that permeate this book. These reflect a tension between, on the one hand, those who see New Labour reforms as broadly positive, although flawed in their implementation, and, on the other hand, those whose perspectives leads them to conclude that the reforms are so fundamentally flawed they must be completely rethought. In noting these two perspectives, we do not seek a resolution. Rather we conclude by contrasting them in order to define an agenda of challenges that needs to be considered by those involved, including our team as we think about the next phase of our work.

Reflecting on reforms: perspectives on the key strands

In 1997 New Labour inherited a number of policies which, rather than rejecting and replacing, it chose to use as a foundation for reform. Therefore, a relentless focus on standards and accountability has formed the linchpin of New Labour education policy. In Chapter 3, Daniel Muijs and Christopher Chapman chart the evolution and development of standardized inspection, league tables and target-setting as levers for school improvement under New Labour. In Chapter 4, Rosemary Webb focuses directly on primary school teachers, making international comparisons with developments in Finland. In Chapter 5, Joanna Bragg and Bill Boyle use a longitudinal dataset to examine the impact of the National Curriculum and testing on curriculum design and how this plays out in children's experiences. Chapters 6, 7 and 8 also focus on reforms implemented by New Labour, many of which are rooted in previous Conservative administrations. In Chapter 6 Gillian Forrester and Helen M. Gunter examine the rise of headteacher leadership as a cornerstone of New Labour reform. In Chapter 7, Charlotte Woods explores the role of school business managers in workforce reform and in Chapter 8 Olwen McNamara provides an overview of the preparation and accreditation of teacher training, and how this is playing out in England, Northern Ireland and Wales. National standards and personal accountability are key features of the New Labour decade; these have been juxtaposed with choice and diversity within this book. In Chapter 9, Denis Mongon and Christopher Chapman examine the restructuring of education in an attempt to create a diverse system that is fit for purpose. In Chapter 10, Andy Howes and Jo Frankham explore the concept of networks, and in Chapter 11, Mel West and Daniel Muijs reflect on personalization and track its development and its use under New Labour governments. The imperative to ensure that all children are safe and central to reform and professional practice is the focus of the final cluster. Here the *Every Child Matters* (ECM) agenda is examined by three chapters, beginning with Chapter 12, in which Alan Dyson, Peter Farrell, Kirstin Kerr and Nadine Mearns examine the construction and operation of multi-agency work in the new children's services. In Chapter 13, Dave Hall and Carlo Raffo tackle the evidence base for the relationship between education and poverty, and how New Labour policy has targeted its resources. Finally, in Chapter 14, Mel Ainscow, Alan Dyson, Sue Goldrick and Kirstin Kerr present their Development and Research approach to working with schools and wider stakeholders.

Most chapters in this book highlight the pressure that New Labour polices have placed on individuals and organizations. In this sense, the government has achieved at least half its aim of creating a high challenge and high support system (Barber 2007). Muijs and Chapman draw attention to the paucity of evidence underpinning some of these policies, especially evidence linking policies to improved outcomes. The chapters in this book begin to question the dogmatic pursuit of developing such a highly pressurized system. Bragg and Boyle argue that the standards agenda, and the National Curriculum in particular, have contributed to a narrowing of the curriculum and teachers 'teaching to the test' in an attempt to hot-house their students. In a similar vein, Webb concludes that primary school teachers are exceedingly constrained by the standards agenda, which has had adverse effects on the affective curriculum, pastoral care and teacher–student relationships. Chapters 3 to 5 suggest that while there is some 'official evidence' of raised standards within the current accountability framework, usually published by the government or its associated agencies, the unrelenting drive for improvement through the standards and accountability agenda has also had a number of unintended negative effects on schools, teachers and perhaps most importantly the students they serve.

A key theme emerging throughout but especially in Chapters 6 to 8 is the changing nature of teachers' roles and responsibilities. This is set within the wider debate of the changing composition of the workforce, particularly the rise of 'professional' managers and how they relate to 'professional' pedagogues. Here it is appropriate to draw parallels with recent developments in the National Health Service, where consultants have seen their broader leadership and management responsibilities eroded, being replaced by an army of professional managers who manage, monitor and direct hospitals, leaving consultants to focus on leading and developing clinical practice. Examples of this phenomenon can be seen emerging in education, where the best is taken from educational practice and combined with the best business management practices, creating a situation where headteachers become responsible for pedagogic development and other professionals such as school business managers lead and manage other aspects of the organization (Chapman et al. 2008). These chapters also go some way to providing an explanation for these changes. Forrester and Gunter focus on the centrality of the headteacher, arguing that New Labour has seduced teachers into leadership positions and then used them as a mechanism for delivering policy within a tight, highly pressurized framework. Woods also draws on the theme of pressure, identifying the unrelenting focus on standards, increased workload and raised expectations as sources of pressure that have made headship a job harder than ever before. It seems that at a time when there are concerns about where the next generation of leaders is coming from, more and more is being added to a headteacher's remit with little being taken away. It is here that workforce remodelling has the potential to redress the balance. The emergence of senior leaders without Qualified Teacher Status (QTS), and some without QTS but with a National Professional Qualification for Headship (NPQH) provides an opportunity for rethinking educational leadership. However, as McNamara cautions, unless policy-makers can move beyond political expediency, resisting short-term and technical rational approaches to reform, deep-rooted change is unlikely. In Chapters 9 to 11, the focus is choice and diversity but the themes of structure and process permeate through the cluster. The content of the chapters is varied ranging from reforms to structural arrangements to the rise of personalization and networking. However, New Labour's commitment to structural reform within the system comes through very clearly. The final cluster of chapters deals specifically with issues related to ECM. This diverse but connected set of chapters draws out a number of important themes, including inter-agency collaboration and the role of inquiry in development and research activity.

Perhaps unsurprisingly, the tensions between the standards and ECM agendas form a common thread throughout this book but they are viewed through alternative lenses depending on the nature of the research and the epistemological position of the researchers undertaking the work. For some, the purpose of their research and development work appears to involve generating knowledge and practice relating to *reform within context*, that is, reform which recognizes the constraints imposed by the broader socio-political context, attempting to influence and change things for the better within the constraints of the system; while for others their work appears more about *reform beyond context*, that is, work which challenges the very nature of the system itself within which the reform is located. As we noted in the introduction to this chapter, this leads us to define two broad overall points of view that seem to run through the book. These reflect a tension between, on the one hand, those who see New Labour reforms as being broadly positive, although flawed by their implementation, and, on the other hand, those whose perspective leads them to argue that the reforms are a product of a fundamentally flawed context, therefore requiring a complete reconceptualization of both priorities and policies.

Reflecting on reform both 'within' and 'beyond' context

A sense of optimism prevailed in school staffrooms the day New Labour took office; it is important not to forget how impoverished the system was in the years running up to 1997. Schools were seriously under-resourced, the physical condition of many schools was deteriorating rapidly and morale within the workforce was in decline. This situation was compounded by a policy position of school improvement through high challenge of national standards to be delivered through the quasi-market and low support on delivery. New Labour's election and the mantra of 'education, education, education' signalled the beginning of one of the most intensive periods of reform experienced in England. Within nine weeks of office New Labour articulated about fifty new policies (Barber and Sebba 1999). This initial energy and commitment has been sustained into subsequent administrations: in 2004/05 alone £1,162 million was spent on national programmes (including Excellence in Cities, Leadership Incentive Grant, Primary and Key Stage 3 National Strategies) and local authority support for school improvement. An additional sum of around £160 million was also spent on the Academies programme (National Audit Office 2006).

From a *within context reform* perspective there is much to praise. The increased investment in the educational system was desperately needed and has been welcomed by the profession. Furthermore, the capital rebuilding programme Building Schools for the Future (BSF) has begun to deliver school buildings that were the preserve of dreams before 1997. Teachers' salaries have risen, as has their morale and standing within society. It has become more common to see professionals from other sectors such as business and law retraining to become teachers and the entry qualifications of those applying for places on postgraduate training courses has also risen. Key Stage, GCSE and the 'gold standard' A level scores have all risen since 1997. The number of low-attaining schools has declined. In 1997 there were over 1500 secondary schools where 30 per cent of students did not achieve five or more A★–Cs at GCSE including English and Maths; now there are 638. In London there have been significant improvements. Students now perform above national average and the rate of improvement in inner London schools since 2001 is twice the national rate. Progress has also been made in narrowing the gap between some groups of learners. For example, in terms of achieving five good GCSEs including English and Maths between 2002 and 2007, the gap between the achievement of Black Caribbean and white students has closed by 7 per cent. Furthermore, OfSTED (2007) has reported improvements in teaching quality across the system, more school leaders are being judged as good or better, rather than satisfactory or worse, and there has also been a reduction of schools being identified as failing since New Labour took office.

However, despite the achievements of reforms within context, there are areas of concern where this approach has been less successful. Here we want to highlight the shortcomings of New Labour's policies by focusing on schools at the bottom of the pile, with the most to gain, that have been subjected to the highest levels of intervention. Surely if New Labour has made a significant difference to our education system, it would be magnified in those schools which it has been most eager to improve? Those calling for reform beyond context would argue that if the government has not managed to make significant gains in this area, then it is likely the system itself requires a radical rethink. In other words we must stop tinkering at the edges, trying to ratchet up performance through policies aimed at squeezing more and more out of the same, and reconsider our fundamental position.

In 2001, about 620 secondary schools were identified as 'facing challenging circumstances' because they were failing to meet government floor targets in 1999/2000. The schools were all 'invited' into the *Schools Facing Challenging Circumstances Initiative* to improve their standards. The initiative involved the provision of additional resources (£70,000 per school) attached to a development planning process and a menu of targeted support for improvement (Chapman 2006). In 2008 the government launched a new *National Challenge*. This involves the injection of £400 million into 638 schools failing to meet these 'moving' floor targets in 2007. These schools will receive specialist advice and be expected to draw up coherent plans for improvement, a strange echo of the *Schools Facing Challenging Circumstances Initiative*. In addition, some of these schools will be expected to restructure as Trusts, Academies or Federations and local authority involvement will be greater than the previous incarnation.

The *National Challenge* provides an opportunity to reflect on New Labour and reform. During a period of such intense reform one might expect to see fewer schools falling below the floor targets. However, the number remains broadly similar. Why is this? Furthermore, if New Labour's reforms have been successful, one might expect to see the schools identified in 2001 to have been improved to a position where they now can meet the floor targets. Is this the case? And if so, who are the schools that are now failing to meet the targets and what might explain this?

To illustrate this situation, as an initial analysis we have selected four diverse and geographically spread local authorities and compared the number of schools failing to meet floor targets based on GCSE performance data from 2000 and 2007. The first authority has a policy of selection where the highest attaining children tend to go to a grammar school. The remaining children are mostly spread between church schools and secondary modern schools. The county is located in a southern coastal region of England. In 2000 there were 27 schools falling below the government floor targets; the average percentage of students gaining five or more A★–C in these schools was 19.5 per cent. By 2007 the number of schools had risen to 33, at least 17 of which were the same schools and the average five or more A★–C GCSE was 20.5 per cent across the schools. The second example we selected was a metropolitan authority with a record for school improvement located in the North West of England. Here in 2000 there were seven schools failing to meet the floor target and by 2007 this number had been reduced to five; the same five schools and the average percentage of students leaving these schools with five or more A★–Cs has fallen from 21.9 per cent to 21 per cent. The third local authority selected was a large urban authority located in the Midlands. In 2000 36 schools in this authority failed to meet the floor targets with on average 22.2 per cent of students in these schools gaining five or more A★–C grades at GCSE. By 2007 this number has fallen to 27 schools with a five or more A★–C average of 23.8 per cent; 22 of the schools failing to meet their targets in 2007 were also present in the group in 2000. Interestingly, if one includes the merger of two schools this provides a total of 23 out of 27. The new entrants failing to meet the floor targets include three schools located near to a school that was in the initial group in 2000 but has demonstrated remarkable progress and is now recognized as an outstanding school. The final local authority was selected as a southern predominantly rural non-selective shire. In 2000 there were two schools in this county not reaching the floor targets. An average of 24 per cent of students left these schools with five or more A★–Cs at GCSE. In 2007 there were three schools, one of which was the same as in 2000.

Clearly, there are a number of limitations regarding this initial analysis. First, we are examining schools only within four local authorities, therefore we have a very limited sample from which it would be unwise to generalize across the system. Second, the measure by which the floor targets are set has changed. The target has risen from 25 per cent to 30 per cent over a period of seven years and now also includes English and Maths, thus making direct comparisons problematic. Furthermore, as in the second example it is likely many of the schools falling short of their floor targets will have been reconstituted as

Academies, Fresh Starts or Collaborative restarts and therefore, because of the name change, not picked up in this preliminary exercise.

Drawing on the above examples we return to the questions posed above. First, as previously noted, the number of schools failing to meet the floor targets is broadly similar. There are two contrasting explanations for this. One, despite a moderate shift in targets, improvement efforts have failed to impact since 2000, leading to minimal change in these schools. Alternatively, in order to maintain challenge within the system there has been a deliberate strategy to move targets to a position where a minority (it would seem about 20 per cent of secondary schools) continue to fall short of the mark. Barber (2007) has argued that if all schools were to meet targets, this would demonstrate a lack of ambition on the part of government. So here we can think about the broad number as either a failure to deliver or a deliberate attempt to maintain challenge on the lowest attaining rump of schools in order to support the development of in Barber's (2007) terms a 'world-class' education system.

Second, if New Labour's reforms have been successful one might expect to see the schools identified in 2001 to have been improved to a position where they now can meet the floor targets. Is this the case? Within our limited sample of four albeit diverse local authorities, two-thirds (66 per cent) of schools failed to reach the government-set floor targets in both 2000 and 2007. If this were to be the case for the whole system, it would suggest there is a rump of over 200 secondary schools that over a seven-year period, New Labour policy has failed to penetrate. Our initial analysis also highlights examples of sleight of hand; in our four local authorities there is at least one example of the merger of two schools failing to meet the floor targets in 2001 which now show as one school in 2007. Such mergers and changes to structural arrangements have been proliferated by the introduction of Academies during the interim period. In a world of headlines reporting the number of underperforming schools, failing schools and schools in crisis, this would seem an expedient solution providing the illusion of progress. There is a particularly interesting example of turnover in our third example. One school has made considerable progress demonstrating significant rises in attainment and has been recognized by OfSTED (in 2007) as outstanding in 23 of 24 areas. The fortunes of this school contrast with three of its neighbouring schools that have slipped below the floor targets between 2000 and 2007. These changes expose some of the challenges of *choice and diversity* in a free market. Some teachers in the improved school have reported shifts in the 'type' of students attending the school; while the student composition remains challenging, changes in the intake are also reflected in a reduction of the percentage of students entitled to free school meals. One explanation may be that it is not possible for all schools within a disadvantaged area to achieve government floor targets. Might it be that as a school begins to improve it attracts more able students, which in turn reinforces improvement, creating an upward spiral of achievement, but destabilizing neighbouring schools, leaving spare places which tend to be filled by the less able from out of the area or by children whose parents or carers are less adept at playing the system than the better educated, more affluent parents moving into the improving school?

So, on the surface, it would seem that seven years on, many of the same schools remain at the bottom of the pile and despite considerable intervention have not significantly improved their levels of attainment. The real issue is not floor targets, it is underperformance within the system. Unfortunately, there has been nothing radical about how we measure and judge the success of our schools. We have not moved beyond a narrow and simplistic measure of performance. Here low attainment, as defined by raw GCSE grades, can easily mask considerable achievements. Indeed, many of the 638 schools have been celebrated by OfSTED, and others have excellent Contextual Value Added (CVA) scores. Rather than being low-achieving or underperforming schools, some of these schools *are* high-performing schools in very difficult contexts. It is clear that a more sophisticated set of measures is needed to identify poorest performing schools within the system; there is nothing radical about relying on the percentage of students attaining five or more good GCSEs. However, this diverse group of schools are to be subjected to a very similar set of interventions to those of 2000. If this approach to improvement had succeeded in the first place, these schools would not have stagnated, and more of the same will not be a recipe for success. More generally within the system, the impact of other initiatives such as the Numeracy and Literacy Strategies (Earl et al. 2003) have also shown to have decreased over time, providing further indications of the dilution of New Labour's reform efforts. Further in-depth analysis comparing like for like and identifying name changes is needed to assess the extent to which our lowest attaining schools have proved impermeable to intervention for improvement. However, this cursory analysis provides little support for New Labour's rhetoric. Rather, it illustrates the inability of central government to effectively intervene at a local level to improve some of the most challenging schools in the country.

From a *reform beyond context* perspective it would seem that New Labour has achieved all that it can by ratcheting up the system in a drive for ever-greater efficiency and effectiveness and for some schools at the bottom of the pile, this approach never really gave them much of a chance anyway. Therefore, following the evidence produced by the contributors in this book, this perspective calls for an 'end to the excesses of the target-driven, punitively accountable and initiative-led programme of reform to which education has been subjected over the last ten years' (Coffield 2007: 75). Rather, the system must engage students in new ways of learning and build capacity at the local level which can foster the leadership and creativity existing within schools and their communites rather than stifling them. This is important because if schools and their communities are to succeed, they must engage with the challenges facing the education system, take ownership of them and work to develop localized solutions from the bottom up, which involves professionals working *with* the community as citizens rather than as consumers. Therefore, a radical rethink is needed.

Such a reconceptualization must reconnect education with a set of democratic values, particularly in relation to politicians' dealings with teachers themselves. To date, the strategy has been to intervene and challenge the professionalism and competency of teachers by subjecting them to unwarranted and unparalleled levels of accountability measures. This is often a difficult argument to develop because the neoliberal response is always 'They would say that wouldn't they?' For example, the reform beyond context perspective would highlight that just because one doctor, Harold Shipman, murdered his patients, it does not mean that automatically all doctors are potential murderers and should be dealt with accordingly in regard to accountability processes. It is essential that professionalism is based on expertise and a defensible model of practice reconstituted, as Marquand (2004) articulates:

> Instead of harassing the professions, a government committed to reinventing the public domain would respect and nurture them. Instead of denigrating the professional ethic, and doing its best to whittle professional autonomy away, it would work with the grain of professionalism, and accept that professionals cannot serve the public interest properly unless they have the space in which to exercise their skills in accordance with their professional judgement. It would also recognize that professionals must be accountable to the public, and acknowledge that in the heyday of the public domain, around the middle of the last century, accountability was often lacking. However, it would approach the thorny problem of how to reconcile accountability with autonomy in a modest, flexible and experimental spirit. It would abandon the suspicious and impatient hectoring and the relentless paper chasing which have done even more to demoralize public-sector professionals than under-funding. It would cease to rely on crude, mechanistic and centrally imposed targets and audits which cannot capture the subtleties of real-world professional practice, and experiment with subtler, qualitative, more specific and more local forms of accountability, based on open-ended dialogue between professionals and their stakeholders.
>
> (Marquand 2004: 141–142)

And this ought to connect with democratic renewal, and government needs to put its own house in order by examining constitutional issues that it has tinkered with but not directly engaged with (e.g. devolution, voting reform, and local governance).

The reform within context perspective recognizes that despite the significant challenges faced in improving these 'tough to move' schools serving the most difficult contexts, we have made some progress and recently there have been particularly encouraging signs. As noted earlier, there have been significant improvements in performance in London, much of which may be attributed to the London Challenge and this type of localized, context-specific intervention and support would seem to offer a positive way forward. Furthermore, it may indicate that New Labour has begun to recognize the limitations of highly prescriptive, one-size-fits-all approaches to change and is prepared (or has no option) to loosen the reins, handing over control to the regional and where capacity exists local level; and where this capacity is lacking to invest resources to generate it from the ground up. The London Challenge has begun to devolve decision-making to the local level, drawn upon local expertise and knowledge to provide sophisticated diagnosis of need and then provided targeted resources and context-specific interventions in these areas. This bespoke localized approach to reform is an encouraging shift in policy, which may be, at least in part, attributed to the experience of development and research activity conducted by those interested in both reform within and beyond context. And let us hope that the lessons will be applied in other settings to bring similar gains in performance to the National Challenge, Greater Manchester, the Black Country and other areas warranting intervention.

Both perspectives call for similar outcomes, and share a similar set of values. For example, both appear to be committed to devolving decision-making and problem-solving to the local level, placing professionals at the centre and involving a broader set of stakeholders. The major fault-line between them rests in the means of achieving the outcomes. From the reform within context perspective the approach tends to involve working with those in the system to improve the implementation of policies for the benefit of those they are designed to serve. The beyond context approach acknowledges the context in which people are working but primarily seeks to work for more fundamental changes to the way the system operates for and against particular interests. In noting these two perspectives, we do not seek a resolution. Rather we conclude by using them to define an agenda of challenges that needs to be considered by those involved, including our team as we think about the next phase of our work.

Reflecting on reforms: key challenges

We would like the work of educational researchers and policy-makers to be revitalized and located in a place where there is significant interplay between reform within and beyond context, where it is the norm for educational researchers and policy-makers to work within the system to improve the prospects of our children of today, but also to challenge, present and debate the big ideas that may limit the prospects for our children of tomorrow. Here we end by outlining five interconnected issues for consideration if we are to move forward together:

- Producing relevant insights
- Challenging accepted norms
- Making connections
- Generating ideas
- Promoting public politics.

Producing relevant insights

By this we mean working with commissioners, and continuing to seek out independent social science funding. While this book has sought to examine the New Labour decade, there is little actual independent research into the realities of what it is like to be in receipt of 'hyper-innovation' (Moran 2003) for children, teachers and the community. As Ainscow et al. (2008: 3) illustrate, there is a range of collaborative activities taking place but little coordinated action regarding inequity, and 'their ability to generate strategy is hamstrung by the perverse consequences of the government's target-setting regime'. Such situations need to be exposed for what they are, and engaged with to find alternatives. Importantly, there is a need to keep building research links with schools and colleges, and enable such educational partnerships to develop new educational research agendas.

Challenging accepted norms

By this we mean challenging and examining what is decided is to be known and by whom. There is a volume of commissioned research and government-funded publications, where there is a discernible pattern of language, design and normative demands to rise to the challenge of New Labour transformation. Notably, there is rhetoric around a science of measurement and evidence. Those who 'know' tend to be a regime made up of politicians, members of non-departmental public bodies (NDPBs), private sector consultants together with some trusted headteachers and professors (Gunter and Forrester 2008). Much of what is decided needs to happen in schools is at a distance from the lives and work of those who are required to make it happen. There is a need to find ways of reinvigorating education from the bottom up in ways that are more humanistic than consumerist, and instead are based on conceptualizations and agreed citizen practices.

Making connections

By this we mean that researchers have an important role to play in bringing people together and stimulating change. Here we have a responsibility to work in both research and developmental capacities to challenge and support policy and practice, create interruptions in schools and government which may lead people to reconsider their values, beliefs and behaviours. We can serve to connect schools, young people and their communities together, to explore how different stakeholders understand these connections and how as a society we may begin to make sense of them. We must resist the temptation to view ourselves only as detached researchers or as a resource for independent validation. Rather, it may be helpful to consider our position as a pivot or a link between policy and practice with the ability to stimulate and perhaps even sustain conversations across the policy–practice divide.

Generating ideas

By this we mean the need to engage in intellectual work and examine the underlying thinking that is producing policy and be involved in generating new ideas. While Giddens (1991) was central to the generation of the Third Way that underpinned the New Labour transformation into an electable party of government, we are asking ourselves how these ideas are sustainable and who is now doing the intellectual work for the next decade. We might ask where are the books from educational thinkers about how governments might revitalize public sector education in ways that does not automatically advantage the market? For example, as we write, the news is being reported that four young men have been attacked in one weekend. One beaten to death, one stabbed to death, and two seriously injured through separate knife attacks. The numbers are stacking up. There is a serious debate unfolding about what it means to grow up in England and how unhappy our children as 'choosers' and 'consumers' are. Our view is that this cannot be handled by elite adults 'in authority' alone, not least what seems to be emerging as the sole emphasis on law and punishment. Children are not the problem but are central to the solution.

Promoting public politics

By this we mean that the market and leadership by a select few has replaced politics, and so it seems that there is nothing to be said except to vision and then sell the solution. It seems to us that children have been made the objects of reform, and must reach the required standards, but at the same time they must be cared for. We need to work on the purposes and practices that are about education and are themselves educational, and we need to open the dialogue with children as active participants in the learning process. They need to make sense of the world they are growing up in, and they need to develop a sense of agency in making a different type of world. In this sense the *radical possibilities* for New Labour, to paraphrase Anyon's (2005) book, have to challenge how the world is being experienced rather than functionally seek to make it work more efficiently and effectively. There is a need to be confident that critical engagement with ideas is not automatically oppositional, even though there are those who seek to characterize it in this way.

In conclusion, the varied perspectives in this book underline our recent calls for a shift from *school* to *educational* effectiveness and improvement (British Educational Research Association (BERA) 2008) and lead us to call for a change in approach where New Labour's commitment to social justice is given primacy. If schools and communities come together in a more authentic fashion, this may begin to challenge the view which tends to define education in a narrow sense, as a mechanism to achieve a level of examination performance which provides access to the next level of formal education or acts to determine at what level one enters the labour market. If we can move to a position where achievement is recognized across a wider range of indicators policy-makers will have to take a more holistic view of social reform, where schools are considered to be an important piece in the jigsaw of society rather than a production line operating to fuel a globalizing economy.

Appendix

Questionnaire to headteachers in the North West of England, May 2007

Daniel Muijs, Christopher Chapman, Helen M. Gunter and Mel West

Characteristics of respondents

We received 144 questionnaires: 60.4 per cent of respondents were female, 39.6 per cent were male. On average, they have been heads for ten years, and head of their present school for seven years. Of the respondents 62.9 per cent are primary heads, 23.6 per cent secondary heads, 6.9 per cent are heads of special schools, 2.8 per cent of nursery and infant schools. The remaining respondents work in three-tier systems. The vast majority of respondents are heads of schools in urban contexts, with 22.7 per cent running inner-city schools, 35.5 per cent urban schools, 31.2 per cent suburban schools and 10 per cent rural schools. Also 18.1 per cent of schools are Specialist Schools, 30.6 per cent faith schools and 1.4 per cent Academies. The vast majority of schools are comprehensive, with 3.5 per cent of respondents saying their school is selective; 1.4 per cent are grammar schools and 5.6 per cent private or independent schools. The vast majority of schools are mixed sex, with just 2.8 per cent boys' schools and 2.5 per cent girls' schools.

Part 1: views on New Labour reforms

1 Curriculum

Respondents were asked to reflect on the impact of government policies relating to aspects of the curriculum on education policy between 1997 and 2007. Results are given in Table A.1.

From Table A.1 it is clear that most of these curriculum-related policies have been positively received by headteachers, with the majority agreeing or agreeing strongly that the policies have had a positive impact for the national strategies, greater flexibility for schools in curriculum development, the move towards personalized learning and the focus on learning rather than teaching. The latter has received the most enthusiastic backing, with almost 90 per cent agreeing on the positive impact of this policy, and almost 40 per cent agreeing strongly. There are two exceptions to this overall positive response. Changes to the 14–19 curriculum were seen as not applicable by almost 60 per cent of respondents.

Table A.1 Impact of curriculum-related policies on the education system (in percentages)

The following strategies and programmes have had a positive effect on improving the quality of education in England	Strongly disagree	Disagree	Agree	Strongly agree	Not applicable
1. The national strategies (e.g. Literacy, KS3)	2.1	11.1	63.2	19.4	4.2
2. Changes to the 14–19 curriculum	4.2	9.0	25.0	2.8	59.0
3. The raising of the school leaving age to 18	20.1	18.8	8.3	1.4	51.4
4. Greater flexibility for schools in curriculum development	6.3	5.6	56.9	30.6	0.7
5. The move towards personalized learning	3.5	19.4	54.2	20.8	2.1
6. A greater emphasis on learning rather than teaching	0.7	7.6	50.0	39.6	2.1

This is a reflection of the dominance of primary schools in the sample of respondents, and almost 70 per cent of heads who did respond were positive about this policy. Over 50 per cent of respondents felt that the raising of the school leaving age was not applicable, again probably partly due to the predominance of primary schools in the sample and partly due to the fact that the policy is very recent. However, the policy clearly worries heads, as 80 per cent of those who did respond disagreed that the policy would have a positive impact.

When asked which two strategies had had the greatest positive impact on their school, the national strategies, with 32.6 per cent of first choices and 16.8 per cent of second choices, the emphasis on learning (27.0 per cent first choices, 35.0 per cent second choices) and greater flexibility in curriculum development (26.2 per cent first choices, 24.8 per cent second choices) were seen as having the greatest positive impact.

In terms of negative impacts, 70.1 per cent of respondents felt that none of the policies had had a negative impact on their school, reflecting the positive view of these policies overall. Of the remaining respondents who indicated at least one policy with negative impact on their school, the national strategies, with 44.2 per cent of first choices, was the most likely to be seen as having a negative impact, with the remainder of choices going to raising the school age, changes to the 14–19 curriculum, and the move towards personalized learning.

The national strategies therefore emerge as the most controversial policy, with the highest number of both positive and negative impact choices, with 46 first (and 23 second) choices for being the policy with the most positive impact, and 19 first (and 4 second) choices for being the policy with the most negative impact on the school. The emphasis on learning rather than teaching and greater flexibility in curriculum development are overwhelmingly positively received, but heads have strong concerns about the raising of the school leaving age.

2 Resources

Respondents' views on policies related to resourcing are collated in Table A.2.

As was the case with the curriculum-related policies, the majority of resource-related policies were positively rated by headteachers. Investment in ICT, with over 90 per cent agreement and over 40 per cent strong agreement, improvements to school buildings, with almost 80 per cent agreement and almost 40 per cent strong agreement, smaller class sizes, with almost 80 per cent agreement, were particularly positively received. The exception to this overall positive view was bidding systems linked to resources, a policy disapproved of by just under two-thirds of headteachers. Only 1.7 per cent strongly agreed that this policy had a positive impact on the education system. Almost one-third of respondents disapprove of policies on pay and conditions of staff.

Asked to name the two strategies that had had the most positive impact on their school, investment in ICT was the first choice of 40.3 per cent of respondents, and the second choice of 35.5 per cent. The other two policies to receive a significant number of mentions were smaller class sizes (29.1 per cent first choices, 19.4 per cent second choices) and improvements to school buildings (23.1 per cent first choices, 29.8 per cent second choices).

Overall 41.7 per cent of respondents did not see any of the above policies as having had a negative impact on their school. Among the other 60 per cent of respondents, the bidding culture was the first choice in terms of having had a negative impact for 58.3 per cent, and the second choice for 50 per cent of respondents. The only other policy to be mentioned by a substantive number

Table A.2 Impact of resourcing-related policies on the education system (in percentages)

The following strategies and programmes have had a positive effect on improving the quality of education in England	Strongly disagree	Disagree	Agree	Strongly agree	Not applicable
7. Smaller class sizes	2.1	9.0	42.4	36.8	9.7
8. Investment in ICT (e.g. electronic whiteboards)	1.4	4.9	49.3	42.4	2.1
9. Pay and conditions of school staff	6.9	23.6	50.7	16.0	2.8
10. Improvements to school buildings	2.1	11.8	40.3	39.6	6.3
11. Bidding systems linking resourcing to specific goals	25.7	41.7	19.4	2.8	10.4

of respondents was pay and conditions, the first negative impact choice for 29.8 per cent of respondents and second choice for over 21.9 per cent.

Overall then, while policies on resourcing are seen as positive, in particular investment in ICT, buildings and reducing class sizes, there is strong opposition to the emphasis on competitive bidding for resources.

3 Standards and accountability

Table A.3 presents heads' views on the impact of policies on standards and accountability on the education system.

Government policies on raising standards and accountability are not as positively received as those on curriculum and resources, with no policies receiving over 80 per cent approval as was the case with some of the curriculum and resourcing policies. Many policies are still approved of by the majority though, with use of PANDA (Performance and Assessment data) being seen by over 75 per cent as having had a positive impact, increased accountability for school performance, reforms in Initial Teacher Training and target-setting receiving over 60 per cent approval. OfSTED inspections are controversial, with

Table A.3 Impact of policies on standards and accountability on the Education System (in percentages)

The following strategies and programmes have had a positive effect on improving the quality of education in England (please tick one box only)	Strongly disagree	Disagree	Agree	Strongly agree	Not applicable
12. Performance tables	45.8	34.0	13.9	2.8	3.5
13. Target setting	11.8	20.1	58.3	7.6	2.1
14. Measures to deal with 'failing' schools	8.3	25.7	42.4	5.6	18.1
15. OfSTED inspections	16.0	29.9	49.3	4.2	0.7
16. Use of Performance and Assessment (PANDA) data	4.9	14.6	67.4	9.0	4.2
17. Specialist School status	9.7	18.8	24.3	7.6	39.6
18. Reforms in Initial Teacher Training	2.1	25.0	52.1	9.7	11.1
19. Encouraging faith schools	22.2	31.3	18.8	10.4	17.4
20. Investment by private individuals into schools, e.g. academies	27.8	33.3	8.3	0.7	29.9
21. Increased accountability for school performance	6.3	23.6	59.0	8.3	2.8
22. The emphasis on parental choice	18.1	47.2	29.2	1.4	4.2

just over half seeing a positive impact and just under half a negative impact on the education system. Measures to deal with failing schools are also controversial, with 48 per cent agreeing that they have had a positive impact, while 34 per cent disagree. Specialist Schools status is similar, with 31.9 per cent seeing a positive impact, 24.5 per cent a negative impact, and 39.6 per cent seeing this as not applicable. Four policies are seen as negative by the majority of respondents: the most negative response was to performance tables, with just under 80 per cent disagreeing that this policy has had a positive impact. Encouraging faith schools was seen as negative by 53.5 per cent, though some heads of faith schools commented that they felt faith schools were being discouraged rather than encouraged. An emphasis on parental choice was seen as not having a positive impact by just under two-thirds of respondents, and while almost 30 per cent of heads found investment by private individuals to be 'not applicable', of those who did comment, the vast majority (87 per cent) did not see a positive impact.

Target setting (27.8 per cent first choices, 13.9 per cent second choices), use of PANDA (22.6 per cent first choices, 26.1 per cent second choices) and increased accountability for performance (12 per cent first choices, 23.5 per cent second choices) were the most likely to have had a positive impact on the school; 32.6 per cent did not mention any policies as having a negative impact. However, of the remainder, performance tables were seen as by far the most likely to have a negative impact, with 56.7 per cent first choices and 27.9 per cent second choices. OfSTED inspections were the second most frequently chosen second option (12.4 per cent first choices, 20.6 per cent second choices). As one head commented: 'Government has squandered so much goodwill, enthusiasm and potential with short-sighted obsession with performance tables and targets.'

Overall, then, use of PANDA data, target-setting and increased accountability for performance are seen as positive policies in terms of impact on the education system and respondents' schools, while the use of performance tables is highly negatively rated.

4 Roles and responsibilities

In Table A.4, we can see heads' views on policies on roles and responsibilities of heads and school staff more generally.

As can be seen in Table A.4, most policies related to roles and responsibilities are judged to have had a positive impact on the education system. Heads particularly value school-to-school collaboration, with over 80 per cent agreeing that this had has a positive impact on the system. The national training programmes for heads, the changing role of the head and remodelling the school workforce all had approval of over 60 per cent of respondents, with the national training programmes receiving over 70 per cent approval. Partnership with the local authority (LA) and performance management were also overwhelmingly positively received. One policy that received a very negative assessment from

Table A.4 Impact of policies on roles and responsibilities on the education system (in percentages)

The following strategies and programmes have had a positive effect on improving the quality of education in England	Strongly disagree	Disagree	Agree	Strongly agree	Not applicable
23. Partnership with the local authority	3.5	20.8	56.3	12.5	6.9
24. Performance management of headteachers and teachers	4.9	27.1	56.9	6.3	4.9
25. General Teaching Council	33.3	47.9	11.8	0.7	6.3
26. Remodelling the school workforce	8.3	18.8	55.6	12.5	4.9
27. Increased school-to-school collaboration	2.8	11.1	56.3	24.3	5.6
28. National training programmes for school leaders	4.9	14.6	59.7	16.7	4.2
29. The change in the role of the headteacher to that of leader	2.8	21.5	54.9	14.6	6.3
30. School Improvement Partners	11.8	23.6	34.0	4.2	25.7

headteachers was the General Teaching Council (GTC), with over 80 per cent of respondents disagreeing that the GTC had had a positive impact. Only one respondent strongly agreed that the GTC had a positive impact. A quarter of respondents saw School Improvement Partners (SIPs) as not applicable. The remainder were split between positive and negative impact.

Increased school-to-school collaboration was also the policy most often mentioned as having a positive impact on respondents' schools, with 27.0 per cent first choices and 24.4 per cent second choices. Workforce remodelling (24.1 per cent first choices, and 15 per cent second choices) was second most likely to be seen to have had a positive impact on the school, followed by partnership with the LA (16.1 per cent first choices, 15 per cent second choices), head training programmes (11.7 per cent first choices, 17.3 per cent second choices) and change in the role of head to leader (10.2 per cent first choices, 14.2 per cent second choices).

About 41 per cent of respondents did not see any policies as having had a negative impact. Among the policies mentioned by the other 58 per cent, the GTC (32.2 per cent first negative choices, 25 per cent second negative choices), workforce remodelling (23.7 per cent first choices, 13.9 per cent second choices), partnership with the LA (15.3 per cent first choices, 5.6 per cent second choices) and SIPs (11.9 per cent first choices, 25 per cent second choices) were most frequent.

Policies on roles and responsibilities were generally positively viewed by heads, especially school-to-school collaboration and national training programmes for heads. One policy received overwhelmingly negative reactions: the GTC, with some respondents adding comments such as 'a damp squib'. Workforce remodelling and partnership with the LA were, while in majority positively seen with regards to their impact on the education system, controversial when looked at with regards to impact on respondents' schools, with mixed views emerging.

5 Equity

As with other policy areas, most policies on equity have been positively judged by heads (see Table A.5). *Every Child Matters* was particularly well received, with over 80 per cent of heads seeing a positive impact on the education system. Student voice, investment in pre-school education and targeting resources at disadvantaged areas have over 70 per cent headteacher approval. The most controversial policy is extended schools, with over 40 per cent disapproval.

Every Child Matters is also by far the most often mentioned policy when heads are asked which policy has had the most positive impact on their school (34.1 per cent first choices, 33 per cent second choices), with investment in pre-school education (22.2 per cent first choices, 10.1 per cent second choices) and student voice (15.1 per cent first choices, 30.1 per cent second choices) the other policies seen as having had a positive impact.

Few respondents report negative impacts of equity-related policies on their school, with 68.8 per cent of respondents not choosing any policies as having had a negative impact. Of the minority who did see some policies as negative,

Table A.5 Impact of policies on equity on the education system (in percentages)

The following strategies and programmes have had a positive effect on improving the quality of education in England	Strongly disagree	Disagree	Agree	Strongly agree	Not applicable
31. Investment in pre-school education	1.4	11.8	47.2	26.4	13.2
32. Extended schools	4.9	35.4	41.7	8.3	9.7
33. Every Child Matters	1.4	13.9	58.3	24.3	2.1
34. Social inclusion initiatives such as Sure Start	5.6	18.1	41.0	14.6	20.8
35. The emphasis on student voice	2.8	13.2	58.3	19.4	6.3
36. Targeting resources to disadvantaged areas	4.2	15.3	49.3	21.5	9.7

extended schools (33.3 per cent) and targeting resources at disadvantaged areas (31.1 per cent) were most frequently seen as negative.

Summary and conclusion

Overall, New Labour's education policies appear to have been seen to have had a positive impact on both the system and heads' individual schools. As one head commented: 'For all its faults, the present Labour government has had an enormous positive effect on education in Britain. Memories are short if those in education can't remember the temporary classrooms and general lack of investment under previous governments.'

Policies such as the emphasis on learning rather than teaching, greater flexibility in curriculum development, the national strategies, investment in ICT, buildings and reducing class sizes, use of PANDA data, target-setting, increased account-ability for performance, school-to-school collaboration, national training pro-grammes for heads, *Every Child Matters*, investment in pre-school education and student voice are all seen as having had positive impacts on the system, while many other policies were also seen as positive by the majority of heads.

However, some negatives do appear. In particular, policies encouraging competition and marketization are seen as problematic. The emphasis on competitive bidding for resources, use of performance tables and private investment in education are negatively assessed. The General Teaching Council is overwhelmingly seen as a failure. Some heads also commented that the sheer volume of policies had been problematic: 'Too many policies in too short a time to ensure that policies that policies are properly embedded' being a typical comment. Similarly, one respondent commented that 'Headteachers feel justifiably "initiative-ed out". Throwing money at disadvantaged families is not the "answer". Parental discipline and social responsibility are equally if not more important.'

Part 2: views on New Labour reforms – differences and similarities

1 Differences by school phase

In these analyses we looked at differences between primary and secondary heads. Statistical significance was tested using the Mann-Whitney U test, a non-parametric test suitable for looking at differences between two groups when the dependent variable is ordinal.

A number of significant differences were found.

- Secondary heads were more likely to strongly agree (secondary 32.1 per cent; primary 11.4 per cent), and primary heads just to agree (primary 75.5 per cent; secondary 57.1 per cent) that the national strategies have had a positive impact on the education system ($U=798$, $p<0.05$).
- Secondary heads were also more likely to strongly agree that a greater impact on learning rather than teaching has had a positive impact (primary:

34.7 per cent; secondary 60.7 per cent), while primary heads were more likely to merely agree with this statement (primary 56.9 per cent; secondary 35.7 per cent) (U=736, p<0.05).

- Secondary heads had a less negative view of performance tables (U=718.5, p<0.05). Among secondary heads, 35.7 per cent strongly disagreed that performance tables had a positive impact on the system, 32.1 per cent disagreed, 28.6 per cent agreed, and 3.6 per cent strongly agreed. Among primary heads 54.9 per cent strongly disagreed that performance tables had a positive impact on the system, 35.2 per cent disagreed, 9.9 per cent agreed, and 0 per cent strongly agreed.

- Secondary heads had a more positive view on target-setting (U=665.5, p<0.01). Among secondary heads, 3.6 per cent strongly disagreed that target-setting had a positive impact on the system, 10.7 per cent disagreed, 67.9 per cent agreed, and 17.9 per cent strongly agreed. Among primary heads 15.5 per cent strongly disagreed that target-setting had a positive impact on the system, 25.4 per cent disagreed, 53.5 per cent agreed, and 5.6 per cent strongly agreed.

- While many primary heads did not respond to the question on Specialist Schools status (45.7 per cent responded), those primary heads who did respond were on average far more negative about the policy than were secondary heads (U=117, p<0.001). Among secondary heads, 3.6 per cent strongly disagreed that Specialist Schools status had a positive impact on the system, 3.7 per cent disagreed, 64.3 per cent agreed, and 28.6 per cent strongly agreed. Among primary heads, 21.9 per cent strongly disagreed that Specialist Schools status had a positive impact on the system, 53.1 per cent disagreed, 25.0 per cent agreed, and 0 per cent strongly agreed.

- Primary heads were more positive regarding the impact of encouraging faith schools on the education system (U=474, p<0.01). Among secondary heads, 50 per cent strongly disagreed that encouraging faith schools had a positive impact on the system, 33.3 per cent disagreed, 8.3 per cent agreed, and 8.3 per cent strongly agreed. Among primary heads, 19 per cent strongly disagreed that encouraging faith schools had a positive impact on the system, 39.7 per cent disagreed, 25.4 per cent agreed, and 15.9 per cent strongly agreed.

- Primary heads had a more positive view of the national training programmes for headteachers (U=714.5, p<0.05). Among secondary heads, 14.8 per cent strongly disagreed that the national training programmes for headteachers had a positive impact on the system, 22.2 per cent disagreed, 59.1 per cent agreed, and 11.1 per cent strongly agreed. Among primary heads, 1.4 per cent strongly disagreed that the national training programmes for headteachers had a positive impact on the system, 14.1 per cent dis-agreed, 66.2 per cent agreed, and 18.3 per cent strongly agreed.

- Primary heads were more likely to strongly agree that ECM has had a positive impact on the education system (secondary 7.4 per cent; primary 29.6 per cent), while secondary heads were more likely to merely agree (secondary 70.4 per cent; primary 56.3 per cent) or to disagree (secondary 22.2 per cent; primary 11.3 per cent).

No significant differences were found on the other items.

2 Differences by urbanicity

Spearman's Rho correlation coefficient was correlated for the relationship between urbanization (treated as a four category ordinal variable) and the items on impact on the education system (a four category ordinal variable).

Only one relationship reached statistical significance, that between urbanicity and the view that targeting resources at disadvantaged areas had a positive impact on the education system, with heads of more urban schools having a more positive view of this policy (Rho = 0.2, p<0.05). Relationships that almost reached significance were those with encouraging private investment (Rho= 0.18, p=0.07), with urban heads having a more positive view, and national training programmes for heads (Rho=-0.15, p=0.07), with urban heads having less positive views.

3 Faith schools

Few significant differences were found between heads of faith schools and non-faith schools. Heads of faith schools were more positive on the move towards greater curriculum flexibility (U=1120, p<0.05), and they were (unsurprisingly) more positive on the impact of encouraging faith schools (U=353, p<0.001).

4 Differences by sex of headteacher

Female heads were more positive on changes to the 14–19 curriculum (U=191.5, p<0.05) and the impact of faith schools (Rho=365.2, p<0.05).

5 Differences by experience

There was a tendency for heads who had been in post longer to have a more negative view of government policies. This tendency reached statistical significance for the variables increased emphasis on learning rather than teaching (Rho=-0.18, p<0.05), the move towards personalized learning (Rho=-0.18, p<0.05), investment in ICT (Rho=-0.16, p<0.05), bidding culture (Rho= -0.19, p<0.05), target-setting (Rho=-0.18, p<0.01), measures to deal with failing schools (Rho=-0.17, p<0.05), use of PANDA (Rho=-0.19, p<0.05), specialist schools status (Rho=-0.27, p<0.01), investment by private individuals (Rho=-0.22, p<0.01), increased accountability for performance (Rho=-0.19, p<0.05), SIPs (Rho=-0.15, p<0.05), ECM (Rho=-0.15, p<0.05), extended schools (Rho=-0.15, p<0.05) and student voice (Rho=-0.23, p<0.05). These differences were unrelated to headteacher age.

Notes

1 A decade of New Labour reform of education

1 When New Labour came to power in 1997, the national ministry in London was called the Department for Education and Employment (DfEE) after reorganization had taken place in 1995. The DfEE became the Department for Education and Skills (DfES) in 2001. In 2007 the DfES was split into two: Department for Children, Schools and Families (DCSF), and the Department for Innovation, Universities and Skills.

2 Education Action Zones (EAZs) were set up in 1998 with resources targeted on underperforming schools in inner city areas. Schools involved in an EAZ could make changes to curriculum provision (e.g. more vocationalism) and to the staffing structure with higher rates of pay.

Excellence in Cities (EiC) was launched in 1999 and focused on achievement and standards in inner city/urban areas. The EAZ programme was discontinued and the most successful Zones merged into the EiC scheme. The EiC scheme had a number of features in order to eradicate underachievement: Learning Mentors, Learning Support Units, Gifted and Talented programme, City Learning Centres and Beacon Schools.

3 Leadership Incentive Grant (LIG) was targeted at secondary schools where the senior leadership was identified as needing to be strengthened in order to enable the school to meet national standards. A LIG consultant would work with the senior leadership to support review of performance and to develop leadership capacity.

4 The National Literacy and Numeracy Strategies were launched in 1998 and 1999 respectively, with speedy change and direct intervention into teaching and learning in primary schools. Specific directions where given to the teacher in regard to the teaching and assessment of literacy and numeracy. These strategies were incorporated into the Primary and Secondary Strategies from 2003.

5 In 2000 the Children's Fund was launched to identify and support children and young people at risk of exclusion and underachievement. *Every Child Matters* was launched in 2003 to bring about inter-agency (local authorities, schools, health, police) working focused around the child in order to secure the following goals: be healthy; stay safe; enjoy and achieve; make a positive contribution; achieve economic well-being. In 2005 a Children's Commissioner was appointed to give children a voice in public matters.

6 Education Improvement Partnerships was launched in 2003 as a means of encouraging collaborations between schools and other organizations. It includes other initiatives such as EiC but has also sought to support other forms of partnership in educational provision. This includes Federations. See Note 7.

7 Federations can be 'soft' where schools work together, e.g. share and jointly plan

14–19 provision, or 'hard' where schools integrate the governance and leadership structures. There are a range of restructurings taking place with job redesign at local level and in schools (see Chapman et al. 2008).

8 Academies are state-funded schools that are run by sponsors. Originally the sponsors were mainly private philanthropists and the Christian churches, with a specific focus on areas of disadvantage where a school or schools who were failing would be closed and replaced with an academy. This has changed with an emphasis now on a range of sponsors and locations. This is a highly controversial strategy (see Beckett 2007; P. Woods et al. 2007).

Trust Schools were established in 2006 and enable schools with partners to formalize the partnership. Trust Schools can employ their own staff, set their admission arrangements, and control their assets.

9 Remodelling the School Workforce was launched in 2003 with a focus on creating a larger non-QTS (Qualified Teacher Status) workforce in schools that could undertake site-based management work. For example, clerical staff, bursar and financial activity, and premises. Central to this has been the employment of non-QTS staff to take on pastoral or student services work, and teaching assistants to support teachers and learners, and to cover lessons for absent teachers. In 2007 the DfES published a report from PricewaterhouseCoopers (DfES/PwC 2007) on school leadership, which presented the scenario of the chief executive of a 'school' or campus including children's services, as not automatically needing QTS. This has been a controversial policy (see Butt and Gunter 2007).

5 Raising standards: What is the evidence?

1 The term 'underachievement' has been used in a range of contexts by journalists, politicians, academics and teachers but there is no consensus on a common agreed definition (see Smith 2003).

2 Specialist School status: the Specialist School Programme (SSP) helps schools, in partnership with private sector sponsors and supported by additional government funding to establish distinctive identities through their chosen specialism and to achieve their targets to raise standards. On the DCSF website, Specialist Schools are described as 'an important part of the Government's plans to raise standards in secondary education'.

3 Key Stage 3 National Strategy: this strategy is aimed at transforming secondary education, designed to support schools to address learning needs of 11–14 year olds, operates across all subjects and supports personalized learning with the overall intention of raising standards through whole school improvement.

4 Healthy Schools: the National Healthy Schools programme promotes a whole school approach to health and is a joint initiative between the Department of Health and the DCSF. It has been in operation since 1999 and targets improvement in health, raised pupil achievement, social inclusion and closer working between health promotion providers and educational establishments.

5 Increased Flexibility Programme: this aims to create enhanced vocational and work-related learning opportunities for 14–16 year olds including provision of the new GCSEs in vocational subjects. Pupils in the programme study off-site at a college or with a training provider for one or two days a week throughout Key Stage 4; they have opportunities to work towards worthwhile vocational and work-related qualifications and have the opportunity to develop their knowledge and under-standing in a work context.

6 14–19 Enterprise (Pathfinders): this programme aims at higher attainment and continues the government's drive to raise standards in schools and colleges, focusing particularly on the quality of teaching and learning. The overall aim is that by the age of 19 every young person should have been prepared by their education to succeed in life.

7 Leading Edge: this programme is about secondary schools working together to address the most critical learning challenges. Partnerships are expected to focus on raising the performance of schools which are struggling to raise standards and on closing the achievement gap by addressing issues of underperformance among groups of pupils from poorer socio-economic backgrounds and from particular ethnic groups. The Leading Edge Partnership programme was aligned with the Specialist Schools programme in 2005 and is one of the options open to high-performing Specialist Schools.

8 Federations: the definition of federation as used in the Education Act 2002 allows for the creation of a single governing body across two or more schools. A federation is a group of schools with a formal agreement to work together to raise standards, promote inclusion, find new ways of approaching teaching and learning and build capacity between schools in a coherent manner.

9 Young Apprenticeships: a Young Apprenticeship (YA) is a route at Key Stage 4 which allows motivated and able 14–16 year olds to study for vocational qualifications, not only in the classroom but also in college with training providers and in the workplace. Pupils are based in school and follow the core National Curriculum subjects, but for two days a week they also work towards nationally recognized vocational qualifications delivered by their local YA Partnership.

10 Aim Higher: this is designed to address the under-representation of students from disadvantaged backgrounds who apply for and enter higher education. It does this by raising aspiration and attainment levels of 13–19 year olds through improved links between universities, colleges and schools in EiC areas, EAZs and some Excellence Clusters. Activities include university tasters, summer schools and the Aim Higher Roadshow.

11 Networked Learning Communities: the National College for School Leadership (NCSL) Networked Learning Communities programme was launched in September 2002. Networked learning takes place when individuals come together in groups from different environments to engage in development activity informed by the public knowledge base, their own experience and by co-constructing new knowledge.

7 Remodelling and distributed leadership: the case of the SBM

1 The National College for School Leadership is a non-departmental public body set up by the New Labour government to build leadership capacity in schools (www.ncsl.org.uk).

2 The *Deployment and Impact of Support Staff* project was commissioned by the then DfES and the Welsh Assembly Government in 2004 (DCFS 2008e). It differentiates seven areas in which school support staff work: Teaching Assistant Equivalents, Pupil Welfare, Technicians, Other Pupil Support, Facilities, Administrative and Site.

3 Research findings on this point remain equivocal. The notion that clear connections can be drawn between remodelling, teacher workload and motivation have been challenged by findings from the *Transforming the Workforce Pathfinder* project (e.g. see Gunter et al. 2005) but are supported in Hammersley-Fletcher (2007).

13 New Labour and breaking the education and poverty link

1 Excellence in Cities has made additional resources available to schools in socio-economically disadvantaged, mainly urban, areas to improve standards of teaching and learning. A particular focus has been upon supporting young people identified within such schools as being 'talented and gifted'.

2 Connexions was launched in 2001 with the aim of helping young people make more informed choices in their transition to adult life. A primary target of the

Connexions service was to reduce the proportion of 16–18 not in education, employment or training.

3 Sure Start aims to improve the life chances of younger children (under 4) through improved services in areas of need. The focus is upon offering better access to early education and play, improved health services for children and their parents and family support in nurturing.

4 The Educational Maintenance Allowance aims to provide assistance to young people from low-income families who are entering post-compulsory education through the provision of a weekly allowance and bonuses for retention and achievement. The weekly allowance is based on a financial assessment of parental income.

5 Full Service Extended Schools. This initiative seeks to support the development in every local authority area of one or more schools which provide a comprehensive range of services on a single site, including access to health services, adult learning and community activities as well as study support.

6 Cultural capital: forms of knowledge, skills and education. Any advantages a person has which give them a higher status in society, including high expectations. Parents provide children with cultural capital, the attitudes and knowledge that makes the educational system a comfortable familiar place in which they can succeed easily.

References

Acheson, D. (1998) *Independent Enquiry into Inequality in Health*. London: The Stationery Office.

Adonis, A. and Pollard, S. (1997) *A Class Act*. London: Penguin.

Ainscow, M. (1999) *Understanding the Development of Inclusive Schools*. London: Falmer.

Ainscow, M. and Howes, A. (2007) Working together to improve urban secondary schools: a study of practice in one city. *School Leadership and Management*, 27(3): 285–300.

Ainscow, M., Booth, T. and Dyson, A. (2004a) Understanding and developing inclusive practices in schools: a collaborative action research network. *International Journal of Inclusive Education*, 8(2): 125–139.

Ainscow, M., Fox, S., Jackson, M. and Moore, M. (2004b) *Manchester Inclusion Standard: Guidance for Schools*. Manchester: Manchester City Council.

Ainscow, M., Booth, T. and Dyson, A. (2006a) Inclusion and the standards agenda: negotiating policy pressures in England. *International Journal of Inclusive Education*, 10(4–5): 295–308.

Ainscow, M., Booth, T. and Dyson, A. with Farrell, P., Frankham, J., Gallannaugh, F., Howes, A. and Smith, R. (2006b) *Improving Schools, Developing Inclusion*. London: Routledge.

Ainscow, M., Crow, M., Dyson, A., Goldrick, S., Kerr, K., Lennie, C., Miles, S., Muijs, D. and Skyrme, J. (2006c) *Equity in Education: New Directions: The Second Annual Report of the Centre for Equity in Education, University of Manchester*. Manchester: Centre for Equity in Education.

Ainscow, M., Dyson, A. and Kerr, K. (2006d) *Equity in Education: Mapping the Territory. The First Annual Report of the Centre for Equity in Education, University of Manchester*. Manchester: Centre for Equity in Education.

Ainscow, M., Crow, M., Dyson, A., Goldrick, S., Kerr, K., Lennie, C., Miles, S., Muijs, D. and Skyrme, J. (2007) *Equity in Education: New Directions*. Manchester: Centre for Equity in Education.

Ainscow, M., Dyson, A., Goldrick, S., Kerr, K. and Miles, S. (2008) *Equity in Education: Responding to Context*. Manchester: Centre for Equity in Education.

Ainsworth, J. and Roscigno, V. (2005) Stratification, school–work linkages and vocational education. *Social Forces*, 84(1): 257–284.

Alexander, R. (1994) *Innocence and Experience: Reconstructing Primary Education*, ASPE Paper no. 5. Stoke-on-Trent: Trentham.

Alexander, R. (2000) *Culture and Pedagogy: International Comparisons in Primary Education*. Oxford: Blackwell.

Alexander, R., Craft, M. and Lynch, J. (1984) *Change in Teacher Education: Context and Provision since Robins*. London: Holt, Rinehart & Winston.

Alexander, R., Rose, J. and Woodhead, C. (1992) *Curriculum Organisation and Classroom Practice in Primary Schools: A Discussion Paper*. London: DES.

Amrein, A.L. and Berliner, D.C. (2002) High-stakes testing, uncertainty, and student learning. *Education Policy Analysis Archives*, 10(18), http://epaa.asu.edu/epaa/v10n18/ (accessed 4 December 2007).

Anderson, D., Brown, M. and Rushbrook, P. (2004) Vocational education and training. In G. Foley (ed.) *Dimensions of Adult Learning: Adult Education and Training in a Global Era*. Crows Nest, NSW: Allen & Unwin.

Anyon, J. (1997) *Ghetto Schooling: A Political Economy of Urban Educational Reform*. New York: Teachers College Press.

Anyon, J. (2005) *Radical Possibilities: Public Policy, Urban Education, and a New Social Movement*. London: Routledge.

Apple, M. (1986) *Teachers and Texts: A Political Economy of Class and Gender Relations in Education*. New York: Routledge & Kegan Paul.

Archer, L. and Yamashita, H. (2003) Knowing their limits? Identities, inequalities and inner city school leavers' post-16 aspirations. *Journal of Education Policy*, 18(1): 53–69.

Argyris, C. and Schön, D.A. (1978) *Organisational Learning: A Theory of Action Perspective*. Reading, MA: Addison-Wesley.

Argyris, C. and Schön, D.A. (1996) *Organisational Learning II: Theory, Method and Practice*. Reading, MA: Addison-Wesley.

Artiles, A. and Dyson, A. (2005) Inclusion, education and culture in developed and developing countries. In D. Mitchell (ed.) *Contextualising Inclusive Education: Evaluating Old and New International Perspectives*. London: Routledge.

Askew, M., Brown, M., Rhodes, V., Johnson, D. and Wiliam, D. (1997) *Effective Teachers of Numeracy*. London: King's College London.

Atkinson, M., Wilkin, A., Stott, A., Doherty, P. and Kinder, K. (2001) *Multi-agency Working: An Audit of Activity*. Slough: National Foundation for Educational Research.

Atkinson, M., Doherty, P. and Kinder, K. (2005) Multi-agency working: models, challenges and key factors for success. *Journal of Early Childhood Research*, 3(1): 7–17.

Audit Commission (1998) *A Fruitful Partnership: Effective Partnership Working*. London: HMSO.

Bagley, C., Ackerley, C.L. and Rattray, J. (2004) Social Exclusion, Sure Start and Organizational Social Capital: evaluating inter-disciplinary multi-agency working in an education and health work programme. *Journal of Education Policy*, 19(5): 595–607.

Baker, M. (2006) Foreword. In A. Parker, A. Duncan and J. Fowler, *Education and Inspections Act 2006: The Essential Guide*. Slough: National Foundation for Educational Research.

Ball, S.J. (1990) *Politics and Policy Making in Education*. London: Routledge.

Ball, S.J. (1993) Education markets, choice and social class: the market as a class strategy in the UK and the USA. *British Journal of Sociology of Education*, 14(1): 3–19.

Ball, S.J. (1994) *Education Reform: A Critical and Post-structural Approach*. Buckingham: Open University Press.

Ball, S.J. (2003) The teacher's soul and the terrors of performativity. *Journal of Education Policy*, 18(2): 215–228.

Ball, S.J. (2007) *Education PLC*. London: Routledge.

Ball, S.J. and Gewirtz, R. (1999) School choice, social class and distinction: the realization of social advantage in education. *Journal of Educational Policy*, 11(1): 21–34.

Balls, E. (2007) Plan for children, Press Notice, 12 December, www.dcsf.gov.uk/pns/DisplayPN.cgi?pn_id=2007_0235 (accessed 22 February 2008).

Barber, M. (1996) *The Learning Game: Arguments for an Education Revolution*. London: Victor Gollancz.

Barber, M. (2001a) The very big picture. *School Effectiveness and School Improvement*, 12(2): 213–228.

Barber, M. (2001b) High expectations and standards for all, no matter what: creating a world class education service in England. In M. Fielding (ed.) *Taking Education Really Seriously*. London: RoutledgeFalmer.

Barber, M. (2007) *Instruction to Deliver*. London: Politico.

Barber, M. and Sebba, J. (1999) Reflections on progress towards a world class education system. *Cambridge Journal of Education*, 29(2): 183–193.

Barker, B. (2005) *Transforming Schools: Illusion or Reality?* Stoke-on-Trent: Trentham.

Bauder, H. (2002) Neighbourhood effects and cultural exclusion. *Urban Studies*, 39(1): 85–93.

BBC (2003) 'Worst school's' GCSE joy, 21 August, http://news.bbc.co.uk/1/hi/england/west_yorkshire/3169429.stm (accessed 16 June 2007).

BBC (2007a) Primary tests results improving, 7 August, http://newsvote.bbc.co.uk/1/hi/education (accessed 10 October 2007).

BBC (2007b) Fewer teens achieve maths target, 14 August, http://newsvote.bbc.co.uk/1/hi/education (accessed 25 October 2007).

BBC (2007c) UK schools slip down in science, 5 December, http://newsvote.bbc.co.uk/1/hi/education (accessed 10 December 2007).

Beck, U. (1992) *Risk Society: Towards a New Modernity*. London: Sage.

Beckett, F. (2007) *The Great City Academy Fraud*. London: Continuum.

Beckett, F. and Hencke, D. (2005) *The Survivor: Tony Blair in Peace and War*. London: Aurum.

Bell, D. (2003) Access and achievement in urban education: 10 years on. Speech to the Fabian Society, London, 20 March.

Bennett, N., Summers, M. and Askew, M. (1994) Knowledge for teaching and teaching performance. In A. Pollard (ed.) *Look Before You Leap? Research Evidence for the Curriculum at Key Stage Two*. London: Tufnell.

Bennett, N., Wise, C., Woods, P. and Harvey, J.A. (2003) *Distributed Leadership: Summary Report*. Nottingham: National College for School Leadership.

Bentley, T., Hopkins, D. and Jackson, D. (2005) *Developing a Network Perspective. What Are We Learning About . . .? Establishing a Network of Schools*. Nottingham: National College for School Leadership.

Bernstein, B. (1996) *Pedagogy, Symbolic Control and Identify: Theory, Research, Critique*. London: Taylor & Francis.

Black, P. and Wiliam, D. (1998) *Inside the Black Box*. London: King's College London.

Black, P., Harrison, C., Lee, C., Marshall, B. and Wiliam, D. (2004) Working inside the black box: assessment for learning in the classroom. *Phi Delta Kappan*, 86(1): 8–21.

Blair, T. (1996) Speech given at Ruskin College, Oxford, 16 December.

Blair, T. (2001) Extracts from Blair's undelivered speech to the Trades Union Congress, *Guardian*, 12 September.

Blair, T. (2005) Higher standards: better schools. Speech on education at 10 Downing Street, 24 October, www.pm.gov.uk/output/Page8363.asp (accessed 17 January 2008).

Blair, T. (2006) 21st century public services speech, 6 June, www.number10.gov.uk/output/page9564.asp (accessed 17 January 2008).

Blair, T. (2007) Education, education, education – 10 years on. In T. Blair, C. Taylor and E. Reid, *Education, Education, Education – 10 Years On*. London: Specialist Schools and Academies Trust.

Blunkett, D. (2000) Remit letter to the National College for School Leadership: tasks and responsibilities, 25 September. London: DfEE.

Bobbitt, P. (2002) *The Shield of Achilles*. London: Penguin.

Bolam, R. (2004) Reflections on the NCSL from a historical perspective. *Educational Management Administration and Leadership*, 32(3): 251–267.

Booth, T. (2003) Embracing the faith, including the community. In P. Potts (ed.) *Inclusion in the City*. London: Routledge.

Bottery, M. (2001) Globalisation and the UK competition state: no room for transformational leadership in education. *School Leadership and Management*, 21(2): 119–218.

Bottery, M. (2007a) New Labour policy and school leadership in England: room for manoeuvre? *Cambridge Journal of Education*, 37(2): 153–172.

Bottery, M. (2007b) Reports from the frontline: English headteachers' work in an ERA of practice centralization. *Educational Management Administration and Leadership*, 35(1): 89–110.

Bourdieu, P. (2000) *Pascalian Meditations*. Cambridge: Polity.

Bourdieu, P. (2003) *Firing Back, Against the Tyranny of the Market*. Cambridge: Polity.

Bourdieu, P. and Passeron, J. (1977) *Reproduction in Education, Society and Culture*. London: Sage.

Bowe, R. and Ball, S.J. with Gold, A. (1992) *Reforming Education and Changing Schools*. London: Routledge.

Bowers, J. (1992) Postmodernity and the globalisation of technoscience: the computer, cognitive science and war. In J. Doherty, E. Graham and M. Malek (eds) *Postmodernism and the Social Sciences*. London: Macmillan.

Bowles, J. and Gintis, H. (1976) *Schooling in Capitalist America*. London: Routledge & Kegan Paul.

Boyd, P., Baker, L., Harris, K., Kynch, C. and McVittie, E. (2006) Working with multiple identities: supporting new teacher education tutors in Higher Education. In S. Bloxham, S. Twiselton and A. Jackson (eds) *Challenges and Opportunities: Developing Learning and Teaching in ITE across the UK*. ESCalate 2005 conference proceedings, Higher Education Academy, www.escalate.ac.uk (accessed October 2007).

Boyd, P., Harris, K. and Murray, J. (2007) *Becoming a Teacher Educator: Guidelines for the Induction of Newly Appointed Lecturers in Initial Teacher Education*. Bristol: ESCalate.

Boyle, B. (2007) Learning through assessment. *Primary Leadership Today*, 2(2): 50–55.

Boyle, B. and Bragg, J. (2005) No science today: the demise of primary science. *Curriculum Journal*, 16(4): 423–437.

Boyle, B. and Bragg, J. (2006) A curriculum without foundation. *British Educational Research Journal*, 32(4): 569–582.

Bracey, G. (2004) The trouble with research, part 2. *Phi Delta Kappan*, 85(8): 635–636.

Bradbury, L. and Gunter, H.M. (2006) Dialogic identities: the experiences of women who are headteachers and mothers in English primary schools. *School Leadership and Management*, 26(5): 489–504.

Bragg, J. and Pearson, D. (2007) *The Impact of KS2 and KS3 Assessment Tests on the Curriculum: Literature Review and Survey*. London: QCA.

Braveman, P. (2003) Monitoring equity in health and healthcare: a conceptual framework. *Journal of Health, Population and Nutrition*, 21(3): 181–192.

Brehony, K.J. (2005) Primary schooling under New Labour: the irresolvable contradiction of excellence and enjoyment. *Oxford Review of Education*, 31(1): 29–46.

Brimblecombe, N., Ormston, M. and Shaw, M. (1996) Teachers' perceptions of inspections. In J. Ouston, P. Earley and B. Fidler (eds) *OfSTED Inspections: The Early Experience*. London: Fulton.

Brisard, E., Menter, I. and Smith, I. (2005) *Models of Partnership in Programmes of Initial Teacher Training: A Systematic Review*. Edinburgh: General Teaching Council of Scotland.

British Educational Research Association (BERA) (2008) Educational effectiveness and improvement, SIG meeting report, 5 December 2007. *Research Intelligence*.

Britzman, D.P. (2003) *Practice Makes Practice: A Critical Study of Learning to Teach*. New York: State University of New York Press.

Broadfoot, P. (2001) Empowerment or performativity? Assessment policy in the late twentieth century. In R. Phillips and J. Furlong (eds) *Education, Reform and the State*. London: RoutledgeFalmer.

Brophy, J. (1992) Probing the subtleties of subject matter teaching. *Educational Leadership*, 49(7): 4–8.

Brophy, J.E. and Good, T.L. (1986) Teacher behaviour and student achievement. In M.R. Wittrock (ed.) *Handbook of Research on Teaching*. New York: Macmillan.

Brown, K. and White, K. (2006) *Exploring the Evidence Base for Integrated Children's Services*, www.scotland.gov.uk/Publications (accessed 30 August 2006).

Brown, M., Woods, C. and Reading, M. (2002) *Report on the Evaluation of the School Business Manager Training Pilot*. Nottingham: National College for School Leadership.

Brown, M., Askew, M., Millett, A. and Rhodes, V. (2003) The key role of educational research in the development and evaluation of the National Numeracy Strategy. *British Educational Research Journal*, 29(5): 655–672.

Brown, P. (1999) Globalisation and the political economy of high skills. *Journal of Education and Work*, 12(3): 233–252.

Brown, T. and McNamara, O. (2005) *New Teacher Identity and Regulative Government: Discursive Formation of Primary Mathematics Teacher Education*. New York: Springer.

Bubb, S., Earley, P. and Totterdell, M. (2005) Accountability and responsibility: rogue school leaders and the induction of new teachers in England. *Oxford Review of Education*, 31(2): 255–272.

Burgess, S. and Wilson, D. (2005) The dynamics of school attainment of England's ethnic minorities. Paper presented at Ethnicity and Education Conference, University of Bristol, 14 October.

Burrell, G. and Morgan, G. (1979) *Sociological Perspectives and Organisational Analysis*. Gower: Aldershot.

Butt, G. and Gunter, H.M. (eds) (2007) *Modernizing Schools: People, Learning and Organizations*. London: Continuum.

Bynner, J. and Joshi, H. (2002) Equality and opportunity in education: evidence from the 1958 and 1970 birth cohort studies. *Oxford Review of Education*, 28(4): 405–425.

Byrne, D. (2005) *Social Exclusion*. Maidenhead: Open University Press.

Cabinet Office (1999) *Modernising Government*, Cm 4310. London: The Stationery Office.

Calder, G. (2003) *Communitarianism and New Labour*, www.whb.co.uk/socialissues/vol2gc.htm (accessed 24 August 2008).

Caldwell, B.J. and Spinks, J.M. (1992) *Leading the Self Managing School*. London: Falmer.

Cameron, A. and Lart, R. (2003) Factors promoting and obstacles hindering joint working: a systematic review of the research evidence. *Journal of Integrated Care*, 11(2): 9–17.

Cameron, A., Lart, R., Harrison, L., MacDonald, G. and Smith, R. (2000) *Factors Promoting and Obstacles Hindering Joint Working: A Systematic Review*. Bristol: School for Policy Studies, University of Bristol.

Campbell, J. and Husbands, C. (2000) On the reliability of OfSTED inspection of Initial Teacher Training: a case study. *British Journal of Educational Research*, 26(1): 39–48.

Carr, W. and Kemmis, S. (1986) *Becoming Critical: Education, Knowledge and Action Research*. London: Falmer.

Carter, P.L. (2003) 'Black' cultural capital, status positioning, and schooling conflicts for low-income African American youth. *Social Problems*, 50(1): 136–155.

Cassidy, S. (2008) Failed! Political interference is damaging children's education, report claims. *The Independent,* 29 February.

Castells, M. (1996) *The Rise of the Network Society.* Oxford: Blackwell.

Caul, L. and McWilliams, S. (2002) Accountability in partnership or partnership in accountability: initial teacher education in Northern Ireland. *European Journal of Teacher Education,* 25(2–3): 187–197.

Central Advisory Council for Education (England) (CACE) (1967) *Children and their Primary Schools* (Plowden Report). London: HMSO.

Chapman, C. (2001) Changing classrooms through inspection. *School Leadership and Management,* 21(1): 59–73.

Chapman, C. (2002) OfSTED and school improvement: teachers' perceptions of the inspection process in schools facing challenging circumstances. *School Leadership and Management,* 22(3): 257–272.

Chapman, C. (2006) *School Improvement through External Intervention.* London: Continuum.

Chapman, C., Ainscow, M., Bragg, J., Gunter, H., Hull, J., Mongon, D., Muijs, D. and West, M. (2008) *Emerging Patterns of School Leadership: Current Practice and Future Directions.* Nottingham: National College for School Leadership.

Charlton, B., Davenport, C. and Elliott, J. (2004) Revising the National Curriculum. *Journal of Education Policy,* 15(2): 247–255.

Chubb, J.E. and Moe, T.M. (1990) *Politics, Markets and America's Schools.* Washington, DC: Brookings Institution.

Clarence, E. and Painter, C. (1998) Public services under New Labour: collaborative discourses and local networking. *Public Policy and Administration,* 13(3): 8–22.

Clark, C., Dyson, A., Millward, A. and Robson, S. (1999) Theories of inclusion, theories of schools: deconstructing and reconstructing the 'inclusive school'. *British Educational Research Journal,* 25(2): 157–177.

Clark, P. (1998) *Back from the Brink.* London: Metro Books.

Clarke, A. (1997) A social worlds research adventure. In A. Strauss and J. Corbin (eds) *Grounded Theory in Practice.* London: Sage.

Clarke, J. and Newman, J. (1997) *The Managerial State.* London: Sage.

Coffield, F. (2007) Improving the quality of the education system. In F. Coffield, R. Steer, R. Allen, A. Vignoles, G. Moss and C. Vincent, *Public Sector Reform: Principles for Improving the Education System,* Bedford Way Papers. London: Institute of Education, University of London.

Coffield, F., Moseley, D., Hall, E. and Ecclestone, K. (2004) *Learning Styles and Pedagogy in Post-16 Learning: A Systematic and Critical Review.* London: Learning and Skills Research Centre.

Coffield, F., Steer, R., Allen, R., Vignoles, A., Moss, G. and Vincent, C. (2007) *Public Sector Reform: Principles for Improving the Education System,* Bedford Way Papers. London: Institute of Education, University of London.

Collarbone, P. (2005) Touching tomorrow: remodelling in English schools. *Australian Economic Review,* 38(1): 75–82.

Connell, N. (1996) *Getting Off the List: School Improvement in New York City.* New York: New York City Educational Priorities Panel.

Connell, R.W., White, V.M. and Johnston, K.M. (1992) An experiment in justice: the disadvantaged schools programme and the question of poverty, 1974–1990. *British Journal of Sociology of Education,* 13(4): 447–464.

Cooper, D. (2006) Collaborating with students in the assessment process. *Orbit,* 36(2): 20–23.

Coopers and Lybrand (1988) *Local Management of Schools: Report to the DES.* London: HMSO.

Cox, C.B. and Boyson, R. (1975) *The Fight for Education*. London: Dent.

Cox, C.B. and Boyson, R. (1977) *Black Paper 1977*. London: Temple Smith.

Cox, C.B. and Dyson, A.E. (1969) *The Black Papers on Education*. London: Davis-Poynter.

Coxon, K. (2005) Common experiences of staff working in integrated health and social care organisations: a European perspective. *Journal of Integrated Care*, 13(2): 13–21.

Craig, J., Huber, J. and Lownsbrough, H. (2004) *Schools Out: Can Teachers, Social Workers and Health Staff Learn to Live Together?* London: Hay.

Creemers, B.P.M. (1994) *The Effective Classroom*. London: Cassell.

Creemers, B.P.M. and Reezigt, G.J. (2005) Linking school effectiveness and school improvement: the background and outline of the project. *School Effectiveness and School Improvement*, 16(4): 359–371.

Cullingford, C. (ed.) (1999) *An Inspector Calls*. London: Kogan Page.

Cummings, C., Dyson, A., Todd, L., with the Education Policy and Evaluation Unit, University of Brighton (2004) *An Evaluation of the Extended Schools Pathfinder Projects*, DfES Research Report 530. London: DfES.

Cummings, C., Dyson, A., Papps, I., Pearson, D., Raffo, C. and Todd, L. (2005) *Evaluation of the Full Service Extended Schools Project: End of First Year Report*, DfES Research Report 680. Nottingham: DfES.

Cummings, C., Dyson, A., Papps, I., Pearson, D., Raffo, C., Tiplady, L. and Todd, L. (2006) *Evaluation of the Full Service Extended Schools Initiative, Second Year: Thematic Papers*. London: DfES.

Cummings, C., Dyson, A., Muijs, D., Papps, I., Pearson, D., Raffo, C., Tiplady, L., Todd, L. with Crowther, D. (2007) *Evaluation of the Full Service Extended Schools Initiative: Final Report*, DfES Research Report 852. London: DfES.

Dadds, M. (1992) Monty Python and the Three Wise Men. *Cambridge Journal of Education*, 22(2): 129–141.

Dadds, M. and Kynch, C. (2004) The impact of RAE 3B ratings on educational research in teacher education departments. *Research Intelligence*, 84: 8–11.

Dale, R. (2000) Globalization: a new world for comparative education. In J. Schriewer (ed.) *Discourse Formation in Comparative Education*. Frankfurt: Peter Lang.

Davies, B. (2006) Subjectification: the relevance of Butler's analysis for education. *British Journal of Sociology of Education*, 27(4): 425–438.

Davies, S.M.B. and Howes, A. (2008) *Prosiect Dysgu Cydradd: Facilitating Teacher Engagement in More Inclusive Practice*, Final Report. London: Economic and Social Science Research Council.

Day, C., Stobart, G., Sammons, P., Kington, A., Gu, Q., Smees, R. and Mujtaba, T. (2006) *Variations in Teachers' Work, Lives and Effectiveness*, DfES Research Report 743. London: DfES.

DCSF (2007) *Extended Schools: Building on Experience*. London: DCSF.

DCSF (2008a) *Education Improvement Partnerships*, www.standards.dfes.gov.uk/sie/si/eips/eips (accessed 16 May 2008).

DCSF (2008b) *Federations*, www.standards.dfes.gov.uk/federations (accessed 23 May 2008).

DCSF (2008c) *What are Academies?*, www.standards.dfes.gov.uk/academies (accessed 23 May 2008).

DCSF (2008d) *What are Trust Schools?*, www.standards.dfes.gov.uk/sie/si/eips/trusts (accessed 23 May 2008).

DCSF (2008e) *Deployment and Impact of Support Staff in Schools and the Impact of the National Agreement (Results from Strand 2 Wave 1 – 2005/06)*, www.dfes.gov.uk/research/ (accessed 3 March 2008).

DCSF (2008f) *Every Child Matters*, www.everychildmatters.gov.uk (accessed 3 March 2008).

DCSF (2008g) Eighty-nine new Specialist Schools announced, Press Notice 2008/0023. London: DCSF.

De Waal, A. (2006) Do targets work? *The Times Educational Supplement*, August: 19.

Dean, C., Dyson, A., Gallannaugh, F., Howes, A. and Raffo, C. (2007) *Schools, Governors and Disadvantage*. London: Joseph Rowntree Foundation.

Demie, F., Butler, R. and Taplin, A. (2002) Educational achievement and the disadvantage factor: empirical evidence. *Educational Studies*, 28(2): 101–110.

DENI (1993) *Review of Initial Teacher Training (ITT) in Northern Ireland: Review of Three Working Groups on Competences, Courses, Cooperation and ITT Structures, and Coordination of ITT and In-service Education*. Bangor, Co Down: DENI.

DES (1978) *Primary Education in England: A Survey by HM Inspectors of Schools*. London: HMSO.

DES (1984) *Initial Teacher Training: Approval of Courses Circular 3/84*. London: HMSO.

DES (1989a) *Initial Teacher Training: Approval of Courses Circular 24/89*. London: HMSO.

DES (1989b) *Licensed Teacher Regulation Circular 18/89*. London: HMSO.

Desforges, C. and Abouchaar, A. (2003) *The Impact of Parental Involvement, Parental Support and Family Education on Pupil Achievement and Adjustment: A Literature Review*, DfES Research Report 433. London: DfES.

DfE (1992) *Initial Teacher Training (Secondary Phase) Circular 9/92*. London: DfE.

DfE (1993a) *The Initial Training of Primary School Teachers Circular 14/93*. London: DfE.

DfE (1993b) *The Government Proposals for the Reform of Initial Teacher Training*. London: DfE.

DfE (1993c) *School-centred Initial Teacher Training (SCITT)*. London: DfE.

DfEE (1997a) *Excellence in Schools*, Cm 2681. London: The Stationery Office.

DfEE (1997b) *The Implementation of the National Literacy Strategy*. London: DfEE.

DfEE (1998a) *teachers: meeting the challenge of change*, Cm 4164. London: DfEE.

DfEE (1998b) New national college for headteachers, Press Notice 1998/0477, 20 October, www.dfes.gov.uk/pns/DisplayPN.cgi?pn_id=1998_0477 (accessed 11 December 2006).

DfEE (1998c) *Teaching: High Status, High Standards Circular 4/98*. London: HMSO.

DfEE (1999a) *The Quinquennial Review of the Teacher Training Agency*. London: DfEE.

DfEE (1999b) *The Standards for the Induction of New Teachers Circular 5/99*. London: DfEE.

DfEE (1999c) *Schools Plus: Building Learning Communities. Improving the Educational Chances of Children and Young People from Disadvantaged Areas: A Report from the Schools Plus Policy Action Team 11*. London: DfEE.

DfES (2000) Blunkett sets out radical new agenda for inner city school diversity and improvement, Press Notice 2000/0106. London: DfES.

DfES (2002) *Qualifying to Teach: Professional Standards for Qualified Teacher Status and Requirements for Initial Teacher Training, Circular 2/02*. London: Teacher Training Agency.

DfES (2003a) *Leadership Incentive Grant*. London: DfES.

DfES (2003b) *Every Child Matters*, Cm 5860. London: HMSO, www.everychild matters.gov.uk (accessed 25 August 2008).

DfES (2003c) *Raising Standards and Tackling Workload: A National Agreement*. London: DfES.

DfES (2003d) *Excellence and Enjoyment: A Strategy for Primary Schools*. London: DfES.

DfES (2003e) *Full Service Extended Schools Planning Documents*. London: DfES.

DfES (2003f) *Full Service Extended Schools: Requirements and Specifications*. London: DfES.

DfES (2004a) *National Standards for Headteachers*. London: DfES.

DfES (2004b) *Smoking Out Underachievement*. London: DfES.

DfES (2004c) *Statistics of Education: Schools in England*. London: DfES.

DfES (2004d) *Department for Education and Skills: Five Year Strategy for Children and Learners*, Cm 6272. London: DfES.

DfES (2004e) *Every Child Matters: Change for Children*. London: HMSO.

DfES (2005a) *Higher Standards: Better Schools for All*. London: DfES.

DfES (2005b) *London Challenge: From Good to Outstanding* London: DfES.

DfES (2006a) *Statistics of Education: School Workforce in England 2006 Edition*. London: The Stationery Office.

DfES (2006b) www.dfes.gov.uk/londonchallenge/docs/Secondary_Families_of_ Schools_2006_V2_KS3.xls no longer available, based on 'Families of Schools May 2005.' London: DfES.

DfES (2007) *The Revised Standards for Qualified Teacher Status*, www.tda.gov.uk/ upload/resources/doc/draft_qts_standards_17nov2006.doc (accessed 20 April 2007).

DfES/PricewaterhouseCoopers (PwC) (2007) *Independent Study into School Leadership*. London: DfES.

Dowling, B., Powell, M. and Glendinning, C. (2004) Conceptualising successful partnerships. *Health and Social Care in the Community*, 12(4): 309–317.

Driver, S. (2006) Modernising the public services. In P. Dunleavy, R. Hefferman, P. Cowley and C. Hay (eds) *Developments in British Politics 8*. Basingstoke: Palgrave Macmillan.

Dunne, M., Lock, R. and Soares, A. (1996) Partnership in Initial Teacher Training: after the shotgun wedding. *Educational Review*, 48(1): 41–53.

Dyson, A. (2007) Department for Education and Skills. In C. Talbot and M. Baker (eds) *The Alternative Comprehensive Spending Review*. Manchester: Manchester University Press.

Dyson, A. and Millward, A. (2000) *Schools and Special Needs: Issues of Innovation and Inclusion*. London: Paul Chapman.

Dyson, A. and Raffo, C. (2007) Education and disadvantage: the role of community-oriented schools. *Oxford Review of Education*, 33(3): 297–314.

Dyson, A., Millward, A. and Todd, L. (2002) *A Study of the Extended Schools Demonstration Projects*. Research report 381. London: DfES.

Dyson, A., Gallannaugh, F. and Millward, A. (2003) Making space in the standards agenda: developing inclusive practices in schools. *European Educational Research Journal*, 2(2): 228–244.

Earl, L., Watson, N., Levin, B., Leithwood, K., Fullan, M. and Torrance, N. (2003) *Watching and Learning 3: Final Report of the External Evaluation of England's National Literacy and Numeracy Strategies*. Toronto: Ontario Institute for Studies in Education, University of Toronto.

Earley, P., Fidler, B. and Ouston, J. (eds) (1996) *Improvement through Inspection*. London: Fulton.

Easen, P. and Bolden, D. (2005) Location, location, location: what do league tables really tell us about primary schools? *Education 3–13*, 33(3): 49–56.

Easen, P., Atkins, M. and Dyson, A. (2000) Inter-professional collaboration and conceptualisations of practice. *Children and Society*, 14: 355–367.

Edwards, A. (1995) Teacher education: partnership in pedagogy?, *Teaching and Teacher Education*, 11(6): 595–610.

Edwards, A., Barnes, M., Plewis, I. and Morris, K. (2006) *Working to Prevent the Social Exclusion of Children and Young People: Final Lessons from the National Evaluation of the Children's Fund*. London: DfES.

Edwards, T. (1994) The Universities Council for the Education of Teachers: defending an interest or fighting a cause? *Journal of Education for Teaching*, 20(2): 143–152.

Ehri, L.C. (2003) Systematic phonics instruction: finding of the National Reading Panel.

Paper presented at the seminar of the Standards and Effectiveness Unit, Department of Education and Skills, London.

Ellenbogen, M.A. and Hodgins, S. (2004) The impact of high neuroticism in parents on children's psychosocial functioning in a population at high risk for major affective disorder: a family-environmental pathway of intergenerational risk. *Development and Psychopathology*, 16: 113–136.

Emerson, C. (2006) *Vital Signs, Vibrant Society*. Sydney: University of New South Wales Press.

Engestrom, Y. (2001) Expansive learning at work: toward an activity-theoretical reconceptualisation. *Journal of Education and Work*, 14(1): 133–156.

Exworthy, M., Stuart, M., Blane, D. and Marmo, M. (2003) *Tackling Health Inequalities since the Acheson Inquiry*. Bristol: Policy Press.

Farrell, P., Woods, K., Lewis, S., Rooney, S., Squires, G. and O'Connor, M. (2006) *A Review of the Functions and Contribution of Educational Psychologists in England and Wales in Light of 'Every Child Matters: Change for Children'*. London: HMSO.

Ferguson, I. (2007) Increasing user choice or privatising risk? The antinomies of personalization. *British Journal of Social Work*, 37: 387–403.

Ferguson, N., Earley, P., Fidler, B. and Ouston, J. (2000) *Improving Schools and Inspection: The Self Inspecting School*. London: Chapman.

Ferlie, E., Ashburner, L., Fitzgerald, L. and Pettigrew, A. (1996) *The New Public Management in Action*. Oxford: Oxford University Press.

Fielding, M. (ed.) (2001) *Taking Education Really Seriously*. London: RoutledgeFalmer.

Fielding, M. (2004a) Transformative approaches to student voice: theoretical underpinnings, recalcitrant realities. *British Educational Research Journal*, 30(2): 295–311.

Fielding, M. (2004b) 'New wave' student voice and the renewal of civic society. *London Review of Education*, 2(3): 197–217.

Fielding, M. (2006) Leadership, radical student engagement and the necessity of person-centred education. *International Journal of Leadership in Education*, 9(4): 299–313.

Fielding, M. (2007) Personalisation, education and the totalitarianism of the market. *Soundings*, 38.

Finkelstein, N.D. and Grubb, W.N. (2000) Making sense of education and training markets: lessons from England. *American Educational Research Journal*, 37(3): 601–631.

Fitz, J., Halpin, D. and Power, S. (1993) *Grant-Maintained Schools: Education in the Marketplace*. London: Kogan-Page.

Fitz-Gibbon, C. (1996) *Monitoring Education: Indicators, Quality and Effectiveness*. London: Cassell.

Fitz-Gibbon, C. (1998) OfSTED: time to go?, *Managing Schools Today*, 7(6): 22–25.

Flecknoe, M. (2001) Target setting: will it help raise achievement? *Educational Management Administration and Leadership*, 29(2): 217–228.

Flynn, J.R. (1987) Massive IQ gains in 14 nations: what IQ tests really measure. *Psychological Bulletin*, 101: 171–191.

Frankham, J. (2006) Network utopias and alternative entanglements for educational research and practice. *Journal of Education Policy*, 21(6): 661–677.

Frankham, J. and Edwards-Kerr, D. (forthcoming) Long story? Beyond 'technologies' of knowing in case study work with permanently excluded young people. *International Journal of Inclusive Education*.

Frankham, J. and Howes, A. (2006) Talk as action in 'collaborative action research': making and taking apart teacher/researcher relationships. *British Educational Research Journal*, 32(4): 617–632.

Franklin, W. (2000) Students at promise and resilient: a historical look at risk. In M.G. Sanders (ed.) *Schooling Students Placed at Risk*. New York: Lawrence Erlbaum.

Freire, P. (1970) *Pedagogy of the Oppressed*. London: Continuum.

Furbey, R., Dinham, A., Farnell, R., Finneron, D., Wilkinson, G., Howarth, C., Hussain, D. and Palmer, S. (2006) *Faith as Social Capital: Connecting or Diving?* Bristol: Policy Press.

Furedi, F. (2006) *Culture of Fear Revisited*. London: Continuum.

Furlong, J. (2001) Reforming teacher education, reforming teachers: accountability, professionalism and competence. In R. Phillips and J. Furlong (eds) *Education, Reform and the State: 25 Years of Policy, Politics and Practice*. London: Routledge.

Furlong, J. (2005) New Labour and teacher education: the end of an era. *Oxford Education Review*, 33(1): 119–134.

Furlong, J. and Kane, I. (1996) *Recognising Quality in Primary Initial Teacher Education: Findings from the 1995–96 OfSTED Primary Sweep*, UCET Occasional Paper no. 6. London: Universities' Council for the Education of Teachers.

Furlong, J., Barton, L., Miles, S., Whiting, C. and Whitty, G. (2000) *Teacher Education in Transition: Re-forming Professionalism?* Buckingham: Open University Press.

Furlong, J., Campbell, A., Howson, J., Lewis, S. and McNamara, O. (2006a) Partnership in English teacher education: changing times, changing definitions – evidence from the Teacher Training Agency National Partnership Project. *Scottish Education Review*, 37: 32–45.

Furlong, J., Hagger, H. and Butcher, C. with Howson, J. (2006b) *Review of Initial Teacher Training Provision in Wales: A Report to the Welsh Assembly Government*. Cardiff: National Assembly for Wales.

Galton, M. and MacBeath, J. with Page, C. and Steward, S. (2002) *A Life in Teaching? The Impact of Change on Primary Teachers' Working Lives*. London: National Union of Teachers.

Galton, M., Simon, B. and Croll, P. (1980) *Inside the Primary Classroom*. London: Routledge & Kegan Paul.

Galton, M., Hargreaves, L., Comber, C., Wall, D. with Pell, A. (1999) *Inside the Primary Classroom: 20 Years On*. London: Routledge.

Geddes, M. (2006) *National Evaluation of Local Strategic Partnerships*, www.communities. gov.uk/documents/localgovernment/pdf/151762 (accessed 8 March 2008).

Gee, J. (2004) *Situated Language and Learning: A Critique of Traditional Schooling*. London: Routledge.

General Teaching Council for Wales (GTCW) (2007) *The Chartered Teacher Standards*, www.gtcw.org.uk/documents/chartered_teacher_standards/GTCW%20Chartered %20Teacher%20Standards%20English.pdf (accessed 6 March 2008).

Gewirtz, S. (2001) Cloning the Blairs: New Labour's programme for the re-socialization of working-class parents. *Journal of Education Policy*, 16(4): 365–378.

Gewirtz, S. (2002) *The Managerial School*. London: Routledge.

Gewirtz, S., Dickson, M. and Power, S. (2002) Governance by spin: the case of New Labour and Education Action Zones in England. In S. Linblad and T. Popkewitz (eds) *Educational Restructuring: International Perspectives on Travelling Policies*. Charlotte, NC: Information Age Publishing.

Giddens, A. (1991) *Modernity and Self-Identity: Self and Society in the Late Modern Age*. Cambridge: Polity.

Giddens, A. (1998) *The Third Way: The Renewal of Social Democracy*. Cambridge: Polity.

Giddens, A. (2000) *The Third Way and its Critics*. Cambridge: Polity.

Giddens, A. (2001) *The Global Third Way Debate*. Cambridge: Polity.

Gillborn, D. (2005) Education policy as an act of White Supremacy: whiteness, critical race theory and education reform. *Journal of Education Policy*, 20(4): 485–505.

Gilroy, P. (1992) The political rape of teacher training in England and Wales: a JET rebuttal. *Journal of Education for Teaching*, 18: 5–22.

Gilroy, P. (1998) New Labour and teacher education in England and Wales: the first 500 days. *Journal of Education for Teaching*, 24(3): 221–230.

Gilroy, P. and Wilcox, B. (1997) OFSTED, criteria and the nature of social understanding: a Wittgensteinian critique of the practice of educational judgement. *British Journal of Educational Studies*, 45: 22–38.

Glendinning, C., Powell, M. and Kirstein, R. (2002) *Partnerships, New Labour and the Governance of Welfare*. Bristol: Policy Press.

Goldstein, H. (2001) Using pupil performance data for judging schools and teachers: scope and limitations. *British Educational Research Journal*, 27(4): 433–442.

Gorard, S. and Smith, E. (2004) What is 'underachievement' at school? *School Leadership and Management*, 24(2): 205–225.

Grace, G. (1995) *School Leadership: Beyond Education Management*. London: Falmer.

Graham, J. and Nabb, J. (1999) *Stakeholder Satisfaction: Survey of OFSTED Inspection of ITT 1994–1999*, UCET Research Paper no. 1. London: Universities' Council for the Education of Teachers.

Gray, J. (2000) *Causing Concern but Improving: A Review of Schools' Experience*. London: DfEE.

Gray, J. (2001) *Success against the Odds: Five Years On*. London: Routledge.

Gray, J. (2004) Frames of reference and traditions of interpretation some issues in the identification of 'under-achieving' schools. *British Journal of Educational Studies*, 52(3): 293–309.

Gray, J. and Wilcox, B. (1995) *Good School, Bad School: Evaluating Performance and Encouraging Improvement*. Buckingham: Open University Press.

Gronn, P. (2000) Distributed properties: a new architecture for leadership. *Educational Management and Administration*, 28(3): 317–338.

Gronn, P. (2002) Distributed leadership. In K. Leithwood and P. Hallinger (eds) *Second International Handbook of Educational Leadership and Administration*. Dordrecht: Kluwer.

Gudykunst, W.B. (ed.) (2005) *Theorizing about Intercultural Communication*. London: Sage.

Gulson, K. (2005) Renovating educational identities: policy, space and urban renewal. *Journal of Education Policy*, 20(2): 141–158.

Gunter, H.M. (2001) *Leaders and Leadership in Education*. London: Paul Chapman.

Gunter, H.M. (2004) Labels and labelling in the field of educational leadership. *Discourse*, 25(1): 21–42.

Gunter, H.M. (2005) Conceptualising research in educational leadership. *Educational Management, Administration and Leadership*, special edition: 'Researching Leadership – A Review of Progress', 33(2): 165–180.

Gunter, H.M. (2006) Knowledge production in the field of educational leadership: a place for intellectual histories. *Journal of Educational Administration and History*, 38(2): 201–215.

Gunter, H.M. (2007) Remodelling the school workforce in England: a study in tyranny? *Journal of Critical Education Policy Studies*, 5(1), www.jceps.com.

Gunter, H.M. and Butt, G. (2007a) A changing workforce. In G. Butt and H.M. Gunter (eds) *Modernizing Schools: People, Learning and Organizations*. London: Continuum.

Gunter, H.M. and Butt, G. (2007b) The challenges of modernization. In G. Butt and H.M. Gunter (eds) *Modernizing Schools: People, Learning and Organizations*. London: Continuum.

Gunter, H.M. and Butt, G. (2007c) Conclusion: wither modernization? In G. Butt and H.M. Gunter (eds) *Modernizing Schools: People, Learning and Organizations*. London: Continuum.

Gunter, H.M. and Fitzgerald, T. (2008) Educational administration and history, Part 1: debating the agenda. *Journal of Educational Administration and History*, 40(1): 5–21.

Gunter, H.M. and Forrester, G. (2008) New Labour and school leadership 1997–2007. *British Journal of Educational Studies*, 56(2): 144–162.

Gunter, H.M. and Rayner, S. (2007) Modernising the school workforce in England: challenging transformation and leadership? *Leadership*, 3(1): 47–64.

Gunter, H.M. and Thomson, P. (2006a) Stories from the field of commissioned research. Paper presented to the British Educational Research Association Conference, University of Warwick, September.

Gunter, H.M. and Thomson, P. (2006b) The makeover: a new logic of practice in policy making? Paper presented to the European Conference for Educational Research, University of Geneva, September.

Gunter, H.M., Rayner, S., Thomas, H., Fielding, A., Butt, G. and Lance, A. (2005) Teachers, time and work: findings from the evaluation of the Transforming the School Workforce Pathfinder Project. *School Leadership and Management*, 25(5): 441–454.

Gunter, H.M., Chapman, C., Ainscow, M., Bragg, J., Hull, J., Mongon, D., Muijs, D. and West, M. (2007) *New Models Project Literature Review: Report to the NCSL*. Manchester: University of Manchester.

Gunter, H.M., Chapman, C., Ainscow, M., Bragg, J., Hull, J., Mongon, D., Muijs, D. and West, M. (2008) *New Models of Leadership: A Literature Review. Report to the National College for School Leadership*. Nottingham: National College for School Leadership.

Guskey, T. (2001) *Evaluating Professional Development*. Thousand Oaks, CA: Corwin Press.

Guthrie, L.F., Guthrie, G.P., Van Heusden, S. and Burns, R. (1989) *Principles of Successful Chapter 1 Programs*. San Francisco, CA: Far West Laboratory for Educational Research and Development.

Haladyna, T. (1992) *Test-score Pollution: Implications for Limited English Proficient Students*, www.ncela.gwu.edu/pubs/symposia/second/vol2/test.htm (accessed 13 May 2008).

Hall, K., Collins, J., Benjamin, S., Nind, M. and Sheehy, K. (2004), SATurated models of pupildom: assessment and inclusion/exclusion. *British Educational Research Journal*, 30(6): 801–817.

Hall, V. (1996) *Dancing on the Ceiling*. London: Paul Chapman.

Hallinger, P. and Murphy, J.F. (1986) The social context of effective schools. *American Journal of Education*, 94(3): 328–355.

Hammersley-Fletcher, L. (2007) Engaging staff in change: experiences in schools in England. *International Electronic Journal for Leadership in Learning*, special edition, 11(16).

Harbin, G. (1996) The challenge of coordination. *Infants and Young Children*, 8(3): 68–76.

Hargreaves, A. (1986) *Two Cultures of Schooling: The Case of Middle Schools*. New York: Falmer.

Hargreaves, A. (1989) *Curriculum and Assessment Reform*. Toronto: OISE Press and Milton Keynes: Open University Press.

Hargreaves, A. (1994) *Changing Teachers, Changing Times: Teachers' Work and Culture in the Postmodern Age*. London: Cassell.

Hargreaves, A. (2003) *Teaching in the Knowledge Society*. New York: Teachers College Press.

Hargreaves, A. and Fink, D. (2006) *Sustainable Leadership*. San Francisco, CA: Jossey-Bass/Wiley.

Hargreaves, A. and Goodson, I. (2006) Educational change over time? The sustainability and nonsustainability of three decades of secondary school change and continuity. *Educational Administration Quarterly*, 42(1): 3–41.

Hargreaves, A., Baglin, E., Henderson, P., Leeson, P. and Tossell, T. (1988) *Personal and Social Education: Choices and Challenges*. Oxford: Basil Blackwell.

Hargreaves, A., Earl, L., Moore, S. and Manning, S. (2001) *Learning to Change: Teaching Beyond Subjects and Standards*. San Francisco, CA: Jossey-Bass and Barcelona: Octaedro.

Hargreaves, A., Halász, G. and Pont, B. (2007) *School Leadership for Systemic Improvement in Finland*. Paris: OECD.

Hargreaves, D. (1982) *The Challenge for the Comprehensive School: Culture, Curriculum and Community*. Boston, MA: Routledge.

Hargreaves, L., Moyles, J., Merry, R., Paterson, F., Pell, A. and Esarte-Sarries, V. (2003) How do primary school teachers define and implement 'interactive teaching' in the National Literacy Strategy in England? *Research Papers in Education*, 18(3): 217–236.

Harris, A. (1998) Improving ineffective departments in secondary schools: strategies for change and development. *Educational Management and Administration*, 26(3): 269–278.

Harris, A. (2005) Distributed leadership. In B. Davies (ed.) *The Essentials of School Leadership*. London: Paul Chapman.

Harris, A. and Ranson, S. (2005) The contradictions of education policy. Disadvantage and achievement. *British Educational Research Journal*, 31(5): 571–587.

Hartley, D. (2007a) The emergence of distributed leadership in education: why now? *British Journal of Educational Studies*, 55(2): 202–214.

Hartley, D. (2007b) Personalisation: the emerging 'revised' code of education? *Oxford Review of Education*, 33(5): 629–642, www.informaworld.com (accessed 8 May 2008).

Harvey, D. (2007) *A Brief History of Neoliberalism*. Oxford: Oxford University Press.

Hastings, A., Flint, J., McKenzie, C. and Mills, C. (2005) *Cleaning Up Neighbourhoods: Environmental Problems and Service Provision in Deprived Neighbourhoods*. Bristol: Policy Press.

Heilbronn, R., Jones, C., Bubb, S. and Totterdell, M. (2002) School-based induction tutors: a challenging role. *School Leadership and Management*, 22(4): 371–387.

Heiskala, R. (2007) Economy and society: from Parsons through Habermas to semiotic institutionalism. *Social Science Information*, 46(2): 243–271.

Herrnstein, R. and Murray, C. (1994) *The Bell Curve*. New York: Simon & Schuster.

Hextall, I. and Mahony, P. (2000) Consultation and the management of consent: standards for Qualified Teacher Status. *British Educational Research Journal*, 26(3): 323–342.

Hextall, I., Mahony, P. and Menter, I. (2001) 'Just testing'? An analysis of the implementation of 'skills tests' for entry into the teaching profession in England. *Journal of Education for Teaching*, 27(3): 221–239.

HMI (1982) *The New Teacher in School*. London: HMSO.

HMI (1983a) *Curriculum 11–16: Towards a Statement of Entitlement*. London: HMSO.

HMI (1983b) *Teaching in Schools: The Content of Initial Teacher Training*. London: DES.

HMI (1991) *School-Based Initial Teacher Training in England and Wales: A Report by HM Inspectorate*. London: HMSO.

HMI (2001) *The Introduction of Newly Qualified Teachers: the implementation of DfEE Circular 5/99*, HMI 270. London: HMSO.

HMI (2002) *The Annual Report of Her Majesty's Chief Inspector of Education 2001/02*. London: The Stationery Office.

Hoggart, L. and Smith, D.I. (2004) *Understanding the Impact of Connexions on Young People at Risk*, DfES Research Report 607. London: The Stationery Office.

Hollins, K., Gunter, H.M. and Thomson, P. (2006) Living improvement: a case study of a secondary school in England. *Improving Schools*, 9(2): 141–152.

Holyoake, J. (1993) Initial Teacher Training: the French view. *Journal of Education for Teaching*, 19(2): 215–226.

Holzman, L. (1997) *Schools for Growth: Radical Alternatives to Current Educational Models.* Mahwah, NJ: Lawrence Erlbaum.

Hood, C. (1991) A public management for all seasons? *Public Administration*, 69(1): 3–19.

Hood, C., Rothstein, H. and Baldwin, R. (2004) *The Government of Risk.* Oxford: Oxford University Press.

Hopkins, D. (2001) *'Think Tank' Report to Governing Council.* Nottingham: National College for School Leadership.

Hopkins, D. (2003) Instructional leadership and school improvement. In A. Harris, C. Day, M. Hadfield, D. Hoplins, A. Hargreaves and C. Chapman (eds) *Effective Leadership For School Improvement.* London: RoutledgeFalmer.

Hopkins, D. and Reynolds, D. (2001) The past, present and future of school improvement: towards the Third Age. *British Educational Research Journal*, 27(4): 459–475.

House of Commons (1998) *The Role of Headteachers. Ninth Report Volume 1 from the Education and Employment Committee.* London: The Stationery Office.

House of Commons (1999) *The Work of OfSTED: Other Inspection Frameworks. Select Committee on Education and Employment, Report from the Education Subcommittee June 1999*, www.publications.parliament.uk/pa/cm199899/cmselect/cmeduemp/62/6213.htm (accessed 20 September 2007).

House of Commons (2002) *House of Commons Debates*, col. 155, 16 July 2002. London: Hansard.

House of Commons (2005a) *Standing Committee A, Second Sitting Report*, col. 66, 22 March 2005. London: Hansard.

House of Commons (2005b) *Education and Skills Committee Report*, HC96. London: Hansard.

Howes, A., Frankham, J., Ainscow, M. and Farrell, P. (2004) The action in action research: mediating and developing inclusive intentions. *Educational Action Research*, 12(2): 239–257.

Howes, A., Booth, T., Dyson, A. and Frankham, J. (2005) Teacher learning and the development of inclusive practices and policies: framing and context. *Research Papers in Education*, 20(2): 131–146.

Hoyle, E. (1982) Micropolitics of educational organisations. *Educational Management and Administration*, 10: 87–98.

Hoyle, E. and Wallace, M. (2005) *Educational Leadership: Ambiguity, Professionals and Managerialism.* London: Sage.

Hyman, P. (2005) *1 out of 10, From Downing Street Vision to Classroom Reality.* London: Vintage.

Jeffrey, B. and Woods, P. (1998) *Testing Teachers: The Effect of School Inspections on Primary Teachers.* London: Falmer.

Jencks, C. (1972) *Inequality: A Reassessment of the Effect of Family and Schooling in America.* New York: Basic Books.

Jesson, D. and Crossley, D. (2008) *Data Driven School Transformation: Educational Outcomes and Value Added by Specialist Schools and Academies 2007 Analysis.* London: Specialist Schools and Academies Trust.

Johnson, P., Wistow, G., Rockwell, S. and Hardy, B. (2003) Interagency and interprofessional collaboration in community care: the interdependence of structures and values. *Journal of Interprofessional Care*, 17(1): 69–83.

Jones, C., Bubb, S., Totterdell, M. and Heilbronn, R. (2002) Reassessing the variability of induction for Newly Qualified Teachers: statutory policy and schools' provision. *Journal of In-service Education*, 28(3): 495–508.

Judge, H., Lemosse, M., Paine, L. and Sedlak, M. (1994) *The University and the Teachers: France, the United States, England.* Wallingford: Triangle Books.

Kalmijn, M. and Kraaykamp, G. (1996) Race, cultural capital, and schooling: an analysis of trends in the United States. *Sociology of Education*, 69: 22–34.

Kellett, M. and Dar, A. (2007) *Children Researching Links between Poverty and Literacy*. York: Joseph Rowntree Foundation.

Kelly, A. (1995) *Free School Meal Contextualisation of GCSE Examination Results: Report of the National Consortium for Examination Results*. Stockport: Stockport LEA.

Kemmis, S. (2001) Exploring the relevance of critical theory for action research: emancipatory action research in the footsteps of Jurgen Habermas. In P. Reason and H. Bradbury (eds) *Handbook of Action Research; Participative Inquiry and Practice*. London: Sage.

Kendall, L., O'Donnell, L., Golden, S., Ridley, K., Machin, S., Rutt, S., McNally, S., Schagen, I., Meghir, C., Stoney, S., Morris, M., West, A. and Noden, P. (2005) *Excellence in Cities: The National Evaluation of a Policy to Raise Standards in Urban Schools 2000–2003*, DfES Research Report 675A. Nottingham: DfES.

King, A. (1976) A problem of overload. In A. King (ed.) *Why is Britain Becoming Harder to Govern?* London: BBC.

Kyriacou, C. and O'Connor, A. (2003) Primary Newly Qualified Teachers' experience of the induction year in its first year of implementation in England. *Journal of In-service Education*, 29(2): 185–200.

Ladson-Billings, G. (1995) Toward a critical race theory of education. *Teachers College Record*, 97: 47–68.

Ladson-Billings, G. (1998) Just what is critical race theory and what's it doing in a nice field like education? *Qualitative Studies in Education*, 11(1): 7–24.

Laming, Lord (2003) *The Victoria Climbié Inquiry: Report of an Inquiry by Lord Laming*. London: HMSO.

Lash, S. and Urry, J. (1994) *Economies of Signs and Space*. London: Sage.

LaVeist, T.A. and Bell McDonald, K. (2002) Race, gender, and educational advantage in the inner city. *Social Science Quarterly*, 83(3): 832–852.

Lawton, D. (2005) *Education and Labour Party Ideologies, 1990–2001 and Beyond*. Abingdon: RoutledgeFalmer.

Leadbeater, C. (2004) *Personalisation through Participation: A New Script for Public Services*. London: Demos.

Leadbeater, C. and Mongon, D. (2009) *Hitting the Target and Making a Point*. Nottingham: National College for School Leadership.

Learmonth, J. (2000) *Inspection: What's in it for Schools?* London: Routledge.

Leithwood, K. (2001) School leadership in the context of accountability policies. *International Journal of Leadership in Education*, 4(3): 217–235.

Leithwood, K. and Levin, B. (2005) *Assessing School Leader and Leadership Programme Effects on Pupil Learning*. London: DfES.

Leithwood, K., Jantzi, D. and Steinbach, R. (1999) *Changing Leadership for Changing Times*. Buckingham: Open University Press.

Leithwood, K., Day, C., Sammons, P., Harris, A. and Hopkins, D. (2006a) *Seven Strong Claims about Successful School Leadership*. Nottingham: National College of School Leadership.

Leithwood, K., Day, C., Sammons, P., Harris, A. and Hopkins, D. (2006b) *Successful School Leadership: What it is and How it Influences Pupil Learning*, DfES Research Report 800. Nottingham: DfES/NCSL.

Leithwood, K., Jantzi, D. and McElherson-Hopkins, C. (2006c) The development and testing of a school improvement model. *School Effectiveness and School Improvement*, 17(4): 441–464.

Levacic, R. and Woods, P.A. (2002) Raising school performance in the league tables

(Part 1): disentangling the effects of social disadvantage. *British Educational Research Journal*, 28(2): 207–226.

Lindsay, G., Harris, A., Muijs, D., Chapman, C., Arweck, E. and Goodall, J. (2007) *Evaluation of the Federations Programme: A Report for the DfES*. Coventry: CEDAR.

Lipman, P. (2004) *High Stakes Education*. London: RoutledgeFalmer.

Lister, R. (2004) *Poverty*. Cambridge: Polity.

Lloyd, M.E. and Lloyd, K.E. (1986) Has lightning struck twice? Use of PSI in college classrooms. *Teaching of Psychology*, 13: 149–151.

Lowe, G. (1998) Inspection and change in the classroom: rhetoric and reality? In P. Earley (ed.) *School Improvement after Inspection*. London: Chapman.

Lupton, R. (2004a) Do poor neighbourhoods mean poor schools? Paper presented at Education and the Neighbourhood Conference, Bristol, January.

Lupton, R. (2004b) *Schools in Disadvantaged Areas: Recognising Context and Raising Quality*, CASE Paper 76. London: Centre for Analysis of Social Exclusion, London School of Economics.

Lupton, R. (2005) Social justice and school improvement: improving the quality of schools in the poorest neighbourhoods. *British Educational Research Journal*, 31(5): 589–604.

Lupton, R. (2006) How does place affect education. In S. Delorenzi (ed.) *Going Places: Neighbourhood, Ethnicity and Social Mobility*. London: Institute of Public Policy Research.

Luthar, S. and Zelazo, L. (2003) Research on resilience: an integrative review. In S.S. Luthar (ed.) *Resilience and Vulnerability: Adaptation in the Context of Childhood Adversities*. Cambridge: Cambridge University Press.

MacBeath, J. (2006) *School Inspection and Self Evaluation*. London: Routledge.

MacBeath, J., Gray, J., Cullen, J., Frost, D., Steward, S. and Swaffield, S. (2007) *Schools on the Edge: Responding to Challenging Circumstances*. London: Paul Chapman.

McCrone, G. (2000) *A Teaching Profession for the 21st Century: The Report of the Committee of Enquiry into Professional Conditions of Service for Teachers*. Edinburgh: Scottish Executive.

McNamara, O., Brundrett, M. and Webb, R. (2008) *Primary Teachers: Initial Teacher Education, Continuing Professional Development and School Leadership Development*, Primary Review Research Survey 6/3. Cambridge: Faculty of Education, University of Cambridge.

McNess, E., Broadfoot, P. and Osborn, M. (2003) Is the effective compromising the affective? *British Educational Research Journal*, 29(2): 243–257.

Maguire, M. (2006) Education and poverty: a matter of complexity. Paper presented at University of Manchester International Seminar on Education and Poverty, Manchester, March.

Mahony, P. and Hextall, I. (2000) *Reconstructing Teaching: Standards, Performance and Accountability*. London: RoutledgeFalmer.

Mansell, W. (2007a) *Education by Numbers: The Tyranny of Testing*. London: Politico.

Mansell, W. (2007b) *Testing has had its day*, www.progressonline.org.uk (accessed 10 May 2008).

Marquand, D. (2004) *Decline of the Public*. Cambridge: Polity.

Marquand, D. (2008) How did we get here? *New Statesman*, 14 April: 54–55.

Marsh, H., Byrne, B.M. and Shavelson, R.J. (1988) A multifaceted academic self-concept: its hierarchical structure and its relation to academic achievement. *Journal of Educational Psychology*, 80: 366–380.

Matthews, P. and Sammons, P. (2005) Survival of the weakest: the differential improvement of schools causing concern in England. *London Review of Education*, 3(2): 159–176.

Matthews, P. and Smith, G. (1995) OfSTED: inspecting schools and improvement through inspection. *Cambridge Journal of Education*, 25(1): 23–34.

Medwell, J., Wray, D., Poulson, L. and Fox, R. (1998) *Effective Teachers of Literacy*. Exeter: University of Exeter.

Meen, G., Gibb, K., Goody, J., McGrath, T. and Mackinnon, J. (2005) *Economic Segregation in England: Causes, Consequences and Policy*. Bristol: Policy Press.

Meiner, D. and Wood, G. (2004) *Many Children Left Behind: How the No Child Left Behind Act is Damaging our Children and our Schools*. Boston, MA: Beacon.

Melhuish, E., Belsky, J. and Leyland, A. (2005) *Early Impacts of Sure Start Local Programmes on Children and Families: Report of the Cross-sectional Study of 9- and 36-Month-Old Children and their Families*, DfES Research Report NESS/2005/FR/013. London: The Stationery Office.

Middleton, S., Perren, K., Maguire, S., Rennison, J., Battistin, E., Emmerson, C. and Fitzsimons, E. (2005) *Evaluation of Education Maintenance Allowance Pilots: Young People Aged 16 to 19 Years*, DfES Research Report 678. London: The Stationery Office.

Milbourne, L., Macrae, S. and Maguire, M. (2003) Collaborative solutions or new policy problems: exploring multi-agency partnerships in education and health work. *Journal of Education Policy*, 18(1): 19–35.

Miliband, D. (2004a) Building success for the Blair generation. Speech to the Annual Meeting of the Secondary Heads Association, Harrogate, 24 March, www.dfes.gov. uk/speeches/latest.cfm (accessed 30 March 2004).

Miliband, D. (2004b) Personalized learning. Address to North of England Education Conference, Belfast, 8 January.

Mills, D., Jepson, A., Coxon, T., Easterby-Smith, M., Hawkins, P. and Spencer, J. (2005) *Demographic Review of the Social Sciences, Report to the Economic and Social Research Council*. Swindon: ESRC.

Ministry of Education (1944) *Education Act (Butler Act)*. London: HMSO.

Ministry of Education (Finland) (2007) *Improving School Leadership, Finland, Country Background Report*. Helsinki: Ministry of Education.

Miron, L. (2006) A response to the Education and Poverty working paper. Joseph Rowntree Foundation International Seminar of Education and Poverty, Manchester.

Mitra, D. (2006) Student voice from the inside and outside: the positioning of challengers. *International Journal of Leadership in Education*, 9(4): 315–328.

Mongon, D. and Chapman, C. (2006) The impact of Specialist School Status on student attainment in London. Unpublished paper.

Montgomery, A., Rossi, R., Legters, N., McDill, E., McPartland, J. and Stringfield, S. (1993) *Educational Reforms and Students Placed At Risk: A Review of the Current State of the Art*. Washington, DC: US Department of Education, Office of Educational Research and Improvement.

Moran, M. (2003) *The British Regulatory State*. Oxford: Oxford University Press.

Morrow, R.A. and Torres, C.A. (2000) The state, globalisation, and educational policy. In N.C. Burbules and C.A. Torres (eds) *Globalisation and Education: Critical Perspectives*. New York: Routledge.

Mortimore, P. (1991) Bucking the trends: promoting successful urban education. The Times Educational Supplement Greenwich Annual Lecture, London.

Mortimore, P. and Whitty, G. (1997) *Can School Improvement Overcome the Effects of Disadvantage?* London: Institute of Education, University of London.

Mortimore, P., Sammons, P., Stoll, L., Lewis, D. and Ecob, R. (1988) *School Matters: The Junior Years*. Salisbury: Open Books.

Muijs, D. (1997) Predictors of academic achievement and academic self-concept: a longitudinal perspective. *British Journal of Educational Psychology*, 67: 263–277.

Muijs, D. (2006) Measuring teacher effectiveness: some methodological reflections. *Educational Research and Evaluation*, 12(1): 53–75.

Muijs, D. and Reynolds, D. (2001) *Effective Teaching: Evidence and Practice*. London: Paul Chapman.

Muijs, D. and Reynolds, D. (2002) Teacher beliefs and behaviours: what matters. *Journal of Classroom Interaction*, 37(2): 3–15.

Muijs, D., Harris, A., Chapman, C., Stoll, L. and Russ, J. (2004) Improving schools in socioeconomically disadvantaged areas: a review of research evidence. *School Effectiveness and School Improvement*, 15(2): 149–175.

Muijs, D., Campbell, R.J., Kyriakides, L. and Robinson, W. (2005) Making the case for differential teacher effectiveness: an overview of research in four key areas. *School Effectiveness and School Improvement*, 16(1): 51–70.

Mullen, C., Gordon, S., Greenler, B. and Anderson, R. (2002) Capacities for school leadership: emerging trends in the literature. *International Journal of Educational Reform*, 11(2): 158–198.

Munby, S. (2006) *The School Leadership Challenges for the 21st Century*. Nottingham: National College for School Leadership, www.ncsl.org.uk/media (accessed 1 February 2007).

Murray, J. (2005) *Investigating Good Practices in the Induction of Teacher Educators into Higher Education*. York: Higher Education Academy.

Murray, J., and Male, T. (2005) Becoming a teacher educator: evidence from the field. *Teaching and Teacher Education*, 21(2): 125–142.

National Audit Office (NAO) (2006) *Improving Poorly Performing Schools in England*. London: HMSO.

National Audit Office (NAO) (2007) *The Academies Programme*. London: HMSO.

National College for School Leadership (NCSL) (2004) *Like no other initiative*. Cranfield: NCSL.

National College for School Leadership (NCSL) (2007) *Bursar Development Programme: Impact and Evaluation Report*. Nottingham: NCSL.

National College for School Leadership (NCSL) (2008) Institutional website, www.ncsl.org.uk (accessed 1 February 2008).

National Curriculum Council (NCC) (1990) *Curriculum Guidance Three: The Whole Curriculum*. York: NCC.

National Evaluation of Sure Start (NESS) (2005) *National Evaluation Report: Early Impacts of Sure Start Local Programmes on Children and Families*, DfES Research Report NESS/2005/FR/013. London: DfES.

National Evaluation of Sure Start (NESS) (2008) *The Impact of Sure Start Local Programmes on Three Year Olds and their Families*, DfES Research Report NESS/2008/FR/027. London: DCSF.

National Strategy for Neighbourhood Renewal (2000) *Report of Policy Action Team 17: Joining It Up Locally*. London: Department of the Environment, Transport and the Regions.

Newman, J. (2001) *Modernising Governance: New Labour, Policy and Society*. London: Sage.

Newman, J. (2002) Changing governance, changing equality? New Labour, modernisation and public services. *Public Money and Management*, January–March: 7–13.

Nias, J. (1989) *Primary Teachers Talking: A Study of Teaching as Work*. London: Routledge.

Nichols, S. and Berliner, D. (2005) *The Inevitable Corruption of Indicators and Educators through High-Stakes Testing*. Tempe, AZ: Educational Policy Research Unit, Arizona State University.

Nichols, S. and Berliner, D. (2007) *Collateral Damage: How High-Stakes Testing Corrupts America's Schools*. Cambridge, MA: Harvard University Press.

Nutley, S., Davies, H. and Walter, I. (2002) *What is a Research Synthesis?* Briefing Note 1. St Andrews: Research Unit for Research Utilisation, University of St Andrews, www.st-andrews.ac.uk/~ruru/Conceptual%20synthesis.pdf (accessed 29 April 2005).

Oancea, A. (2004a) The distribution of Educational Research expertise: findings from the analysis of RAE 2001 submissions (I). *Research Intelligence*, 87: 3–8.

Oancea, A. (2004b) The distribution of Educational Research expertise: findings from the analysis of RAE 2001 submissions (II). *Research Intelligence*, 88: 3–6.

OECD and Programme for International Student Assessment (PISA) (2000) *Measuring Student Knowledge and Skills: The PISA 2000 Assessment of Reading, Mathematical and Scientific Literacy*. Paris: OECD.

Office for National Statistics (ONS) (2007) *Office for National Statistics Population Projections 2003–2028*, www.statistics.gov.uk (accessed 20 March 2007).

OfSTED (1994) *A Focus on Quality*. London: HMSO.

OfSTED (1995) *Inspection Quality 1994/1995*. London: HMSO.

OfSTED (1996) *Framework for the Inspection of Schools*. London: HMSO.

OfSTED (1997) *From Failure to Success*. London: HMSO.

OfSTED (1999a) *Lessons Learned from Special Measures*. London: HMSO.

OfSTED (1999b) *Inspection of Initial Teacher Training Primary Follow-up Survey 1996–1998*, HMI 193. London: OfSTED.

OfSTED (2000) *Improving City Schools*. London: HMSO.

OfSTED (2003a) *Excellence in Cities and Education Action Zones: Management and Impact*, HMI 1399. London: OfSTED.

OfSTED (2003b) *The National Literacy and National Numeracy Strategies and the Primary Curriculum*, HMI 1973. London: OfSTED.

OfSTED (2003c) *Annual Report of HMCI 2001–2*. London: HMSO.

OfSTED (2003d) *Quality and Standards in Initial Teacher Training*, HMI 547. London: OfSTED.

OfSTED (2006) *Annual Report of Her Majesty's Chief Inspector of Schools 2005–6*. London: The Stationery Office.

OfSTED (2007) *Annual Report of Her Majesty's Chief Inspector of Schools 2006–2007*. London: The Stationery Office.

OfSTED (2008) Office for Standards in Education Children's Services and Skills Portal, www.ofsted.gov.uk/portal/site/Internet/menuitem.455968b0530071c4828a0d8308 c08a0c/?vgnextoid=e99c8587fd24a010VgnVCM1000008192a8c0RCRD (accessed 25 January 2008).

OfSTIN (1997) *A Better System of Education?* Hexham: Office for Standards in Inspection.

Ogawa, R.T., Crowson, R. and Goldring, E. (1999) Enduring dilemmas of school organization. In J. Murphy and K. Seashore-Louis (eds) *Handbook of Research on Educational Administration*. San Francisco, CA: Jossey-Bass.

Osborn, M., McNess, E. and Broadfoot, P. with Pollard, A. and Triggs, P. (2000) *What Teachers Do: Changing Policy and Practice in Primary Education*. London: Continuum.

Ozga, J. (2000) *Policy Research in Educational Settings*. Buckingham: Open University Press.

Painter, C. and Clarence, E. (2000) New Labour and inter-governmental management: flexible networks or performance control? *Public Management*, 2(4): 477–498.

Palmer, P. (2007) A new professional: the aims of education revisited. *Change*, November–December.

Passmore, B. (1998) Headship novices learn the creed. *The Times Educational Supplement*, 23 October, www.tes.co.uk/search/story/?story_id=79615 (accessed 11 December 2006).

Payne, J. (1998) The attractions of joined up thinking. *Adults Learning*, 10(4): 12–14.

Percy-Smith, J. (2005) *What Works in Strategic Partnerships for Children?* Barkingside, UK: Barnardo's.

Phillips, M. (1996) *All Must Have Prizes*. London: Time Warner.

Plewis, I. (2007) Income effects and educational progress: methodological puzzles, statistical problems and substantive findings. Centre for Census and Survey Research (CCSR) Seminar, University of Manchester, October.

Plomin, R. and Spinath, F.M. (2004) Intelligence: genetics, genes, and genomics. *Journal of Personality and Social Psychology*, 86: 112–129.

Pollard, A. and Triggs, P. with Broadfoot, P., McNess, E. and Osborn, M. (2000) *What Pupils Say: Changing Policy and Practice in Primary Education*. London: Continuum.

Powell, M. (1999) *New Labour, New Welfare State*. Bristol: Policy Press.

PriceWaterhouseCoopers (2001) *Teacher Workload Study*. London: DfES.

PricewaterhouseCoopers (2007) *Independent Study into School Leadership*. London: DfES.

Prime Minister's Strategy Unit (PMSU) (2006) *The UK Government's Approach to Public Service Reform*. London: PMSU.

Quality Assurance Agency (QAA) (2001) *The Framework for Higher Education Qualifications in England, Wales and Northern Ireland*, www.qaa.ac.uk/academicinfrastructure/fheq/EWNI/default.asp (accessed 6 March 2008).

Raffe, D., Brannen, K., Croxford, L. and Martin, C. (1999) Comparing England, Scotland, Wales and Northern Ireland: the case for 'home internationals' in comparative research. *Comparative Education*, 95(1): 9–25.

Raffo, C. (2006) Disadvantaged young people accessing the new urban economies of the post-industrial city. *Journal of Educational Policy*, 21(1): 75–94.

Raffo, C. and Gunter, H.M. (2008) Leading schools to promote social inclusion: developing a conceptual framework for analysing research, policy and practice. *Journal of Education Policy*, 23(4): 363–380.

Raffo, C., Dyson, A., Gunter, H.M., Jones, L. and Kalambouka, A. (2007) *Education and Poverty: Mapping the Terrain and Making the Links to Educational Policy*, Report to the Joseph Rowntree Foundation. York: Joseph Rowntree Foundation.

Rainwater, L. and Smeeding, T. (2003) *Poor Kids in a Rich Country: America's Children in Comparative Perspective*. New York: Russell Sage Foundation.

Ravitch, D. (2000) *Left Back: A Century of Failed School Reforms*. New York: Simon & Schuster.

Rawnsley, A. (2001) *Servants of the People: The Inside Story of New Labour*. London: Penguin.

Reid, E. (2007) For schools by schools – progress in the past year, prospects for the future. In T. Blair, C. Taylor and E. Reid, *Education, Education, Education – 10 Years On*. London: Specialist Schools and Academies Trust.

Reynolds, D. (1999) School effectiveness, school improvement and contemporary educational policies. In J. Demaine (ed.) *Contemporary Educational Policy and Politics*. London: Macmillan.

Reynolds, D. and Farrell, S. (1996) *Worlds Apart? A Review of International Surveys of Educational Achievement Involving England*. London: HMSO.

Reynolds, D., Sammons, P., Stoll, L., Barber, M. and Hillman, J. (1996) School effectiveness and school improvement in the United Kingdom. *School Effectiveness and School Improvement*, 7(2): 133–158.

Reynolds, D., Potter, D. and Chapman, C. (2002) School improvement for schools facing challenging circumstances. *School Leadership and Management*, 23(3): 242–256.

Ribbins, P. (ed.) (1997) *Leaders and Leadership in the School, College and University*. London: Cassell.

Ribbins, P. and Marland, M. (1994) *Headship Matters: Conversations with Seven Secondary School Headteachers*. Harlow, UK: Longman.

Ribbins, P., Bates, R. and Gunter, H.M. (2003) Reviewing research in education in Australia and the UK: evaluating the evaluations. *Journal of Educational Administration*, 41(4): 423–444.

Richards, C. (2005) *Standards in English Primary Schools: Are They Rising?* London: Association of Teachers and Lecturers.

Richards, C., Simco, N. and Twiselton, S. (1998) *Primary Initial Teacher Education, High Status? High Standard?* London: Falmer.

Riddell, R. (2005) Government policy, stratification and urban schools: a commentary on the five-year strategy for children and learners. *Journal of Education Policy*, 20(2): 237–241.

Riley, D. and Mulford, B. (2007) England's National College for School Leadership: a model for leadership education? *Journal of Educational Administration*, 45(1): 80–98.

Rizvi, F. and Lingard, B. (2000) Globalisation and education: complexities and contingencies. *Education Theory*, 50(4): 419–426.

Robertson, R. (1995) Glocalization: time-space and homogeneity-heterogeneity. In M. Featherstone, S. Lash and R. Robertson (eds) *Global Modernities*. London: Sage.

Rose, J. (2006) *Independent Review of the Teaching of Early Reading: Final Report*. London: DfES.

Rubie-Davies, C., Hattie, J. and Hamilton, R. (2008) Expecting the best for students: teacher expectations and academic outcomes. *British Journal of Educational Psychology*, 76(3): 429–444.

Rudduck, J. and Flutter, J. (2003) *Involving Pupils, Improving Schools*. London: Continuum.

Rushmer, R. and Pallis, G. (2002) Inter-professional working: the wisdom of integrated working and the disaster of blurred boundaries. *Public Money and Management*, 23(1): 59–66.

Sahlberg, P. (2007) Education policies for raising student learning: the Finnish approach. *Journal of Education Policy*, 22(2): 147–171.

Sammons, P., Hillman, J. and Mortimore, P. (1995) *Key Characteristics of Effective Schools: A Review of School Effectiveness Research*. London: OfSTED and Institute of Education, University of London.

Schoon, I. and Bynner, J. (2003) Risk and resilience in the life course: implications for interventions and social policies. *Journal of Youth Studies*, 6: 21–31.

Scottish Executive (2007) *Teacher Induction Scheme 2007–08*, www.scotland.gov.uk/Resource/Doc/157036/0042250.pdf (accessed 20 May 2007).

Seaman, P., Turner, K., Hill, M., Stafford, A. and Walker, M. (2006) *Parenting and Children's Resilience in Disadvantaged Communities*. York: Joseph Rowntree Foundation.

Seldon, A. (ed.) (2007) *Blair's Britain 1997–2007*. Cambridge: Cambridge University Press.

Sellgren, K. (2007) Too many new initiatives – heads, 5 May, http://news.bbc.co.uk/1/hi/education/6627947.stm (accessed 12 November 2007).

Sennett, R. (1998) *The Corrosion of Character: The Personal Consequences of Work in the New Capitalism*. New York: Norton.

Shepherd, J. (2008) Diplomas off to a halting start. *Education Guardian*, 8 January.

Shirley, D. and Hargreaves, A. (2006) Data-driven to distraction: why American educators need a reform alternative. *Education Week*, 26(4): 32–33.

Shonkoff, J.P. and Phillips, D.A. (eds) (2000) *From Neurons to Neighbourhoods: The Science of Early Childhood Development*. Washington, DC: National Academy Press.

Sibley, D. (1995) *Geographies of Exclusion*. London: Routledge.

Simco, N. and Wilson, T. (2002) *Primary Initial Teacher Training and Education: Revised Standards, Bright Future?* Exeter: Learning Matters.

Sinnott, S. (2007) Test results conceal the downside of tests, targets and tables, 7 August,

National Union of Teachers (NUT), www.teachers.org.uk/resources/pdf/pr4807 v2.pdf (accessed 12 October 2007).

Sloper, A. (2004) Facilitators and barriers for co-ordinated multi-agency services. *Child Care, Health and Development*, 30(6): 571–580.

Smith, E. (2003) Understanding underachievement: an investigation into the differential attainment of secondary school pupils. *British Journal of Sociology of Education*, 24(5): 575–586.

Smith, E. (2005) Raising standards in American schools: the case of No Child Left Behind. *Journal of Education Policy*, 20(4): 507–524.

Smith, F., Hardman, F., Wall, K. and Mroz, M. (2004) Interactive whole class teaching in the National Literacy and Numeracy Strategies. *British Educational Research Journal*, 30(3): 395–411.

Smith, T. and Nobel, M. (1995) *Education Divides: Poverty and Schooling in the 1990s*. London: Child Poverty Action Group.

Smyth, J. (2006) Educational leadership that fosters 'student voice'. *International Journal of Leadership in Education*, 9(4): 279–284.

Smyth, J. (2007) Toward the pedagogically engaged school: listening to student voice as a positive response to disengagement and 'dropping out'. In D. Thiessen and A. Cook-Sather (eds) *International Handbook of Student Experience of Elementary and Secondary School*. Dordrecht: Springer Science.

Smyth, J. (2008a) The elusive search for social justice in educational policy: could this be the end of state education? Inaugural lecture as Simon Visiting Professor, School of Education, University of Manchester, 6 March.

Smyth, J. (2008b) Listening to student voice in the democratization of schooling. In E. Samier with G. Stanley (ed.) *Political Approaches to Educational Administration and Leadership*. London: Routledge.

Smyth, J., Dow, A., Hattam, R., Reid, A. and Shacklock, G. (2000) *Teachers' Work in a Globalizing Economy*. London: Falmer.

Social Exclusion Unit (1998) *Bringing Britain Together: A National Strategy for Neighbourhood Renewal*, Cm 4045. London: The Stationery Office.

Social Exclusion Unit (2001) *A New Commitment to Neighbourhood Renewal: National Strategy Action Plan*. London: Social Exclusion Unit.

Southworth, G. (1995) *Looking into Primary Headship*. London: Falmer.

Specialist Schools and Academies Trust (SSAT) (2008) *Our Principles*, www.specialist schools.org.uk/about/valuesandmission/default.aspa (accessed 12 May 2008).

Spillane, J.P., Halverson, R. and Diamond, J.B. (2001) Investigating school leadership practice: a distributed perspective. *Educational Researcher*, 30(3): 23–28.

Stahl, S.A. (1999) Different strokes for different folks? A critique of learning styles. *American Educator*, 23(3): 27–31.

Steer, R. and Coffield, F. (2007) Introduction. In F. Coffield, R. Steer, R. Allen, A. Vignoles, G. Moss and C. Vincent, *Public Sector Reform: Principles for Improving the Education System*, Bedford Way Papers. London: Institute of Education, University of London.

Stevenson, H. (2007) Changes in teachers' work and the challenges facing teacher unions. *International Electronic Journal for Leadership in Learning*, special edition, 11(13).

Stewart, A., Petch, A. and Curtice, L. (2003) Moving towards integrated working in health and social care in Scotland: from maze to matrix. *Journal of Interprofessional Care*, 17(4): 335–350.

Stoker, G. (2006) *Why Politics Matters, Making Democracy Work*. Basingstoke: Palgrave Macmillan.

Stoll, L. and Fink, D. (1996) *Changing our Schools*. Buckingham: Open University Press.

Strain, M. and Simkins, T. (2008) The legacy of the Education Reform Act 1988. *Educational Management Administration and Leadership*, special edition, 36(2).

Stronach, I., Corbin, B., McNamara, O., Stark, S. and Warne, T. (2002) Towards an uncertain politics of professionalism: teacher and nurse identities in flux. *Journal of Education Policy*, 17(1): 109–138.

Suchman, L. (1995) Making work visible. *Communications of the ACM*, 38(9): 56–64.

Sugrue, C. (ed.) (2005) *Passionate Principalship: Learning from the Life Histories of School Leaders*. London: RoutledgeFalmer.

Taylor, C. (2002) *ESRC Teaching and Learning Research Programme Research Capacity Building Network – The RCBN Consultation Exercise: Survey Report*. Cardiff: University School of Social Science.

Taylor, C. (2007) Something for something: challenges and opportunities for specialist schools and academies in the future. In T. Blair, C. Taylor and E. Reid, *Education, Education, Education – 10 Years On*. London: Specialist Schools and Academies Trust.

Taylor, J. (2007) *The Impact of the Specialist Schools Programme on Exam Results*. Lancaster: Department of Economics, Lancaster University.

Taylor, W. (2000) The role of the providers. In I. Reid (ed.) *Improving Schools: The Contribution of Teacher Education and Training. An Account of the Joint UCET/HMI Symposium, Edinburgh*, December. UCET Occasional Paper no. 13. London: Universities' Council for the Education of Teachers.

Teacher Training Agency (TTA) (1998) *National Standards for Headteachers*. London: TTA.

TeacherNet (2007) TeacherNet, www.teachernet.gov.uk (accessed 1 February 2008).

Teddlie, C. and Reynolds, D. (eds) (2000) *The International Handbook of School Effectiveness Research*. London: Falmer.

Teddlie, C. and Stringfield, S. (1993) *School Matters: Lessons Learned from a 10-year Study of School Effects*. New York: Teachers College Press.

Tesla, N. (1934) *Radio Power Will Revolutionize the World: Modern Mechanics and Inventions*. Robbinsdale, MN: Fawcett.

The Primary Review (2007) *How Well are We Doing? Research on Standards, Quality and Assessment in English Primary Education*, www.primaryreview.org.uk/Downloads/Int_Reps/2.Standards_quality_assessment/Primary_Review_Standards-quality-assessment_overview_briefing_071102.pdf (accessed 4 March 2008).

Thomson, P. (2001) How principals lose 'face': a disciplinary tale of educational administration and modern managerialism. *Discourse: Studies in the Cultural Politics of Education*, 22(1): 2–22.

Thomson, P. (2002) *Schooling the Rustbelt Kids: Making the Difference in Changing Times*. Stoke-on-Trent: Trentham.

Thomson, P. and Gunter, H.M. (2006) From 'consulting pupils' to 'pupils as researchers': a situated case narrative. *British Educational Research Journal*, 32(6): 839–856.

Thomson, P. and Gunter, H.M. (2008) Researching bullying with students: a lens on everyday life in an innovative school. *International Journal of Inclusive Education*, 12(2): 185–200.

Thrupp, M. (1999) *Schools Making a Difference: Let's Be Realistic! School Mix, School Effectiveness and the Social Limits of Reform*. London: Taylor & Francis.

Thrupp, M. (2005) *School Improvement: An Unofficial Approach*. London: Continuum.

Tisdall, K., Wallace, J., McGregor, E., Millen, D. and Bell, A. (2005) *The Provision of Integrated Services by Family Centres and New Community Schools*. York: Joseph Rowntree Foundation.

Tomlinson, S. (2005) *Education in a Post-Welfare Society*. Maidenhead: Open University Press.

Totterdell, M., Heilbronn, R., Bubb, S. and Jones, C. (2002) *Evaluation of the Effectiveness of the Statutory Arrangements for the Induction of Newly Qualified Teachers*. London: DfES.

Training and Development Agency (TDA) (2000/2006) *ITT Place Allocations*, www.tda.gov.uk/partners/funding/allocations.aspx (accessed 13 March 2007).

Training and Development Agency (TDA) (2000/2007) *QTS Skills Test in Numeracy, June and July 2000: National Results Summary for Initial Training Providers*. London: TDA.

Tymms, P. (2004) Are standards rising in English primary schools? *British Educational Research Journal*, 30(4): 477–494.

Tymms, P. and Merrell, C. (2007) *Standards and Quality in English Primary Schools Over Time: The National Evidence, Primary Review Research Survey 4/1; Primary Review Interim Reports*. Cambridge: University of Cambridge.

Universities' Council for the Education of Teachers (UCET) (2007) *ITE Inspection Burdens*. London: UCET.

UNICEF (2007) *Child Poverty in Perspective: An Overview of Child Well-Being in Rich Countries*, Report Card 7. Florence, Italy: Innocenti Research Centre, UNICEF, www.unicef.org/media/files/ChildPovertyReport.pdf (accessed 4 September 2008).

Välijärvi, J., Linnakylä, P., Kupari, P., Reinikainen, P. and Arffman, I. (2002) *The Finnish Success in PISA and Some Reasons Behind It*. Jyväskylä, Finland: Institute for Educational Research, University of Jyväskylä.

Van Eyk, H. and Baum, F. (2002) Learning about interagency collaboration: trialling collaborative projects between hospitals and community health services. *Health and Social Care in the Community*, 10(4): 262–269.

Vulliamy, G. (2006) Primary teacher professionalism. In R. Webb (ed.) *Changing Teaching and Learning in the Primary School*. Maidenhead: Open University Press.

Vulliamy, G. and Webb, R. (2006) Education policy under New Labour. In R. Webb (ed.) *Changing Teaching and Learning in the Primary School*. Maidenhead: Open University Press.

Waks, L.J. (2007) The concept of fundamental educational change. *Educational Theory*, 57(3): 277–295.

Walberg, H.J. (1986) Syntheses of research on teaching. In M.C. Wittrock (ed.) *Handbook of Research on Teaching*. New York: Macmillan.

Walford, G. (2005) Introduction: education and the Labour Government. *Oxford Review of Education*, 31(1): 3–9.

Warren House Group at Dartington (2004) *A Research Perspective on Reforms to Children's Services in England*, www.dartington.org.uk/documents/reformsand20toand20 childrenand27sand20services.pdf (accessed 4 March 2008).

Wasoff, F., MacIver, S., McGuckin, A., Morton, S., Cunningham-Burley, S., Hinds, K. and Given, L. (2004) *A Baseline Study of Outcome Indicators for Early Years Policies in Scotland*, www.scotland.gov.uk/library5/education/eybaseline.pdf (accessed 30 August 2006).

Waterman, C. (2006) *Sins of Admission*. London: Institute for Research in Integrated Strategies.

Watkins, C. and Mortimore, P. (1999) Pedagogy: what do we know? In P. Mortimore (ed.) *Understanding Pedagogy and its Impact on Learning*. London: Paul Chapman.

Webb, R. and Vulliamy, G. (1996) *Roles and Responsibilities in the Primary School: Changing Demands, Changing Practices*. Buckingham: Open University Press.

Webb, R. and Vulliamy, G. (1999a) Changing times, changing demands: a comparative analysis of classroom practice in primary schools in England and Finland. *Research Papers in Education*, 14(3): 229–255.

Webb, R. and Vulliamy, G. (1999b) Managing curriculum policy changes: a comparative analysis of primary schools in England and Finland. *Journal of Education Policy*, 14(2): 117–137.

Webb, R. and Vulliamy, G. (2001) Joining up solutions: the rhetoric and practice of inter-agency cooperation. *Children and Society*, 15: 315–332.

Webb, R. and Vulliamy, G. (2004) *A Multi-Agency Approach to Reducing Disaffection and Exclusions from School*, DfES Research Report 568. Nottingham: DfES.

Webb, R. and Vulliamy, G. (2006) *Coming Full Circle? The Impact of New Labour's Education Policies on Primary School Teachers' Work*. London: Association of Teachers and Lecturers.

Webb, R., Häkkinen, K., Hämäläinen, S. and Vulliamy, G. (1998) External inspection or school self-evaluation? A comparative analysis of policy and practice in primary schools in England and Finland. *British Educational Research Journal*, 24(5): 539–556.

Webb, R., Vulliamy, G., Hämäläinen, S., Sarja, A., Kimonen, E. and Nevalainen, R. (2004) A comparative analysis of primary teacher professionalism in England and Finland. *Comparative Education*, 40(1): 83–107.

Webb, R., Vulliamy, G., Sarja, A. and Hämäläinen, S. (2006) Globalization and leadership and management: a comparative analysis of primary schools in England and Finland. *Research Papers in Education*, 21(4): 407–432.

Weindling, D. (2004) *Funding for Research on School Leadership*. Nottingham: National College for School Leadership, www.ncsl.org.uk (accessed 18 May 2007).

West, A. and Pennell, H. (1997) Educational reform and school choice in England and Wales. *Education Economics*, 5(3): 285–305.

West, M. (2003) *Inspection in Malawi*, Final Report. Manchester: University of Manchester.

West, M., Muijs, D. and Ainscow, M. (2007) Improving schools in challenging circumstances: a study of school-to-school collaboration. Paper presented at the Australian Association for Research in Education Conference.

Whitty, G. (2001) Education, social class and social exclusion. *Education and Social Justice*, 1: 2–9.

Whitty, G. (2002) *Making Sense of Education Policy*. London: Paul Chapman.

Wikeley, F., Bullock, K., Muschamp, Y. and Ridge, T. (2007) *Educational Relationships Outside School: Why Access is Important*. York: Joseph Rowntree Foundation.

Wilcox, B. and Gray, J. (1996) *Inspecting Schools: Holding Schools to Account and Helping Them to Improve*. Buckingham: Open University Press.

Wilkin, A., White, R. and Kinder, K. (2003) *Towards Extended Schools: A Literature Review*, Research Report RR432. London: DfES.

Wilkin, M. (1996) *Initial Teacher Education: The Dialogue of Ideology and Culture*. London: Falmer.

Wilkin, M. (1999) *The Role of Higher Education in Initial Teacher Education*, UCET Occasional Paper no. 12. London: Universities' Council for the Education of Teachers.

Wood, A.D. (1982) A training college for headteachers of secondary schools: some thoughts and considerations. *School Organisation*, 3(3): 287–296.

Wood, L., O'Sullivan, F. and Rix, S. (2007) *School Business Managers' Baseline Study: Interim Report* (unpublished). Nottingham: National College for School Leadership.

Woods, C., Nicolaidou, M. and Horrocks, K. (2003) *Report on National Rollout of Certificate of School Business Management, Cohort 1* (unpublished). Nottingham: National College for School Leadership.

Woods, C., Gunter, H.M. and West, M. (2007) *School Business Director Scoping Study: Final Report* (unpublished). Nottingham: National College for School Leadership.

Woods, P. and Jeffrey, B. (2002) The reconstruction of primary teachers' identities. *British Journal of Sociology of Education*, 23(1): 89–106.

Woods, P., Jeffrey, B., Troman, G. and Boyle, M. (1997) *Restructuring Schools*

Reconstructing Teachers: Responding to Change in the Primary School. Buckingham: Open University Press.

Woods, P., Woods, G. and Gunter, H.M. (2007) Academy schools and entrepreneurialism in education. *Journal of Education Policy*, 22(2): 263–285.

Wragg, E.C., Haynes, G.S., Wragg, C.M. and Chamberlin, R.P. (2004) *Performance Pay for Teachers: The Experiences of Heads and Teachers*. London: RoutledgeFalmer.

Wyse, D. (2003) The National Literacy Strategy: a critical review of empirical evidence. *British Educational Research Journal*, 29(6): 903–916.

Wyse, D., McCreery, E. and Torrance, H. (2008) *The Trajectory and Impact of National Reform: Curriculum and Assessment in English Primary Schools*, Primary Review Research Survey 3/2. Cambridge: University of Cambridge.

Yarker, P. (2005) On not being a teacher: the professional and personal costs of workforce remodelling. *Forum for Promoting 3–19 Comprehensive Education*, 47(2–3): 169–174.

Yarker, P. (2008) Personalised corruption: testing, cheating and teacher integrity. *Forum for Promoting 3–19 Comprehensive Education*, 50(1): 113–125.

Youdell, D. (2006) Subjectivation and performative politics – Butler thinking Althusser and Foucault: intelligibility, agency and the raced-nationed-religioned subjects of religion. *British Journal of Sociology of Education*, 27(4): 511–528.

Young, M.F.D. (2008) *Bringing Knowledge Back In*. London: Routledge.

Yukl, G.A. (2002) *Leadership in Organizations*, 5th edn. Upper Saddle River, NJ: Prentice Hall.

Zachariou, M. (2008) Inspection in Cyprus: a case study, unpublished PhD thesis, University of Nottingham.

Index